COMMUNICATION, DEVELOPMENT & the THIRD WORLD

The Global Politics of Information

Robert L. Stevenson

UNIVERSITY
PRESS OF
AMERICA

Lanham • New York • London

University Press of America®, Inc.
4720 Boston Way
Lanham, Maryland 20706

3 Henrietta Street
London WC2E 8LU England

This book was reprinted in 1993 by
University Press of America
by arrangement with Longman Publishing Group

Library of Congress Cataloging-in-Publication Data

Stevenson, Robert L.
Communication, development, and the Third World :
the global politics of information / Robert L. Stevenson.
p.   cm.
Originally published: New York : Longman,
©1988, in series: Communications.
Includes bibliographical references (p.   ) and index.
1. Communication—Developing countries.
2. Mass media—Developing countries.
3. Communication—International cooperation.
4. Communication, International.   I. Title.
P92.2.S7   1992   302.2'09172'4—dc20   91–42579 CIP

ISBN 0–8191–8488–8 (pbk. : alk. paper)

Contents

Foreword

For all those who have tried to follow the ebb and flow of the international debate on information and communication issues during the past quarter century there has been altogether too much of the former and too little of the latter: information galore; communication limited and faulty. The comprehensive bibliography at the end of this volume reflects only a minuscule part of the flood of newspaper and magazine articles, books, monographs, and speeches bearing on various aspects of this fascinating and frustrating field. That we live in the age of information and communication is evidenced by this fact alone.

International conferences on these issues sponsored by governments, international organizations, foundations, and academic institutions proliferate to the extent that some of the regular participants must have to live out of suitcases for months on end as they jet from one conference site to another. With all this movement and all the words generated thereby, however, there has been very little illumination of the basic issues and even less meaningful communication among those involved.

The frustrations of well-meaning professionals on all sides of these issues increase and the tone of their discussions becomes more strident as they find themselves unable to harness what they perceive as the enormous potential of information and communication for the accomplishment of that most noble and sought-after of goals — a world of peace and plenty for all.

The plaint of all concerned is still best expressed by the oft-cited verses of T. S. Eliot, written more than half a century ago in his liturgical drama, *The Rock*:

"Where is the wisdom we have lost in knowledge?
Where is the knowledge we have lost in information?"

In this slim volume Dr. Stevenson, utilizing both wisdom and knowledge, applies his keen observer's ability to get at the heart of the issues of information and communication. He combines this with his social scientist's respect for empirical research to present a clear and concise review of the origins and development of what has become one of the major items on the international agenda, East and West, North and South. Information and communication are and will continue to be motives of international concern well into the next century.

International cooperation on the resolution or management of the problems of information and communication is vital. Yet it must be accomplished against formidable odds. Traditional patterns of cultural behavior, nationalisms, jealously guarded illusions of personal and national security, and cherished ideological commitments all militate against meaningful communication and genuinely fruitful negotiations. Whether the issues are discussed between individual communications professionals in informal academic settings or among representatives of blocs or nations at the U.N. General Assembly, Unesco, or the World Administrative Radio Conference, the first step must be an agreement on a clear presentation of the issues.

This is precisely what Dr. Stevenson has attempted to do in this book. And I think he has succeeded. His presentation of the factual basis of the information controversy is straightforward both in terms of what can and what cannot be ascertained and what can be expected. His analyses of available data is clear and calm and his conclusions reasonable.

Slogans and catch phrases — the "free flow of information" and the "New World Information and Communications Order" — or the esoteric language of Unesco debates cannot help us to approach the very basic problems of the coexistence of glut and scarcity in world information flows, the overcrowding of the radio spectrum and the geostationary orbit, the role of telecommunications in national development, or the regulation or nonregulation of direct broadcast satellites, to mention only a few of the issues befogging the information and communication scene. Careful scholarship and clear, expository writing such as we find in this book can.

Dr. Stevenson has made a very positive contribution to the presentation of the fundamental issues of the information and communication debate. His research findings and modest appraisals deserve careful attention from everyone who wants to be informed on this issue.

This work puts a most thorny subject into perspective. Although it will not be without detractors from various positions on the ideological spectrum, it will be a valuable guide to the reader seeking a documented and factual foundation on which to base his or her own conclusions.

Hewson A. Ryan
Edward R. Murrow Professor
of Public Diplomacy

The Fletcher School of Law & Diplomacy
Tufts University, Medford, MA 02155

Introduction

This book is the product of nearly a decade's observation of a complex, contentious problem that will not go away. From my comfortable spectator's seat in Chapel Hill, far from the debating forums in Paris and New York and even farther from the developing countries that are the focus of the debates, I have tried to keep track of the problem as it moved from one argument to another, one forum to another. It was not easy.

At first the problem seemed to encompass all sorts of disparate issues: the dominance of the West in international news flow and other aspects of communication; the role of mass media in Third World development; the developing nations caught in (and sometimes exploiting) the geopolitical struggle between the superpowers; the North-South debate between the rich and poor nations. Then it occurred to me that the debate, as it grappled with obscure concepts such as *cultural imperialism* and *new world information order*, really dealt with aspects of a single question: What is the purpose of journalism?

Most of the debate was over the question of transferring the Western concept of journalism — independent of government, aloof and critical — to the developing nations. But also at issue was the performance of the Western mass media, clearly the engine that drove a rapidly expanding global communication system that comprised technology, popular culture and language as well as news and, some argued, the values that threatened the integrity of the developing nations as well.

The global debate reached its peak about 1980 (the approval of the Unesco Declaration on Mass Media in 1978 might be the single most important turning point), but the debate went on. And the question that spawned it — the purpose of journalism — is as complex and contentious now as it was a decade ago. I see nothing to suggest any change in the 1990s.

I have tried to show how the different pieces of the problems of communication, development, and the Third World fit together; how the global debate developed, and what might be done to alleviate the real challenge of an information-poor Third World in an information age still dominated by the West. I assume that the reader is familiar with the broader issues of East-West, North-South relations and the Western (or American) concept of the press, but that he or she is puzzled by phrases such as *cultural imperialism* and *new world information order* and doesn't understand why they arouse such an impassioned attack on what we consider a cornerstone of liberty.

On the whole, I defend Western (and American) mass media for two reasons. First, I believe (as Churchill said of democracy) that they represent the worst form of journalism — except for all the others. In recent years I have had the chance to travel in many parts of the world and to see firsthand what passes for journalism under the banner of alternative press theories. The reader who finds the critique of Western mass media appealing is encouraged to spend some time with Marxist journalism, development journalism, or protocol journalism, all of which have been put forward as appropriate to "authentic" Third World development.

A second reason for defending Western journalism is that the debate has largely belonged to the critics. This has occurred partly by default. Government and journalists are uncomfortable bedfellows at best — certainly when sitting together at Unesco arguing for a wall of separation between them or cooperating on a training program that stresses the importance of keeping a distance between them. They are also unused to defending themselves with the kind of passion advocates of the new global order invoke. The academic participants, some of them my professional colleagues and personal friends, have also been mostly on the side of critics of Western press performance. I think it is time for a critical searchlight to be turned on them, their arguments, and their evidence.

Still, I hope Western journalists and their supporters will not find this book too flattering. Because Western (and especially American) media have the resources, freedom, and professionalism to do so, they also have the obligation to do a better job in two areas. One is to share their wealth and knowledge and to support their Third World colleagues. Efforts of the Center for Foreign Journalists, World Press Freedom Committee, and International Press Institute are encouraging. The other is to improve their coverage of the world, especially the developing countries. On the whole, the national news media in the United States do a better job than they get credit for, but not as good a job as they could. Local media do a terrible job. They especially, it seems to me, need to recognize that readers, listeners, and viewers are interested in the rest of the world. Readership studies show it consistently, but editors continue to ignore the evidence. They also need to recognize that events in Africa, Asia, or Latin America can have as much influence on their own community as the city council and to report them accordingly. Projects such as that sponsored by Sigma Delta Chi (Hamilton, 1986) demonstrate that Main Street America is closer to — and more interested in — the Third World than most journalists realize. Reporting of the links between local communities and the rest of the world needs to be expanded; it is good journalism and good for circulation.

Many students and professional colleagues over the years contributed to the development of the argument I make in this book, but two deserve special mention. Shailendra Ghorpade did most of the number collection and number crunching on the growth of communication in the Third World; Dale Gardner contributed the section on communication development in Venezuela and Mexico. They got a doctoral dissertation and a master's thesis respectively; I got the benefit of their insights and expertise.

Robert L. Stevenson
Chapel Hill, North Carolina

1

New Issues and Old Problems

THE NEW INTEREST IN COMMUNICATION

In the 1980s, an old question assumed a new urgency. The old question was how the Western ideal of press freedom could be transferred to the developing nations of the Third World. The new urgency resulted from a collision between a 30-year history of using mass media to assist economic and social development and new voices that defined development in radical political terms demanding the mobilization of mass media to support a new global order.

At stake for the rest of the 1980s and the 1990s were both the future of mass media in the Third World and an international legitimacy for the popular argument that Western press freedom and its commitment to a free flow of information were merely old imperial domination in new dress.

How had a generation of development assistance efforts in the tradition of agricultural extension and press freedom become the object of such scorn and anger? Western journalists and diplomats were often more puzzled than angry as they listened to a decade of rhetoric demanding a vaguely defined new world information order. Yes, Westerners agreed, the Third World had gaping needs in everything from telecommunications to printing presses and even typewriters that Western assistance should meet. And yes, Third World governments might be more directly involved in mass media than Western journalists preferred. But why discard an ideal as central to human liberty as a free

1

flow of information for a global order nobody could define? That was too much.

When the political issue burned itself out after the approval of an ambiguous declaration on the role of mass media at the Unesco General Conference in 1978, the real problem remained: how to reduce the wide and expanding gap between the information-rich West and the information-poor Third World where most still lived in poverty and ignorance.

Tanzania's President Julius Nyerere dramatized both the plight of many struggling with squalor and the frustration of underdevelopment when he complained that the West was reaching for the moon while the Third World was still trying to reach the countryside.

COMMUNICATION AS MULTIPLIER

A generation earlier, mass communication had promised to speed the transition of rigid, centuries-old cultures of Africa, Asia, and Latin America into the open, wealthy societies of the industrialized West. What the West had done in centuries, the emerging Third World hoped to achieve in decades with the aid of modern mass media, especially radio, and later, television.

In the years after World War II when the Western colonial powers were preparing to dismantle their empires, evidence of change was everywhere. Daniel Lerner, an MIT sociologist, was one of the first to note how the old patterns of life in an arc of countries at the eastern end of the Mediterranean were changing. First it was physical contact with urban dwellers and people from different villages that gave hope that the future could be different and better. But more than anything, even in a small Turkish village in the mid-1950s, it was radio that challenged the authority of tradition.

Examples of how mass media disrupted old ways, raised hopes for a better future, and often fomented frustration were repeated in all parts of the Third World. In 1964, Wilbur Schramm wrote a book for Unesco that made rapid economic and social growth, spurred on by mass media, seem realistic, exciting, and relatively simple. The dust jacket of the book, virtually the bible for a generation of development efforts, showed rural villagers clustered around a bulky, old-fashioned community radio receiver somewhere in South Asia. The radio, as Daniel Lerner had noted in the Middle East, ended centuries of isolation and stability and gave people a glimpse of what their future could be, not what it inevitably must be. The villagers around that radio could be hearing of new agricultural techniques or learning about ways of reducing disease.

Perhaps they were listening to arguments in a national political campaign.

In fact, when Schramm's book appeared India already had been using rural radio forums for almost a decade to promote improvements in village life. A decade after Schramm's book, the Indian government undertook an ambitious program using a borrowed American satellite to broadcast directly to television sets in thousands of villages. Pictures added a dramatic dimension to worthy projects designed to reduce illiteracy, increase agricultural production, promote family planning, and improve health and sanitation. The dazzling space-age technology allowed the world's largest democracy to reach out to its 700 million people with messages of help and hope. The familiar extension agent from the American heartland was transformed into a long-distance teacher reaching millions of people in a thousand villages.

The medium had changed, but not the message. Encouraged by Western development assistance programs and a generation of scholars who accepted the optimistic scenario advanced by Lerner and Schramm, efforts to use mass media as the great multipliers of knowledge, experience and inspiration continued. Even those whose vision of the future was not Western capitalism — Nyerere, for example — embraced the basic assumption of what had become known as the dominant paradigm: that mass media could help Third World countries accelerate toward the future of their choice, capitalist or socialist, industrial or agrarian, democratic or totalitarian.

THE FAILURE OF COMMUNICATION

In those heady days, development meant either the creation of stable democratic government to replace traditional, authoritarian regimes or, more frequently, government programs to improve social conditions, agriculture, and literacy. In both cases, mass media were assumed to be capable of compressing the time required for change and of multiplying the impact of development programs. But even as efforts to mobilize mass media in support of development were gathering strength, objections were heard.

It is not easy to fix the time when the vision of communication and development embraced by a generation of development planners lost its nearly universal appeal. The disenchantment gained strength and legitimacy, however, during the Vietnam war when, in the wake of assassinations and racial violence, America's short-lived invincibility and innocence in world affairs ended.

The war gave ammunition to those who later argued that the

"Western model" of development was merely a smokescreen for a new style of colonialism in which multinational communication organizations, operating behind the facade of freedom, served as advance strike forces for a coalition of political and economic interests intent on maintaining exploitive control of Third World resources. But the denunciations of this new "cultural imperialism" that permeated so much of the Unesco debate in the 1970s came later. The problem with national development efforts around 1970, two decades after World War II and nearly a decade after mass communication promised so much, was that they had produced so little.

The changes that had occurred throughout the vast continents where three-quarters of the world's population lived seemed not only to tear up the old ways but to leave in their wake mostly chaos and dashed hopes. The vision of modernity that development had promised — industrial, material, democratic — often seemed as incongruous and inappropriate in the Third World as an English cottage in an African plain or an American sitcom televised to a Latin American barrio.

In 1975, Everett Rogers, an early disciple of the Lerner-Schramm school and Schramm's successor at Stanford University's influential communication development program, brought together the growing doubts, questions, and worries about the course of Third World development. In some cases change had produced unexpected consequences, usually negative. Lerner, for example, had argued that urbanization could create a critical mass of people and resources out of which could come rapid growth in literacy and mass media. Rapid industrialization had seemed a worthy goal in itself and the only way to create the wealth for health, education, and other social projects.

By the time of Rogers' writings, Third World cities in Latin America, Asia, and even in Africa had become among the world's largest, most crowded, and least habitable. Industrialization had produced some of the world's worst pollution, but not much in the way of a better life. More important, the fruits of the new way of life were going not to workers who toiled in conditions and for wages appropriate to a Dickens novel, but to the tiny elites who already controlled most of the wealth and, worse, to the multinational corporations, which had discovered that Third World factories meant cheap production costs and fast returns on investments.

Meanwhile, the problems of the Third World that had motivated so much of the development effort remained unresolved. Schramm, at a 1975 conference to assess the record of development programs, noted that while the percentage of Third World illiteracy declined between 1960 and 1970, the total number of illiterate adults increased by 65 million because of the rapid growth of population. In other areas —

health, food production, even media statistics such as newspaper circulation and radio receivers — absolute gains were reduced and sometimes completely absorbed by a population explosion that threatened to undo everything that the most successful development programs had accomplished. It was not much to show for a decade of work.

The biggest failure of all was political. Democratic government, which Lerner had called "the crowning institution of the participant [i.e., modern] society," had fared poorly in most Third World countries. As the fragile political institutions modeled on those in London, Paris, and Washington collapsed, occasionally into structures and rhetoric suggestive of Moscow but more often into new versions of old tribalism, it became a reasonable argument, and to many a matter of faith, that the template of modern Western industrial democracy was simply inappropriate for the rest of the world. Something else was needed as guide and inspiration.

As Rogers noted, the inspiration for many Third World countries in the 1970s was China, which had recently emerged from more than two decades of isolation to bedazzle Western reporters and scholars, who saw behind the smiles and well-fed bodies "a miracle of modernization." Rogers ticked off China's accomplishments: . . . "a public health and family planning system that was envied by the richest nations. Well-fed and -clothed citizens. Increasing equality. An enviable status for women." Most of all, China provided a vision of what Third World countries could do for themselves without foreign assistance or inter- ference. China now claimed to represent the emerging Third World, mimicking neither the capitalism of the industrialized West nor the grim socialism of the Soviet Union and her European satellites. (The difference between a Soviet vision of national development and a Third World vision, which was usually cloaked in Marxist rhetoric but privately as critical of the Soviet Union as it was of the United States, was subtle. The distinction eluded many journalists and politicians in the West who saw the developing nations separating into two tidy camps, the "free" and the "communist" nations.)

Of course, the linking of a non-Western philosophy of development to Soviet-style communism was strengthened when the Non-Aligned Movement itself became an active political organization with rhetoric and sometimes politics that smacked more of simple anti-Americanism than any neutral ground between the super power cold warriors. When Cuba, which had as much claim to non-aligned status as, say, Canada, became a leader of the movement, it was inevitable that many in the West would see almost any criticism of Western development efforts as radical and dangerous.

It was sometimes difficult to remember that criticism of early communication development efforts contained two intertwined but separate strands. One was built on the real and frequent failures of early development assistance programs and the vision of a truly self-sufficient and non-aligned Third World. The other, which dominated the new world information order debate at Unesco throughout most of the 1970s, was radical, dangerous, and quite different.

COMMUNICATION AS IMPERIALISM

Just when doubts about the power of mass media to compress centuries of Western industrial and political evolution into decades in the Third World were challenging early optimism, several intellectual forces combined to produce a radical critique of the original optimistic ideas. Most of the new ideas grew out of the fertile atmosphere of university campuses, first in Europe and Latin America where Marxism was traditionally fashionable and in some places mandatory. Then they spread to the United States where the intellectual hegemony of the so-called dominant paradigm also came under fire.

In Latin America, a school of thought defined the failure of Third World development in terms of dependency. Dependency theory viewed the world as a single system and found "imperial centers," notably the United States, which controlled the flow of goods, services, and capital between themselves and nations on the periphery of the system. Economic development at the periphery, which included most of the Third World, was used to strengthen the dominance of the center nations and to maintain the peripheral nations's position of dependence.

In this theory, twentieth century multinational or transnational corporations (MNCs or TNCs) performed the same functions as eighteenth and nineteenth century imperial armies. It was the MNCs and TNCs that came, saw, and conquered through the manipulation of wants, needs, and desires and made the Third World *believe* that development could come only through the continuation of the existing global system.

Because dependency theory argued that domination was maintained through persuasion rather than armies, mass media — or communication TNCs — were especially important. The articulation of a cultural/information imperialism component of dependency theory was the work of a North American, Herbert Schiller. His explanation of cultural domination in the early 1970s spread from his home base at the University of California at San Diego to universities, development centers, and occasionally even government offices around the world. His influence seemed to expand even as American economic and military power declined in the 1970s because he argued that the West, especially the United States, was all-powerful in information, the coin of the new information age, and that information was increasingly the business of the MNCs and TNCs.

European theorists in the 1970s also became critical of the development model. They argued that North American theories had looked in the wrong place to find the causes and cures for Third World poverty and instability. The traditional emphasis in U.S. communication development scholarship was on the individual, not the political and economic system in which he or she lived. To make countries modern, Lerner had argued, people had to be made modern. Both he and Schramm seemed to assume — naively, as it turned out — that rigid and often oppressive Third World governments would change to accommodate the "modern" ideas and aspirations of their newly modern populations.

In fact, the European scholarship argued, the existing system, including American-style development programs, simply served to strengthen the already exploitive imbalance between the neo-imperialists and the Third World. The legions of scholars and program planners mobilized in the first generation of development assistance programs were not part of the solution to Third World underdevelopment; they were a large part of the problem.

The solution? Disengagement from the global system and something close to revolution. China, of course, had shown that it could be done, and countries such as Cuba and Tanzania were also held up as models of an authentic, non-Western, noncapitalist development. Even when many of the impressive gains were the result of brute force (China's birth control program) or even stronger dependency on other countries (Cuba's economic dependence on the Soviet Union), the argument for an "alternative" vision of development, decoupling the Third World from the West, held sway.

Dependency theory and its corollaries also relieved people and Third World governments from responsibility for their actions. Why were "Dallas" and Disney cartoons as popular in the Third World as they were in the United States? Not because of the universal appeal of fantasy programming, but because the communication TNCs first created the demand for it, then sold the programs to satisfy the demand. Why did Third World countries rely so heavily on the Western news agencies? Not because the Western agency files were fast, reliable, and interesting, but because the TNCs that controlled the news prevented the development of alternative organizations to challenge their hegemony.

Cultural dependency was a tidy and appealing explanation for the sad state of the Third World a decade or two after liberation from colonialism and it flourished in the hospitable environment of Unesco.

GROPING FOR A NEW ORDER

The United Nations Educational, Scientific and Cultural Organization (Unesco), ironically, had been created after World War II in the image of Western ideals and ideology. One of its divisions, called the Free Flow of Information, enshrined that very Western principle, and Schramm's influential study of mass media and national development, of course, was commissioned by Unesco and represented a synthesis of Unesco-sponsored meetings in the late 1950s.

A decade later the organization again sponsored a series of meetings devoted to the issue of communication and national development, but this time things were different. For one thing, Third World countries constituted a majority of the membership and that meant a caucus of developing countries could, if properly organized and controlled, dominate the organization. Western nations, responding to Third World rhetoric with some sense of collective responsibility for the plight of the Third World, were mostly absent or silent when radical new orders were put forward as the solution to Third World dependency.

The first new order was economic. With a resolution worded in the vocabulary of dependency theory approved in 1975, Unesco decreed that the gap between the wealth of the West and poverty of the Third World, the heritage of colonialism, ought to be redressed as a matter of justice by a massive transfer of economic resources from the rich nations to the poor. In the typical rhetoric of international diplomacy, the statement was ambiguous and subject to differing interpretation. The West paid little attention.

The second new order was related to communication. Because information was acknowledged to be a new medium of wealth, attention turned toward a declaration on a new world information order (NWIO). Regional meetings in Latin America, Africa, and Asia in the early 1970s came to identical conclusions about the new order, all phrased in language derived from the ideology of dependency. Because of cultural imperialism, the Third World deserved to receive vast quantities of information resources from the information-rich West. And those resources should be used to create an authentic Third World communication system appropriate for "Third World reality," a recurring phrase that suggested somehow that reality was different in the developing countries.

The NWIO debate was at the time something like a shell game.

Ideas that were clearly anathema to the West — licensing of journalists, government responsibility for mass media, an undefined national right to communicate — were part of the new order, but when pressed, advocates of the NWIO could point out that Unesco statements had never advocated such ideas.

They were right, but in a narrow sense. In some cases, objectionable phrases were removed at the insistence of Western delegates or blurred to the point where they became code words for whole schools of thought. In others, Unesco officials simply said different things to different audiences. Where did Unesco call for an end to the free flow of information? Where did it advocate licensing of journalists? Nowhere, although among the debaters were people who defined the new order in precisely those terms.

The heated debate over a resolution that would recognize the legitimacy of a new world information order — at the insistence of the West it was always "a" new order, never "the" new order — served about the same function as the stick the farmer used to hit the mule between the eyes to get its attention. In the early years of the debate the Western nations and particularly the United States, which had never attached much importance to the United Nations system, were often absent, usually silent and never forceful in defending their own very modest record of aid to Third World development or their belief in the universal value of independent, critical mass media.

By the time a draft declaration on the NWIO was presented to the Unesco general conference in 1976, however, the debate had come to the attention of Western governments and media, and they said no. The draft called for nations to be responsible for the activities of mass media operating under their flag and argued that mass media had a positive responsibility to assist in the creation of a new global order. When it was clear that no agreement on the draft was possible, it was sent back for redrafting and more study.

A watered-down resolution, stripped of its most odious provisions but still subject to mischievous interpretation, was approved two years later amid recognition that an equitable distribution of the world's information resources would not be accomplished by simply willing it so. Yes, work toward the goal of a balanced flow of information, said the West to the Third World, but do it by expanding your own communication capabilities, not by restricting the free flow from the powerful, information-rich West. Out of the wreckage of the debate came a small area of common understanding between the West and the Third World that pointed the way toward a renewal of interest in pragmatic communication development efforts in the 1980s.

The debate over old and new global orders had obscured the very real and serious needs of the Third World. The kinds of growth that mass media were supposed to facilitate — political stability, economic development, improvement in the lives of the millions of ordinary people in the developing countries — were still elusive. The gaps between the "have" and the "have not" nations were large and growing, particularly in information.

The one area of common agreement between the defenders of Western press ideals and their Third World critics was the need to do something about the Third World's lack of communication capabilities. The promise of assistance was the West's strong card in the Unesco sweepstakes, and despite a characteristic lack of organization, diplomatic skill, and common purpose that plagued the Western caucus during these years, it was played effectively.

The rich information resources available in the West and the promise to share them helped turn the NWIO question into a two-way debate between the West and the Third World, with the Soviet bloc the odd man out. Although the rhetoric still contained a heavy dose of Soviet influence and the Soviet Union itself and its Third World allies remained active in the debate, the NWIO debate was more and more between the Third World and the West because the West had what the Third World needed: technology.

In return for elimination or blurring over of the more troubling aspects of the new world information order debate, the West promised to help the Third World with its massive and obvious communication needs. The tactic worked. By the time a declaration on mass media was approved at the Unesco general conference in 1978, most of the debate participants seemed ready to turn from rhetoric to real problems. The United States at various points had promised to help by providing a satellite (an experiment in India was promising), setting up training centers (nothing ever came of the offer) and, finally, proposing a clearinghouse to match all of the diverse needs and wants with existing and promised offers of help.

The International Program for the Development of Communication (IPDC), a stepchild of Unesco not quite part of the organization but living there, was born in 1980 as the one practical outcome of the decade-long debate. From the beginning it was a sickly child, but represented the one point where the West and the Third World found common agreement.

The original proposal to Unesco in 1980 was to make IPDC a clearinghouse for a wide range of communication development needs and resources. If country A wants help improving its radio network, list it with IPDC; if country X is prepared to train 20 journalists, record the offer; then match the needs and resources. It did not work out that way.

Over the objections of the Soviet Union and other countries, IPDC did accept participation by nongovernment organizations (read privately owned mass media) and parallel programs (read bilateral aid projects). But it was not content to be merely a clearinghouse, a codeword meaning that donor countries would have the final say on the selection and details of each project. Instead the organization called for generous contributions without strings so that Third World countries themselves could decide the priorities among competing projects and allocate the money.

IPDC did not get much. The American delegation, probably with an eye toward explaining to Congress why IPDC wanted to support a training school in Cuba or a news agency for the Palestine Liberation Organization, two early project ideas that were quickly discarded, announced that its contributions would be limited to parallel programs in existing agencies and limited funds in trust. That meant that existing programs might be increased a bit and that IPDC could keep the books on several others, but that no generous check — and certainly no blank check — would be forthcoming.

Most other donors followed suit. When the organization met in Acapulco in January 1982 it had more than 50 proposals for projects, from which a review committee selected 19 with a lifetime cost of more than $7 million. At the time IPDC had pledges of only $6 million, most of it designated for specific projects, coordinated bilateral funding, or soft currency. It could allocate less than $1 million as seed money for the approved projects and development of future projects. It was a modest beginning for an ambitious idea, but a hesitant step toward the redemption of a pledge to reduce the information gap.

COMMUNICATION DEVELOPMENT RENEWED

In a way, communication development came full circle from the publication of Schramm's optimistic and enthusiastic book in 1964 to the creation of IPDC almost 20 years later. The early promise had given way to disappointment, then to radical alternatives which burned brightly but briefly, then back to the harsh reality of lingering Third World needs and the even bigger gap between the West and the Third World. But communication development in the 1980s did not mean using new tools to tackle old problems. In two decades, some things had changed.

The most apparent difference between communication in the 1960s and the 1980s was technology. Schramm had written hopefully of the cheap transistor radio and the potential of satellites. The transistor, of course, was made obsolete by even cheaper microchip technology, and satellites became commonplace. Getting information to a receiving dish anyplace in the world, even in the remotest areas, was no problem; getting it from the dish into homes and offices was a different matter. The communication revolution, which was no tired cliche to a Third World struggling to join it, had produced the technology to put together just about any kind of communication structure the developing countries wanted.

And costs had plummeted so rapidly that it was within the range of possibility — and for some already a reality — to build a system for mass media and telecommunications rivaling that of the most advanced industrial society. Even in the most depressed countries, pocket-sized radios, TVs, and cassette players were commonplace. Is any rural village still beyond the reach of radio? a Texas researcher asked after looking at recent changes in several of the world's poorest countries. Probably not.

If the problems of communication development in the 1980s were only technical they would be easy to solve and the information-rich West would be a more enthusiastic participant. The important difference between communication development in the hopeful 1960s and the skeptical 1980s was not technology so much as the purposes to which the technology would be put.

A residue from the NWIO debate that permeated IPDC was the lingering suspicion that Western principles of press independence were out of place in the Third World. As long as rapid national development was still the overriding goal of Third World countries, a media system that promoted development was the dominant need for the 1980s. An aloof, critical, independent press would not do.

Even the definition of development had changed. In IPDC, Third World spokesmen typically defined national goals in political terms; not the comforting idea of stable, participatory democracy that Lerner had written about, but cultural sovereignty, independence from existing global systems, and a sense of nationhood to replace divisive tribal loyalties.

To support such goals, a new definition of news was needed along with new structures to produce and disseminate it. The idea that mass media could support national development was not new, of course. After all, that was the premise of Schramm's early work, and it had the enthusiastic endorsement of the West. Furthermore, a model for early development programs was the extension service, which was as reassuring a symbol of trustworthy values as one could find.

The 1980s' definition of development was different, however, more political, calling for independence of the West and often hostility toward the values the West cherished. The new definition of development included a concept of *development news*. The term seems to have originated in Asia as an outgrowth of rural development programs, precisely the focus of early development efforts. Development news was that which *promoted* development, everything from literacy and personal hygiene to agricultural practices and family planning. But it also was defined as that which *reflected* development, that is, the "good news" of development. That could include slow but significant progress in raising literacy, the implementation of a land reform program, the opening of a factory or school, precisely the positive events that the Western news agencies and media usually ignored. It was a short leap from that to the kind of good news that had filled the pages and airwaves of dictatorships for generations, and to the West, "development news" sounded more and more like a new international justification for blatant political control of the news.

Why did the president's picture appear on the front page day after day? Why did his routine, public appearances lead off every newscast? Why was there never a hint of corruption, incompetence, or other shortcoming? Because *political* development demanded that the symbol of nationhood be shown in a light that would inspire trust and confidence. Because ribbon cutting and cornerstone laying were important symbols of nation building. And most of all, because international leadership was the keystone of Third World coming of age.

"Protocol news," the ceremonial comings and goings of public officials, was an offshoot of development news. It included the endless clips of airport arrival and departure ceremonies, the dreary photos of world leaders making small talk around conference tables, and the columns of small type devoted to congratulatory telegrams, banquet toasts, and high-sounding communiques. Meanwhile, for their own use, Third World leaders relied on Western media even when they denied the same access to their own citizens.

Western media, particularly the "Big Four" news agencies from the United States, Britain, and France, had little time for development news and even less for protocol news. Of all the Western institutions that came under attack in the new world information order debate, it was the major Western news agencies that took the most criticism. In the forums devoted to communication issues, speaker after speaker took the floor to denounce the news agencies for ignoring the Third World, for reporting only disruptions and upheavals, for seeing the Third World through a Western cultural bias, and for monopolizing the world flow of information.

Even when research and common sense argued against many of the accusations, the creation of new structures to distribute information supportive of the new definition of development was the top priority of communication development in the 1980s. In its first years, IPDC emphasized regional networks to improve the flow of news and other information within the Third World and, in the few countries without them, national news agencies to plug into the international systems. Many in the West were still skeptical. For every grant to an independent (privately owned) newspaper in Botswana there were a half dozen grants for government-controlled news agencies or politicized regional exchanges.

The need to strengthen Third World countries' ability to communicate within and among themselves was the one very important point of common agreement between Third World leaders and Westerners who were skeptical of the new journalism. Some of the new organizations, such as the Non-Aligned News Agencies pool and the Pan African News Agency, were blatantly political and immediately got tangled in the politics of their sponsoring organizations. Others, such as Inter Press Service, an independent news agency devoted to Third World events but retaining a sense of independence and skepticism, and regional exchanges in Latin America and Asia, could claim a modicum of success by complementing the major agencies and filling in the gaps in the global flow.

On the whole these early, halting efforts to use mass media to promote a new style of national development had a salutary effect. Third World journalists often shared Western suspicions about development and protocol journalism and the justification for mobilizing mass media to support national political objectives. Reporters and editors who had to assemble news files, newscasts, and newspapers minimally acceptable to an audience day after day appreciated the value of professional judgment and independence. They also understood that most of the catalog of journalistic sins of omission and commission of which the Western media were accused reflected the universal limits of the media and human failure, not a Western conspiracy.

Many Third World journalists also stood in awe of their Western counterparts' freedom to report critically without fear of retribution and were often as skeptical as Western journalists of the pious rhetoric of a new world information order. The old-fashioned Western values of journalistic independence and responsibilty had far greater acceptance in the Third World than the rhetoric at Unesco implied. The idea of journalism as watchdog, not cheerleader, of the powerful is still alive in the Third World. The West and the Third World still seem to have something to say to each other in the 1990s.

COMMUNICATION DEVELOPMENT IN THE FUTURE

After a decade of harsh debate over the role of mass media and the disillusionment with early efforts to use communication to speed modernization, it is easy to despair. It is tempting to say "enough!" and to walk away as the United States did from Unesco, where so much of the battle over the role of mass media had taken place. If Western journalism collectively turns its back on the Third World and its real, urgent, and growing needs, it will be a mistake. Both the West and the Third World will lose.

The developing countries will lose an opportunity to move, however slowly and painfully, toward stability, growth, and independence, goals as valid and urgent as they were three decades ago. The West will lose an opportunity to retain influence in areas that are vital to its future. And beliefs about the universal worth of individual liberties and responsibilities that served the West well over several centuries will be diminished. What is to be done? Where to begin?

Despite a resurgence of interest in communication and national development in the wake of the new world information order debate, many questions remain unanswered. The debates in the 1970s were long on rhetoric but short on evidence. Obviously the availability of mass media, particularly radios and televisions, increased dramatically everywhere in the Third World; but were they an incentive to economic and political change or a product of it? Or did they flourish independent of the upheavals that swirled around them? For that matter, even questions of changes in social, economic, and political conditions remain at issue. We do not know for sure, even after all the debate, what happened to Third World economic and social development in the turbulent decade of the 1970s, and how much, and even whether, communication was involved.

Is the new journalism of national development merely a new face on old-fashioned political control? How can Western journalists, committed to independence from government, support new Third World institutions that by definition and sometimes necessity are agents of government? These, too, are questions for which no clear answers are evident, even though they are at the heart of the problem of communication development for the 1990s and beyond.

The West in general cannot escape responsibility for assisting Third World communication development, and Western journalism in particular must assert more effective leadership in defending the universality of its ideals and honoring its commitment to provide technical assistance. By tradition Western media try to keep a critical spotlight trained on the institutions of power; they should keep a spotlight turned on themselves as well to see how they could report the struggles and aspirations of Third World peoples as thoroughly as their failures. Introspection is needed as much as self-defense and aid.

These are not easy tasks and require understanding of issues that have been argued more with ideology than evidence and with history that has been presented more as hyperbole than chronology. The path of communication development twists and turns through three decades of hope and disillusionment, stagnation and upheaval. It begins with an optimistic prediction of how mass media could help developing countries compress centuries of development into decades, then moves to a pessimistic acknowledgment of the failure of many early efforts. Beyond that is a radical interpretation of the problem and a call for an equally radical solution. But the path of communication must be understood if what Nyerere called the "terrible ascent" of Third World nations to stability, economic growth, and democracy is to be smoother and straighter in the decades ahead. It begins in an isolated rural village in Turkey in the 1950s.

The Magic Multiplier

2

THE VILLAGE OF BALGAT

The village of Balgat lay only eight kilometers from Ankara, but in 1950 a trip to the Turkish capital took two hours by car over trails that did not qualify as roads. Few of the residents had visited Ankara and most had never heard the one radio in the village. Balgat was a traditional village, isolated from the rest of the world and governed by a stern chief who had left the village only twice, both times to fight in war. The villagers lived out their lives as their ancestors had before them.

Balgat, however, was about to experience more change in a few years than it had seen in the previous century. The residents of Balgat and millions of other people like them in Africa, Asia, the Middle East, and Latin America were beginning to move toward a modern life that exchanged the security and rigidity of traditional culture for the uncertainty and opportunity of the twentieth century industrial age.

An observer of this rupture of history was Daniel Lerner, the MIT sociologist who was a director of a pioneering study of the clash between tradition and modernization in seven countries that formed an arc around the eastern Mediterranean. The study dealt mostly with the role of mass media and opinion formation in these traditional societies. When the study's questionnaires were tabulated, however, unexpected evidence of change appeared, and Lerner began to piece together the outline of a theory about how and why these countries were changing so fast.

Four years after the first interviews in Balgat, Lerner himself visited the village at the end of a trip through the Middle East testing his theory. By then Balgat had been incorporated as a district of Greater Ankara, but the changes that seemed to affect village life most were not administrative. A road now linked the village to Ankara and hourly bus service cost the equivalent of four cents. Most buildings had electricity and a pipe to import clean water was under construction. In four years the number of houses had grown from 50 to more than 500 and the number of radios from one to more than 100.

The real transformation of Balgat, however, was not immediately visible. Most of the able-bodied men had left their farms for factory work in Ankara, where daily wages were more than twice the inflated rate of two lira that farm workers now earned. The chief himself had sold or rented most of his land and his two sons, heirs to generations of landowners, had become shopkeepers. The elder son owned a grocery store in the village and his younger brother owned Balgat's first clothing store.

In Lerner's phrase, Balgat had "entered history." Ties to generations of stability were broken when villagers could see life outside Balgat and begin to imagine a different and better future. Lerner's book, *The Passing of Traditional Society*, documented the changes in Balgat and theorized about how other parts of the emerging Third World were undergoing similar disruptions. It influenced a generation of thinking about what was happening throughout the Third World and how that change could be channeled toward rapid political and economic growth.

Ironically, many of the social forces that had opened Balgat to change became new sources of misery for the generation that followed. Metropolitan Ankara grew from a population of 287,000 in 1950 to 2.5 million in 1980, as roads broke the isolation of other villages whose inhabitants moved to the capital in search of food, shoes, and jobs. By most standards of measurement life was better for the city's inhabitants, but the stability and strength of traditional village life were gone. For too many people in too many places, the "revolution of rising expectations," Lerner's phrase describing the psychological effects of modernization, had given way to a revolution of rising frustrations. The gap between what the villagers of Balgat wanted and what they and their governments could provide was larger in 1980 than in the heady days of 1954, when the path to a modern future seemed to require only a dirt road, a water pipe, electricity, and a few radios.

Balgat in 1980, only one generation after it entered history, had become part of the sprawl of greater Ankara, indistinguishable by any political or cultural identity. If the chief's grandchildren could have returned to the Balgat of 1950 they would have found his village as strange and alien as he had found the world beyond the village that disappeared in his lifetime. Similar ruptures of traditional life, the product of centuries of cultural evolution, were taking place throughout a band of countries and colonies that sweep across the tropics and southern hemisphere.

THE EMERGING THIRD WORLD

The millions of Balgats began their terrible ascent after World War II, at a time when the industrialized nations were caught in a cold war, divided into two opposing ideologies, and committed to the extension of their political and economic influence as much as colonial powers had been in earlier centuries. The developing nations formed a third world, as the architects of the new Non-Aligned Movement argued, belonging to neither camp. From its organizational meeting in Indonesia in 1955, the new Non-Aligned Movement became a third player on the world stage, balancing East against West, often playing one against the other.

This Third World contained three-quarters of the world's people in a bewildering assortment of free states and colonies, subcontinents, and ministates. Some had been politically independent of the European colonial powers for more than a century; a few had never been colonized. In Asia and Africa most were on the brink of political independence. All shared the miseries of underdevelopment: illiteracy, early death, and poverty. Most of all, poverty.

Lerner's study appeared at a time when Third World development was becoming an urgent issue. Britain, France, and the minor European colonial powers were dismantling their empires with promises to atone for past exploitation. The United States, as leader of the Western alliance, viewed the emerging Third World in terms of both idealism and world politics. On one hand, the postwar policy of containing communism was extended to the developing countries after the Chinese revolution demonstrated that Marxism could fire the imagination in the Third World as well as it could the industrialized North. On the other, New Frontier programs such as the Alliance for Progress and the Peace Corps reflected a naive optimism about America's ability to deal with world problems.

On all fronts, a way of focusing and guiding the new forces in the Third World was needed, and Lerner's study of the Middle East seemed to provide it. The pieces of the development process he sketched out were straightforward and direct, so obvious that the theory seemed beyond question. It is hard to overestimate the importance of Lerner's book. It shaped a generation of thought on how communication could help in national development efforts, not just in the Middle East, but throughout the rising nations of Africa, Asia, and Latin America as well.

It is not surprising that Lerner and those who followed saw communication as an almost magic machine to speed the process of change. In the 1950s, when he was writing, the United States had experienced firsthand the revolutionary influence of a new mass medium. At the start of the decade television was a curiosity; at the end, it was a ubiquitous presence, changing and often dominating people's lives. Television was still the exception in most Third World countries, but most had in place an extensive radio network that was ready made for the job of development. To the new nations of the Third World, it seemed communication could propel them toward the takeoff point where, as Rostow had argued from his influential history of Western industrialization, development would become self-sustaining and accelerating.

As development programs themselves accelerated in the 1960s, Lerner's theory that mass media could multiply and speed change was applied to a wide range of development objectives, from birth control and sanitation to changes in centuries-old social patterns. By the time the issue became the focus of international debate in the 1970s, the phrase *national development*, like the Queen of Hearts' words, could mean anything a speaker wanted it to mean. In the Unesco debates in the 1970s it usually meant disengagement from the West and precisely the opposite of what early writers, such as Lerner, had intended. Lerner, however, was quite precise in his definition of development. He used the word to mean stable democracy and defended it as the heart of "modernity," not so much on moral grounds as on the pragmatic argument that only participatory democracies could absorb the rapid social change that swept through all countries in the last part of the twentieth century.

THE GREAT MULTIPLIER

The model of development that Lerner sketched from his study of the Middle East is notable both for its precision and for its ambiguity. Among middle-range social theories, it is one of the most detailed and explicit. Yet nowhere in *The Passing of Traditional Society* is there a single statement defining a theory of modernization. What Lerner does offer is a careful definition of several key factors in the modernization process and some attention to the order in which they occur.

As was characteristic of American social science research at the time, Lerner focused on individuals rather than the social, political, and economic system in which they lived. Lerner saw individuals as the key to social change. To change society, people must change. To create a modern (stable) society, men and women must be modern.

The key that set into motion the modernization process was *empathy*, defined simply as "the capacity to see oneself in the other fellow's situation." How did one learn empathy? For Lerner the key was travel or the modern-day equivalent, vicarious encounter through the mass media:

> Radio, film and television climax the revolution set into motion by Gutenberg. The mass media opened to the large masses of mankind the infinite *vicarious* universe. Many more millions of persons in the world were to be affected directly, and perhaps more profoundly, by the communication media than by the transportation agencies. (Lerner 1958, 53)

Thus, mass media became a crucial link in the modernization process, replacing personal experience as the font of new ideas. But before mass media could grow, a developing nation had to concentrate its human resources enough to form a critical mass of people. This meant that urbanization was the first step toward national development. Once about 10 percent of a national population was urbanized, Lerner argued, urbanization and literacy increased together until they reached 25 percent, a takeoff point beyond which literacy continued to rise independently of the growth of cities.

So far, so good. Lerner seemed to encourage the movement of people from rural areas to cities, an ironic twist given the enormity of the problem of urban sprawl and decay in the 1970s and 1980s. But in the 1950s, problems looked less formidable and negative consequences of rapid change in the Third World were overlooked.

Literacy, according to Lerner, was closely followed by, and often confounded with, a rapid growth of mass media use or, in Lerner's phrase, "media participation." The power of mass media at this stage of development lay in their ability to focus the forces of change into other forms of democratic participation.

Democratic government, "the crowning institution of the participant society," came late in the development process. In a survey of the world's nations testing the patterns first observed in Balgat, it was the "modern" nations — urban, literate, democratic — that were capable of incorporating continuing social change into existing institutions. "In a century that has reinstated revolution as a method of social change," Lerner commented, "they have managed to adapt their own accelerated growth mainly by nonviolent procedures."

Lerner's book was not written as a guide for development planners, of course, and was certainly not a how-to instruction manual for transforming a traditional society into a developed nation. But it did suggest that the wealth, power, and stability of the West could be attained by the poor, weak, and unstable nations. And more than anything else available at the time, *The Passing of Traditional Society* provided a way of looking at the disparate nations of the vast Third World and seeing in them a coherence and order that pointed to a better future.

For the institutions committed to the struggle for a better future, the Lerner study was virtually the only beacon. The Chinese version of development, which a decade later became an appealing alternative model, was at this time either unknown or rejected as an extension of Soviet-style totalitarianism. It was to the West that leaders of emerging nations looked for aid and ideas. The responsibility for translating theory into action fell heavily onto two groups: one was the United Nations system; the other was a group of American academics who were enlisted to carry out research and to train Third World development communicators.

FROM THEORY TO ACTION

The first concerted effort to define mass media's power to promote national development came, ironically, from Unesco. In the 1970s it was the organization that promoted a radical definition of development in the context of new global orders, but in the early 1960s the ideological balance was different. Although the original definition of national development expanded to include all sorts of political, social, and economic change, the inspiration for the mobilization of a mass media crusade was a combination of Lerner's early optimism and the familiar extension agent who had helped modernize rural America.

The publication of *The Passing of Traditional Society* in 1958 was propitious. In the same year the United Nations General Assembly called for a program to help developing nations expand their mass media. From a series of regional meetings attended by representatives of mass media, government, and other professional organizations, Unesco prepared a survey of information needs and resources in Africa, Asia, and Latin America.

After considering the survey, in 1962 the General Assembly encouraged its member governments to include mass media in their economic development plans. At the same time Unesco, along with other public and private agencies, was urged to support the effort to expand mass media. The assembly resolution noted hopefully that "information media have an important part to play in education and in economic and social progress generally and that new techniques of communication offer special opportunities for acceleration of the education process."

At the end of the same year the Unesco General Conference authorized a study "to help give practical effect to the mass media development program." Wilbur Schramm, then director of the Institute for Communication Research at Stanford University, had participated in the three regional meetings that produced the original Unesco survey and had already distinguished himself in the infant discipline of communication research with thoughtful and readable analyses of a variety of topics related to mass media.

The Schramm study, published jointly by Stanford University Press and Unesco as *Mass Media and National Development*, appeared in 1964. The timing was superb. The 1960s had been proclaimed the United Nations Decade of Development; newly independent nations in Africa and Asia were expanding the roster of United Nations member states; and in several Western countries, but particularly the United States, scholars and development program administrators were ready to join the crusade to liberate the three-quarters of the world's population bound by poverty and illiteracy.

Like Lerner, Schramm began his book by focusing on the human expression of underdevelopment. Schramm, however, described two families, one in Africa and one in Asia, which together demonstrated that villagers in rural Turkey shared many of the same problems, constraints, and aspirations with villagers in other parts of the Third World. The Ife family, living somewhere in west central Africa, was rich in human values but unable to escape a marginal existence that tied them to small, dusty plots of land worked by homemade tools. In one year the family might see $50 in cash. Almost nothing that affected their lives and nothing they talked about took place more than 10 miles from their village. Yet Schramm also praised "the warmth of their life together, the affection they seem to feel for each other, and in particular the kindness they show the old and useless grandfather."

Several thousand miles away in southern Asia, the Bvani family was also struggling for survival. There were differences between the two families. The Bvanis were better fed than the Ifes and had a better sense of their own history. They were conscious of their nation's heritage of religion, philosophy, poetry, and art. And the government of this emerging nation was actively reaching out to encourage better agricultural practices.

The problem for the Bvani family was not the gap between people eager for change and a government that lacked the resources or willingness to innovate. The problem was the clash between tradition and change:

Change comes hard in that village. The old men are the decision makers, and they usually make conservative decisions. There is a tight caste system, which limits the kinds of jobs any man can aspire to. There are rather rigid customs as to what kind of work a woman can do and what her influence can be. The government has been trying to break down these rules, but it is hard to do by law; the old customs linger. The whole village system tends to enforce what has been, and to oppose what might be. (Schramm 1964, 7)

Wasn't this exactly the situation Lerner had found in Balgat a decade earlier, before the road to Ankara was built? Couldn't mass media, multiplying the efforts of an army of extension agents, break down the barriers to change as effectively here as in the Great Plains in the 1930s? It was an exhilarating idea.

Schramm went on to describe the dismal state of communication in the developing nations and reviewed research in various parts of the world on the contribution of communication to modernization. His conclusion was a call to arms to mobilize the mass media in support of national development:

But we must remember that the full power of mass communication has never been used, in any developing country, to push economic and social development forward. This is the really exciting question: how much could we increase the present rate of development, how much could we smooth out the difficulties of the "terrible ascent," how much further could we make our resources go, how much more could we contribute to the growth of informed, participating citizens in the new nations, if we were to put the resources of modern communication skillfully and fully behind economic and social development? (Schramm 1964, 271)

The Schramm book, which by 1985 had sold 14,000 copies, shifted the focus of the Lerner argument in two ways. One was to emphasize economic development as the outcome of the modernization process rather than political stability. The other was to raise the question, albeit in obscure language, of the relationship between mass media and government that was to split the West and supporters of a radical definition of national development in the NWIO debates.

Schramm typically wrote about economic *and* social development, as in the paragraph above. His research data focused on the former, but the latter was a common theme throughout the book:

It is very hard to argue against change based on assumptions that, other things being equal,

- knowledge is better than ignorance;
- health is better than disease;
- to eat is better than to be hungry;
- a comfortable standard of living is better than poverty;
- to participate actively in one's nation is better than to be isolated from it (Schramm 1964, 35).

Critics were later to reject *economic* growth as the main development goal in favor of vaguely defined objectives such as *social transformation, spiritual growth,* and *equity.* But Schramm's brief litany emphasized the necessity of creating wealth as an antecedent for any other kind of development. Hungry people cannot live on spiritual values and an inadequate economic pie will not advance development, no matter how evenly sliced.

Schramm's second change in emphasis was a consideration of how mass media could be mobilized to support the development process. None of the countries Lerner examined had a system of press and broadcasting that would be considered "free" by Western standards, a circumstance that has changed little in 30 years. But there is an assumption, more implicit than explicit, that competitive newspapers independent of government would emerge at a late stage of development along with multiple parties and free elections.

For Schramm, however, government was the prime force in directing national development efforts and that meant, inevitably, government involvement in mass media. The question was not whether government would promote and control mass communication, but what kind of control it would exercise and how it would involve itself in the development of mass media. In an essay on legal aspects of mass media and national development by Fernand Terrou, the director of the French Institute of the Press, written for the Schramm book, the issue was raised delicately:

> This mobilization [for development] sometimes means, inescapably, the taking over the management by the state of the great mass communication media. It is at this price that these techniques, especially radio, can be fully utilized, not only under the conditions analyzed in this book, for economic and social development, but also (for all these tasks go together) for political unification and the creation of a real "public opinion." (Schramm 1964, 239)

"Political unification" and "real public opinion" were precisely the buzzwords that advocates of radical new global orders used later to defend their definition of national development, which seem to have nothing in common with Schramm's vision. But Schramm inventoried the catalog of mass media — radio, television, newspapers, films, even news agencies — and found some role for government in each. From the perspective of the 1980s, the question is how Schramm was able to advocate a role for mass media in national development in which government ownership or influence was the norm.

The answer is partly in the changed character of the issues. At that time few challenged the assumption that Western-style institutions were the goal of newly independent countries, and controlled media were seen as a temporary staging point along the route of development in the same way that authoritarian governments can be supported as part of an evolution toward democracy.

A second and more important reason for Schramm's advocacy of media development even where government dominated the mass media was that the model of government media cited in these forums was not a dictatorship but the more familiar and successful United States agricultural extension service. In fact, many of the studies of innovation — exactly the kind of changes in attitude and behavior that made up the core of "modernization" as Lerner and Schramm defined it — were carried out originally in the United States. Getting farmers in the Midwest to adopt new varieties of seed and new techniques of planting and erosion control was not much different from getting the Bvani family to increase rice production. In both societies the government was the force pressing for change and mass media were a key link in the effort.

The link between academics and policy makers was well established in the United States. In the context of communication development that link grew directly out of the experience of agriculture extension, where local agents working for the great state universities had written newspaper columns, produced radio programs, and distributed pamphlets that offered guidance for more efficient farming and homemaking, improved health and safety and, above all, education.

It was not surprising that some of these same universities took the lead in research in Third World communication development and in training a generation of Third World leaders committed to helping their nations ease the terrible ascent to modernity. From Michigan State and Wisconsin to Stanford and on to the new East-West Center at the University of Hawaii, the Lerner and Schramm volumes served as a guide for research and a beacon for action.

And there was action. In Latin America, Asia, and Africa, the bureaucracy of international aid — the new United States Agency for International Development (USAID), the United States Information Agency (USIA), and Peace Corps, the agencies of the United Nations system and a host of private international organizations — set out to harness the power of mass media to create in decades the kind of stable, comfortable democracies that had emerged in the Northern Hemisphere over centuries.

COMMUNICATION DEVELOPMENT IN ACTION

Despite the extravagant promises of the Lerner model and the emphasis given to communication development in United Nations resolutions, printing press and radios never replaced guns and surplus butter in aid programs. In fact communication never was — and still is not — a major component of development programs. Transport and communication combined, mostly the former, represented only 13 percent of the United Nations Development Program $669 million expenditure in 1980. World Bank loans for telecommunications maintained a steady $100 million a year through the decade, but as a percentage of total bank loans dropped to slightly more than one percent. According to a Unesco estimate, communication development to Third World countries totaled $267 million in 1978–1979, a figure that represented only one percent of all aid commitments. The total seems impressive until one remembers that it had to be apportioned among more than 100 countries and applied to immediate requirements totaling $15–20 billion.

For the United States, communication development presented a dilemma. On one hand, most of the national efforts were administered by government agencies and, of course, paid for by public funds. But the strong tradition of separation between government and mass media made it difficult to provide government support for mass media overseas that would be unconstitutional at home. As a result, most of the American efforts, which totaled several million dollars a year, went into development of support communication rather than mass media directly. Support communication added a communication component to development projects in health, education, agriculture, and family planning. Projects typically followed the extension service model and concentrated more on expanding existing media to carry a message encouraging "modern" behavior than on the construction of new media systems.

Other nations, however, were less sensitive about breaching the wall between government and mass media, if a wall even existed, and were willing to direct their aid efforts to the establishment or expansion of newspapers, radio, and television systems, and news agencies. Unesco itself, which became the major United Nations agency concerned which communication development, contributed advice, but not much money. In conferences, consultations, resolutions, and country studies, Unesco continued to hammer away at the need to develop mass media and to integrate communication into overall national development projects.

Meanwhile, in the United States, the modest and sometimes hesitant commitment of aid money to development projects was overshadowed by the nation's continuing academic influence. Major universities carried out research, usually with government grants, and continued to train Third World students who returned to their own countries to apply the development model to countries as disparate as Venezuela, India, and Egypt. But enthusiasm was beginning to wane, especially in academia.

By 1970 the results of a decade of communication development efforts were in. They were mixed at best and, at worst, interpreted as evidence of the failure of mass media to accelerate economic and political development. In retrospect it is surprising that the essentially Western model of development lasted as long as it did. By the time the Schramm book was published in 1964, the glittering promise of Kennedy's New Frontier was already lost and about to be replaced by the series of tragedies that seemed to make the decade of the 1960s a watershed in so many ways: political assassinations, civil rights violence and, of course, Vietnam.

So much had changed in the United States and the world between 1960 and 1970 that it is not surprising to find the model of communication development that inspired Third World leaders in 1960 turned on its head a decade later. Now the Western virtues of free expression were seen as a disguise for a new form of colonialism and Western efforts to aid communication development were interpreted as a ruse to maintain an economic and political system that exploited Third World countries as much as eighteenth and nineteenth century colonialism. What was called for in 1970 was not the continuation of expansion of the old Western communication model into the Third World, but a new world information order built on a new economic order.

RETHINKING DEVELOPMENT

The early crusaders against Third World underdevelopment were naive, of course. Schramm, reflecting on the history of communication development for the MacBride Commission, which was appointed by Unesco to assess the very political issues of international communication in the 1970s, noted how simple the problem had appeared two decades earlier. Then, rapid growth seemed to require only the judicious investment of money here and there in key sectors of the society and its effects would be multiplied and extended by mass media.

Part of the frustration that grew among development theorists and practitioners resulted from the failures of early programs. It was not always easy to change old ways of life, but sometimes the Bvani and Ife families were more than ready to accept change; it was the rigid political, social, and economic system that would not allow them to achieve their new goals.

At other times, the new, "modern" practices, which were transplanted from the West in the development programs, seemed out of place. They disrupted — but could never fully replace — the old ways. The result was an uprooting of traditional society and its replacement with bits and pieces of modern Western society scattered unevenly over the wreckage. It was the incongruity of urban slum dwellers watching American television programs in shacks where the only electricity flowed through a jerry-built line to the TV set. It was the ubiquity of Coca-Cola in countries where most of the population lacked access to clean water.

These frustrations were fertile ground for sweeping criticisms later, but in the mid-1960s, the critics were still faint voices. At this point there was enough dissatisfaction with the real and alleged failures of development programs and the growing sense that the Third World was paying a high price for a style of modernity that did not fit.

In 1964, the same year Schramm's *Mass Media and National Development* appeared, a conference at the East-West Center in Hawaii provided a forum for the faint voices of criticism. Part of the frustration resulted from the failure of newly independent Third World regimes to accomplish much in the first heady years of freedom; however, the frustration represented something more than growing pains. At one level it was a yearning for a definition of modernity that did not center on industrialization; at another, it was the posing of a counter model to the "materialist" West by extolling the "spiritual" East.

At the conference, the burden of arguing the irrelevance of the Western model was carried by Chaudry Inayatullah, a Pakistani development official then at the East-West Center. His arguments were not new but contained a stridency that had not appeared in the development debate. He argued that the first generation of Third World leaders, most of them trained in the West, had been duped:

> The intellectuals [of emerging countries] ... hold now their own society and culture responsible for its decadence and are ready to reject it, transform it, change it, and in extreme cases destroy it. The political and bureaucratic elite, forcibly modernized (Westernized?) earlier by colonial regimes and alienated from the traditional society, equipped with powers of the state, unhindered by democratic processes, resting on a narrow political base, comfort their guilty conscience and seek legitimacy for their newly acquired power in transforming these societies into powerful and respectable ones. (Lerner and Schramm 1967, 100)

Inayatullah argued that the charge of cultural imperialism — an early use of the phrase that became a code word in the 1970s — could not be levied as long as Third World leaders themselves promoted the Western model. Authentic Third World development, he argued vaguely, was built on emancipation of Third World countries from control of other nations, even at the price of severing the kind of links that aid programs fostered.

A Utopian view of society? A romanticized picture of the Third World? Lerner seemed to think so. While acknowledging the frustrations and failures of the first decade of development, he refused to acknowledge the split between East and West claimed by Inayatullah. He called it a false dichotomy that "serves merely to camouflage apathy and fatalism. . . . What I reject is the equation of spirituality with poverty, disease, ignorance, and apathy among the helpless peoples of Asia."

Western observers at the conference were perplexed to hear Third World advocates talk of a separate "Third World reality," as though the principles of science changed at national borders or rules of logic operated differently in the Southern Hemisphere. But the idea gained strength. On one hand, it expressed the distaste for the negative consequences of rapid development that early advocates had not anticipated; on the other, it was a harbinger of the new world information order debate that called Western communication resources incompatible with Third World reality, then demanded their transfer to the Third World as a matter of right.

The issues of how Third World development should be defined and how communication resources should be mobilized in its support became the central questions of debate as the 1960s wore on and formed the centerpiece of a second conference in Hawaii in 1974.

There, Schramm noted some of the dramatic events that had taken place since the first conference: men had walked on the moon, China had become a major player in world politics, OPEC had upset the old economic order, the United States had begun to extricate itself from Vietnam, and Third World countries had become a majority in the United Nations General Assembly. After reviewing economic progress in the Third World (mixed) and growth of radio and TV (dramatic), participants turned again to the central question that had perplexed the first two decades of concerted communication development efforts: How, if at all, did communication contribute to development? By this time, however, even the definition of development was in question.

If anything, the conference participants seemed to be groping for new ways to address the development issue. The phrases "new model," "new paradigm" and the like were heard frequently. Lerner himself was ready to accept the obsolescence of his own pioneering research. But he cautioned against the temptation to make too much of the notion of varieties of development or culture-specific models. He urged a global perspective and denied any kind of unique Third World "reality" that demanded a non-Western theory of development.

His main antagonist at the earlier conference, Inayatullah, had also mellowed. He acknowledged the Western model was less rigid and overlapped more with what he saw as the outline of an authentic Asian model of communication development. Probably the most important contribution was made by Everett M. Rogers, by then Schramm's successor at Stanford. In a long look at the history and findings of research in the diffusion of innovations, Rogers pulled together the threads of the new definition of development for which the conferees were groping.

Rogers' presentation was especially important because it articulated many of the concerns that others had tried to express. Beyond that, it gave them authority. Rogers was a leading figure in communication development research and had been strongly identified with the Lerner-Schramm approach. His acknowledgment of much of the criticism of the old way of looking at development, although not a complete renunciation of it, helped make the more radical critics respectable.

After retracing how the first generation of researchers and policy makers had approached development — capital-intensive technology, economic growth, quantification — and some of the intellectual criticisms of it, Rogers noted events in the late 1960s and 1970s that challenged their faith. The first was evolution of environmental pollution in the industrialized world as a major social issue. It raised the question whether heavy industrialization supported by high technology was the appropriate engine for Third World development.

The second event was the world oil crisis in 1973, which showed that a favored few Third World countries fortunate enough to be located over oil reserves could humble the industrialized nations to a degree not even the most radical critics of the West had dreamed of.

The third event, and probably the most important politically in the 1970s, was the reestablishment of normal relations between the People's Republic of China and the rest of the world. By this time much of the Third World had identified with the growing Non-Aligned Movement, rejecting both the capitalist model of Western development and the socialist model of the Soviet Union. China, which had challenged the Soviet Union's claim to leadership of revolutionary communism a decade earlier, now offered a new vision for development. China had set about modernization independent of both the West and the Soviet Union. Its approach to the task of rapid development was very different from that advanced by Lerner and Schramm, and from the outside it looked like a success story. Rogers put it this way:

> Here was one of the poorest countries, and the largest, that in two decades had created a miracle of modernization. A public health and family planning system that was envied by the richest nations. Well-fed and -clothed citizens. Increasing equality. An enviable status for women. And all this was accomplished with very little foreign assistance and presumably without much capitalistic competition. China, and to a lesser extent Cuba, Tanzania and Chile (in the early 1970s), suggested that there might be alternatives to the dominant paradigm. (Rogers 1976, 129–130)

In contrast, Rogers pointed to the unimpressive record of development under Western tutelege: "further stagnation, a greater concentration of income and power, high unemployment and food shortages in these nations." If Lerner found that the product of the first decade of development was mostly a revolution of rising frustrations, Rogers' assessment was even more bleak. Was it time to redefine development?

The Rogers paper sketched the elements of a new definition of modernity:

1. Emphasis on the equality of distribution of information and socioeconomic benefits with priority in development plans to rural areas and the urban poor;
2. Popular participation in self-development planning and execution and decentralization of authority and responsibility;
3. Self-reliance and independence in development, relying on local resources;
4. Integration of traditional and modern systems and values, such as the use of both acupuncture and antibiotics in Chinese medicine.

Finally, Rogers attempted a new definition of *development* itself. Repeating what Inayatullah had said at the first conference, Rogers argued that development should emphasize the idea of control: people getting control of their own lives, nations getting control over their own destinies. Such a goal, Rogers noted delicately, might require developing nations "to forego certain advantages of liberal democracy for the tighter government control that they thought to be necessary to maintain nationhood over tribal, religious, or regional factions," a point that Schramm also had made in his still influential book.

By the time the Rogers paper was presented, the old approach to

Third World development was clearly on the defensive. What had been a distrust of a too-Western model had opened the floodgates to a major ideological issue: Were Western values and politics being used to replace the imperial armies with a new form of cultural imperialism?

Even before the second Hawaii conference, in fact, all the pieces for an frontal assault on the original idea of how communication could promote development were in place: the frustration from the failure of early efforts to promote rapid growth, the unexpected negative effects of rapid change in the Third World, and the growing acceptance of voices that openly rejected the West as a model for the rest of the world.

The doubts and hesitations that plagued the original development theorists strengthened the hand of advocates of a radical alternative, who became the dominant architects of a new world information order in the 1970s. Built on a foundation of Marxist theology and a redistribution of global economic resources as part of a new economic order, the call for new world information order demanded not only a redistribution of the world's information resources but also a full mobilization of mass media in support of the new, radical definition of Third World development.

In the new order, development was defined as disengagement from the existing information system and its replacement with something that would promote the still undefined authentic Third World realities. News was information that promoted the new order, and the new agents of change were not the extension worker and teacher but journalists.

Not surprisingly, the arena where the new global information order took form was not the conference rooms in Hawaii or lecture halls at Stanford or even the villages of the Third World where the fight against poverty and illiteracy continued. The communication development debate shifted from villages like Balgat to Paris and the modern building that houses Unesco.

Collision with a New Order

THE RADICAL ALTERNATIVE

Jeremy Tunstall, a British sociologist who has written extensively on the dominance of Anglo-American mass media in the world, argued that the emergence of Unesco as a leading advocate of a new information order rejecting many of the principles that had guided its activities into the 1970s, was a takeover of the organization less by Moscow or Havana than by France itself. Unesco's leap leftward, he wrote, was "a leap from the communication schools on the right bank of the Ohio River to the cafes on the left bank of the River Seine."

The allusion was clever and contained a good bit of truth. When the confidence of the first generation of nation builders faltered it was a generation of Marxist intellectuals who seized the banner of development, but as Tunstall notes, it was a style of Marxism "that goes down better in Belgrade or Boston than in Moscow." The coalition of Western and Third World intellectuals, like their forebears who made pilgrimages to the Soviet Union in the 1930s, were still looking for a leftist future that worked. The takeover of the development debate occurred when the old vision of development, already losing legitimacy, was overrun by the intellectual Marxist vision of the future that was picking up speed in the academy and, most of all, in Unesco.

It was probably inevitable that communication development would be overtaken by neo-imperialism, which is at the core of what Tunstall defines as French literary Marxism, and that the center of gravity would slide to Paris. "Unesco," he argued, "after long residence as an

American-in-Paris, has finally gone native and become simply a Parisian in Paris.'' In communication development, however, most of the leading voices were not French and a surprising number were American. The accent of the new rhetoric was less Parisian than Californian with an overlay of Latin American Spanish.

Three strands, all critical of various aspects of the traditional approach to communication development and all relying on Marxist analysis, formed the basis of the new and radical approach to the problem of communication development. Together they provided the groundwork for calls for the restructuring of the world's economic and information systems that occupied Unesco for most of the 1970s.

CULTURAL IMPERIALISM

The first strand was represented by Herbert Schiller who articulated the tenets of a theology of an American information empire. Schiller's perspective allied him with an impressive list of Marxists and neo-Marxists, people like Kaarle Nordenstreng, the Finnish president of the International Organization of Journalists; Mustapha Masmoudi, the Tunisian minister of information who, more than anyone else, brought the new world information order issue before the Unesco; and Juan Somavia, a Chilean who was executive director of the leftist Latin American Institute for Transnational Studies in Mexico City.

In a series of books, Schiller linked major segments of the American economy to a conscious effort to use mass media and other forms of communications to stride across the world in a way reminiscent of the imperial armies of earlier centuries:

> Unavailable to expansionists of earlier times, modern mass communications perform a double service for their present-day controllers....
> Abroad, the antagonism to a renewed though perhaps less apparent colonial servitude, has been quite successfully (to date) deflected and confused by the images and messages which originate in the United States but which flow continuously over and through local informational media....
>
> Expanding across all continents, the sphere [of American investment and trade] grows significantly larger year by year. A powerful communications system exists to secure, not grudging submission by an open-armed allegiance in the penetrated areas, but by identifying the American presence with freedom — freedom of trade, freedom of speech and freedom of enterprise. (Schiller 1971, pp. 2–3)

Over the years Schiller and a growing band of supporters moved away from the simple view that the U.S. government was the guiding force behind this new colonialism and toward the transnational corporation (TNC) or multinational corporation (MNC) as the chief villain. By the mid-1970s, a new element was added to this argument — the conceptualization of the United States as an "information society" or "information economy." In this view, the decline of Western or American political and economic power was offset by information, the new medium of wealth and influence. Schiller, like many other contemporary critics of the United States, found abuse of the First Amendment:

> Any attempts by foreign countries to regulate the flow of information across their borders are regarded as interference with the 'free flow of information." . . . By conferring on billion-dollar private combines the [First Amendment] right of the individual to free speech, the government is weakening legitimate concern for genuine individual liberties. And its attempt to impose American laws and institutions on other countries encourages chauvinism abroad and at home. (Schiller 1982, 33)

Such a view came as a shock to those who came of age on the Lerner-Schramm approach to communication development and even more to those who assumed that the libertarian principles of the First Amendment represented a universal ideal. The arguments advanced by Schiller and others of the "cultural imperialism" school were more than an embellishment of Inayatullah's contention at the Hawaii conferences about the difference between the "spiritual" East and "material" West. They linked the information order debate to the broader issue of national development that defined development not as emulation of the industrial West but as disengagement from it.

DEPENDENCY AND DEVELOPMENT

The arguments of cultural imperialism struck a responsive chord among those who argued against the irrelevance or malediction of the early idea of communication development. Here was more than evidence of the failure of early efforts to use mass media; here was an argument that explained why traditional development was bound to fail. And why a revolutionary solution was needed.

Schiller's early work on mass communication does not bear any acknowledgment of influence by a group of mostly Latin American Marxist development theorists, but the similarity is strong. His dependency theories examined the global economic system and found "imperial centers," notably the United States, which controlled the flow of goods, services, and capital from those centers to nations on the periphery of the system. Economic development at the periphery — mostly Third World countries — was shaped to strengthen the dominance of the center nations and to maintain the peripheral nations' positions of dependence.

Although the original formulations of the dependency arguments were mostly by economists and political scientists who examined traditional components of international trade and politics, the framework fit neatly around the arguments generated by the advocates of information imperialism. In fact the two schools were almost symbiotic because the communications approach emphasized information as the new medium of power, thus accounting for the relative decline of Western economic and military power but continued dominance in world affairs. For those more attuned to the *cultural* dominance issue, the failure of advocates of a new order to generate any plausible alternative to the West could also be explained by assertions that dependent development required subjugation and even extermination of indigenous cultures that could threaten the dominant powers or offer alternative models.

Careful reading of the dependency development literature is hard going. Most of it is notable for an absence of clear definitions of fundamental terms like *imperialism* and an almost total lack of empirical evidence to support the arguments. Of course, it is based on dialectical reasoning, which is unfamiliar and foreign to many of the participants in the communication development debate. In fact the very research methods by which the issues of communication development were pursued also became a part of the challenge to the dominant paradigm and represent the third strand in the debate that brought academics and policymakers together at Unesco in the 1970s.

THE UNIVERSITY CONNECTION

As good American social scientists, Lerner and Schramm were cautious in assessing mass media's impact on economic and social change, attentive to the quantity and quality of evidence and, for the most part, reliant on statistics. Not so when the call for a new approach to communication development came to the fore.

It is curious that a research methodology could be an element of disagreement over a substantive area like communication development. Physicists often argue over theory, but seldom over data. Social science is different. Part of the problem is that communications, as Schramm once put it, is less a discipline than a crossroads where scholars from many disciplines pass but seldom linger. And even among those who do stay, different intellectual backgrounds produce different ways of looking at the world. In the highly politicized atmosphere of communication development research, there was disagreement over evidence and even more disagreement over where one ought to look to find the causes of and cures for the unhappy state of Third World development.

Was American-style research looking in the wrong place, or worse, helping to strengthen the existing global system, which was responsible for the problem in the first place?

In the United States, where the first generation of scholarship on communication development grew, the main roots of communication research were psychology and social psychology. Both shared the intellectual traditions of Anglo-American science, which emphasized reduction as a goal, empiricism as a method, and attention to reliability and validity of observation as protection against false inferences. Caution and intellectual conservatism are the hallmarks of this largely Anglo-American tradition, both of which are apostasy to Marxism with its literary generalizations, dialectical reasoning, and contempt for empirical testing. Many of the new communication scholars, particularly the second generation that accepted cultural imperialism and dependency theory as elements of a political creed, found the old, cautious methods inadequate.

Their first objection was that the traditional methods of social science — the sample survey, content analysis of news media, and the controlled experiment — removed people from the broad social environment that was precisely the most influential factor. Luis Beltran was typical of the new breed. A native of Bolivia, Beltran earned a doctorate at Michigan State, one of the most impregnable of the empirical research fortresses, before he embraced the new model of development.

In an impassioned critique of "alien" — that is, American — communication research, he argued that by focusing on the individual, research missed the context in which individual behavior occurred. He meant the very economic and political underpinnings of the nation and indeed the global system into which it was integrated. The argument that American communication science addressed the wrong questions was raised by others as well. The criticism was not merely that research in the tradition of Lerner and Schramm was irrelevant; radical critics such as Beltran argued that the theories and methods of American communication science were part of an ideology it could not escape.

Beltran, often citing American scholars for support, even argued that the Anglo-Saxon Protestant ethic and spirit of capitalism influenced what he called the "within-individual" approach that put most of the responsibility for underdevelopment on the individual rather than on the political and economic social system within which he struggled for survival.

Beltran's prescription called for scientists to recognize the ideology of their theories and to throw off the pretenses of dispassionate scholarly objectivity. A new generation of development researchers in Latin America was responding to this call, he said, some committed to revolution, some merely committed to research in support of political objectives: "The scientist should not disguise his militant convictions in scientific garments." Beyond the rhetoric, though, the radical critics shared more with the disciples of Lerner and Schramm than they acknowledged. Both camps believed that mass media could multiply efforts to induce social change. Both believed that new communication technology from the West could speed the process. And when development projects from both groups were laid out in detail, they looked a lot alike: governments or some representatives of them made use of some system of mass media to promote some kind of social change among individuals. Neither the most conservative nor most radical regime allowed communication development to support a revolution against itself.

The "revolutionary" researchers were, of course, committed to revolution against the old style of communication development and the mostly capitalist system on which it was based. Therefore they tended to focus their research on that part of the global system. A continuing embarrassment was the failure of those regimes already organized around Marxist ideology to demonstrate a superior record of development and certainly to demonstrate that the blatant and harsh propaganda that passed as development information had any power to mobilize people or even to hold their attention.

Beltran's call to arms was characteristic of a new style of research and a new generation of researchers who openly disdained the neutrality of traditional methods and the cooperation — they might say complicity — of academics in Western government and private sector development programs. Although the new style of "critical analysis" research, openly ideological and Marxist, sweeping in scope, and generally contemptuous of empirical evidence, became fashionable with a small but significant segment of American development researchers in the early 1980s, it was in the political debates of Unesco in the 1970s that critical analysis research first found a hospitable reception.

UNESCO AND THE NEW ORDER

The Unesco debate over the dominance of Western influence in world news flow, communication technology, and popular culture — the issues that collectively defined the new world information order debate — had little to do with communication development as it had been defined and promoted in the 1950s and 1960s. But the call for transfer of information resources as a part of a new order inescapably raised questions of what was meant by development and how mass media could promote it. From the American and European academies and Left Bank cafes where the theories of dependency and cultural imperialism were now flourishing came very different answers than those heard a generation earlier.

When the issue of communication development arose in the Unesco debates over new global economic and information orders, development was defined as the creation of true sovereignty and independence from the West. That meant the disengagement of Third World mass media from the existing Western-dominated system and rejection of some of its most cherished ideals. For Unesco this was a complete turnabout from its founding after World War II and its sponsorship of Schramm's study.

The United Nations and Unesco, one of its many specialized agencies, from their founding were involved in communication issues, even the political aspects of communication. The original emphasis, however, was purely Western, and at the time the few developing-nation members were firmly in the Western camp. Both the United Nations' Declaration of Freedom of Information and its Universal Declaration of Human Rights, passed in the late 1940s, included strong statements about the right to seek and transmit information and the importance of a free flow of information.

The Unesco constitution, adopted when the organization was formed in 1945, contained similar language. Within the bureaucratic structure a Division of Free Flow of Information was established to carry out the organization's obligation "to promote the free flow of ideas by word or image."

Dissatisfaction with the free flow emphasis predated the 1970s, of course, but the complaints were muted because the West dominated the United Nations system in numbers and ideas in its early days. During the 1960s, as new nations joined the U.N., the voices of a militant Third World coalition, nurtured on theories of dependency and cultural imperialism and sympathetic to the alternative models of development in China and Cuba, found a hospitable forum. It is hard to trace the origins of this shift, but a starting point was a 1969 Unesco-sponsored meeting of communication experts in Montreal that acknowledged Western domin-ance of information flow and called for efforts to achieve a "two-way circulation of news" and "balanced circulation of news." Those two phrases became code words in the next decade for much of the debate on a new world information order.

The code words introduced new elements into the issue of commu-nication development. For one thing, they made it clear that communi-cation development did not mean simply using mass media to promote social and economic development in the image of the Western model. The notion of a "balanced circulation" of news implied that Western media needed to change as well as to give more coverage to the emerging nations that were shifting the voting power of the United Nations. The use of the word *news* also expanded the scope of communication development from an emphasis on mostly technical information related to health, agriculture, etc., to the politically sensitive question of what should be reported about a nation and who should decide. Finally, the broadened definition of development implied — even demanded — a full mobilization of national resources in support of national objectives, including, of course, the harnessing of any critical or even independent mass media.

In the decade of the 1970s, when the first generation of development theory came under attack from several directions, Unesco became the main forum at which communication development issues were defined and debated. In 1970 the Unesco General Conference, the biennial meeting of all Unesco members, authorized the secretary general to assist member states in the formation of their mass communication policies, an extension of earlier exhortations to Third World countries to plan their development and to coordinate various aspects of development.

The statement was vague and open to diverse interpretations. From the Western perspective it could refer to the development of a national system of telecommunictions or the kind of communication development efforts that had been going on for more than a decade. Western delegations seemed to choose those interpretations rather than the more inflammatory ones about harnessing the media to achieve narrow political goals.

Two years later, at the next General Conference, the Soviet Union stepped into the middle of the issue by introducing a resolution calling on the director general — the usual way for General Conferences to express the wishes of member states — to prepare a declaration on "the Fundamental Principles Governing the Use of the Mass Media with a View to Strengthening Peace and Understanding and Combating War, Propaganda, Racialism and Apartheid." Although the Soviet Union was not known for sophistication in public relations, the title of the proposed declarations was clever. It put the advocates of a new world information order on the side of peace and understanding. And those who argued against the resolution were lumped together with advocates of war, racism, and apartheid. The resolution drew together those who were unhappy about the way the Third World was presented in the dominant Western media, those who were frustrated about the failure of Third World development efforts to date, and those who saw the problem in the simple outlines of dependency theory and cultural imperialism.

This resolution became the focal point for the international debate over most of the rest of the decade. The issue was again debated at the 1974 General Conference, but no consensus was reached. Because most general conference resolutions are adopted by consensus rather than recorded vote, the conference took the only action it could. It postponed action and called for more study. After the 1974 meeting, the radical voices dominated the political maneuvering. A preliminary meeting of experts was held in Paris in December 1975, to draft a compromise resolution for consideration at the General Conference the following year. Thirteen Western delegations walked out of the meeting after a resolution equating Zionism with racism was adopted. That left the way open for the approval of a draft resolution introduced by the Soviet Union that would make governments responsible for the activities of mass media operating under their jurisdiction.

A similar tone was in evidence at a Unesco-sponsored regional meeting in Costa Rica in July 1976, where advocates of the dependency school pushed for recommendations compatible with those in the draft resolution adopted in Paris. At the Costa Rica meeting, however, was a delegation of observers from the Inter American Press Association (IAPA), a hemispheric organization most of whose members were publishers strongly committed to private ownership of mass media and hostile to any hint of government control. The IAPA delegation formed an ad hoc lobby that toned down some of the stronger proposals but was most influential in raising a warning cry to the U.S. news media industries about the philosophical and practical implications of the resolutions under discussion. The result was the formation of a 36-member umbrella group of independent journalistic organizations called the World Press Freedom Committee.

By this time, the debate had taken on a new name and a new ideological premise. The phrase *new world information order* — or sometimes new international information order or new international information and communication order — was shorthand for the complex arguments over the purpose of mass media as well as the efforts to promote communication development in the Third World. The phrase linked the information debate to a companion Unesco debate over the inequitable distribution of the world's economic resources. That debate had produced a Unesco declaration on a new world *economic* order in 1975 that called for a redistribution of economic resources as a matter of reparation for the exploitation of much of the Third World by colonial powers in earlier centuries. The new world information order called for a similar redistribution of information and communication resources for similar reasons. It recognized information as the coin of the new information age and argued from the premises of cultural imperialism that Western dominance in information was as much the result of exploitation of the Third World as North-South economic disparities.

The new world information order debate absorbed communication development issues into the broader question of the political role of mass media in the developing countries and, indeed, within the Western nations as well. An old argument was that an aloof, critical press was a luxury a fragile Third World democracy could not afford early in its ascent to modernity, but would evolve later along with a stable participatory political system. That, of course, was Lerner's vision. In the NWIO debate, however, an independent, critical press was considered a sham, a tool of the MNCs and TNCs that ran the global economic and political system.

Why are we even debating the value of press freedom? some Western media organizations asked, and they urged their governments to walk away from the issue. When the Reagan Administration, in the wake of a decade of such talk, announced its intention to withdraw from Unesco, it was cheered by an unusual assembly of newspapers that were critical of the administration's record in most other areas, especially its efforts to control information.

The politicization of the issue of communication development by subsuming it in the broader, more ideological, and certainly more public new world information order debate obscured the real needs of the Third World to improve its media systems. And it also clouded legitimate concerns about the meager and often uninformed attention the Western media paid to the developing world. It took a decade before the NWIO issue burned itself out enough for the real issues that faced the Third World and the West to reassert themselves.

When Unesco delegations assembled for their 1976 General Conference in Nairobi (the first time in the Third World), prospects for agreement on any statement of Third World needs or the uses of mass media were not good. On the table was the draft resolution from Paris with the clause making states responsible for news media. The Third World delegations, strong in number and considerably more assertive than at previous conferences, were more vociferous in their criticism of Western dominance and more willing to adopt the rhetoric of cultural imperialism. And the Western delegations had to accommodate aroused mass media organizations that were in the uncomfortable position of demanding their governments support resolutions that recognized the separation of state and media.

In the heated rhetoric of Nairobi it was clear that an acceptable compromise resolution could not be found. The director general of Unesco, the anticolonial revolutionary-turned-statesman from Senegal,

Amadou-Mathar M'Bow, especially wanted to avoid a collapse of the Third World's first general conference. Solution? More study.

The draft resolution was tabled and M'Bow was invited to undertake a review of "the totality of the problems of communication in modern society." Perhaps here, outside the contentious politics of the Unesco General Conference, a panel of dispassionate experts could define the new order and a new role for mass media in national development.

After four years of often heated argument, Unesco had still not been able to define the role of mass media, but the Nairobi conference was important. If nothing else the rhetoric of the issue seemed to consume itself; afterward, Western and especially Third World delegates seemed anxious to compromise and to grope their way toward common ground. At the same time, the new world information order debate became even less of an East-West issue and almost entirely a North-South issue, that is, an issue between the industrialized nations, mostly in the Northern Hemisphere, and the Third World countries, mostly in the Southern Hemisphere. In the shift the influence of the Soviet Union waned because the technology needed for communication development was available only in the West and because the ideals of Western democracy and independent journalism still commanded respect from many Third World journalists if not from many of the politicans who represented the developing nations in public forums.

For M'Bow and the small circle of advisers who directed Unesco's communication policies, the resolution of the communication issue became crucial even though communication activities represented a small part of the organization's varied and mostly apolitical programs. Some said his future at the organization depended on it. And there was even the question of the organization's future health because of rumblings in the U.S. Congress that it might suspend its contribution (as it had done in 1974 over treatment of Israel) or even withdraw. Unesco's active involvement in the international communication issues resulted in the congressional mandate for the State Department to determine periodically whether Unesco had taken any action to restrict the free flow of information or interfere with the activities of journalists. It was also a major — but probably not decisive — factor in the Reagan Administration's decision at the end of 1983 to withdraw entirely from Unesco.

For the 1978 General Conference, Unesco returned to its headquarters in Paris. For more than a month delegations worked in occasional plenary sessions and in five committees to grind out resolutions that had no force in any nation except the meager power of international public opinion. Most attention in Paris and in the press was on the committee that was assigned the responsibility of preparing an acceptable compromise resolution on the role of mass media. To begin its deliberations, it had a draft written at Unesco headquarters that endorsed the principle of government responsibility for mass media. The draft did not find favor with the Western delegations, however, and certainly not with the World Press Freedom Committee, which had nongovernment observer status at Unesco.

The picture that emerges from accounts of the conference reveals bitter high-stakes negotiations that are unusual for an organization like Unesco, whose proclamations commit no nation or person to anything. Thomas L. McPhail, whose account captures some of the drama of the Paris conference, concludes that M'Bow backed off his earlier support of the more radical draft resolution because of a fear that Western withdrawal from the organization or suspension of financial support could bring Unesco — and his career — crumbling around him. M'Bow himself took the chair at the crucial committee meeting where a compromise resolution was finally approved after considerable delay and all-night negotiating sessions. M'Bow's presence in the chair made it clear to the delegates that he expected them to accept the compromise, which was a vague, equivocal statement that pleased no one. The approval of the resolution by consensus at a final plenary was a formality.

The resolution was officially known as the Declaration on Fundamental Principles Concerning the Contribution of the Mass Media to Strengthening Peace and International Understanding, the Promotion of Human Rights and to Countering Racialism, Apartheid and Incitement to War. It contained 11 fairly short articles that, in typical compromise prose, were vague and even contradictory. Without knowledge of the earlier drafts and compromises behind the scenes, one could miss the importance of several code words. The "responsibilities" of mass media had been replaced with "contributions." The "balanced" flow of information and the "free" flow, which had been pitted against each other as code words for the two opposing positions on the role of mass media, were linked. The resolution called for "a free flow and wider and better balanced dissemination of information." The new code words were "free *and* balanced flow."

It is hard to know what the declaration on mass media accomplished aside from derailing an inevitable collision between two member camps with opposite ideas on the purpose and function of mass media and possibly paralyzing Unesco itself. The catch phrase "new world information order," which the resolution was supposed to embody, remained undefined.

The Unesco debates, however, did make communication development a political issue rather than a technical one. Questions about the "responsibilities" or "contributions" of mass media in areas as Pollyanna-ish as opposing war and racism did not come up in Lerner's work or even in Schramm's Unesco book. They also seemed to have little to do with real issues of national development, such as literacy and rural develop-ment. By the late 1970s, however, the issue was openly ideological and development itself had taken on a political meaning. No longer was development focused on Indian villages and African farmers; now it had to do with global and economic power and the purposes of mass media. Under the circumstances, it was not surprising that the only compromise Unesco's contentious membership could agree on was ambiguous to the point of saying everything to everyone. As a result, it also said nothing.

Two other items on the Unesco agenda at the end of the 1970s did contribute significantly to the issue of communication development. The first was the International Commission for the Study of Communication Problems, the MacBride Commission, which examined the state of global communications and development needs more thoroughly than anyone had ever done before. The second was the International Program for the Development of Communication, a new mechanism to channel renewed efforts to speed the unfinished job of communication develop-ment when the ideological debate finally diminished, a victim of excess and boredom. Both had important implications for communication development in the 1980s and 1990s.

THE MACBRIDE COMMISSION

The deadlock over communication at the 1976 General Conference in Nairobi was noted earlier. In the absence of any compromise statement on the topic, the conference invited M'Bow to undertake a review of "the totality of the problems of communication in modern society." M'Bow responded by naming a commission of 16 "wise men" and appointed Sean MacBride as chairman. MacBride had won both the Nobel Peace Prize and Lenin Peace Prize and had a distinguished career of service to the United Nations and his native Ireland.

Commission members were as diverse as Elie Able, of Stanford University, and Sergei Losev, director general of Tass. Inevitably, there were complaints about the commission's makeup: the Latin Americans were too leftist; the Asians were too rightist; Britain, whose contribution to a Western philosophy of liberty was immense, was not represented. Tunstall described the commission's key members as "a Tunisian, a Yugoslav, and an Irishman, a typical Left Bank trio." But despite the suspicions and lack of a clear mandate, the commission proceeded. It met for a total of 42 days, commissioned more than 100 papers, and rehashed the new world information order issues, including communication and development, more thoroughly than any previous forum had done. Its interim report was circulated for comment in more than 7,000 copies and was submitted to the Unesco General Conference in Paris in 1978.

The final draft represented a modest improvement in syntax but not much clarification in substance over the preliminary version; both were written mostly by the Unesco staff assigned to the commission. Like most compromise Unesco statements, the report acknowledged all arguments and all points of view. In some cases it read as though two drafts representing the two basic positions in the debate had been woven together with the phrase "But on the other hand" thrown in as a transition.

The report, aptly titled *Many Voices, One World*, was important, even if it did not give the kind of clear direction to a new definition of communication development that many had hoped for. It endorsed the traditional Western values of the free flow of information and freedom of speech and press, even though some U.S. broadcasters were critical of the commission's preference for noncommercial broadcasting. It also made a strong argument for the need to improve Third World mass media, a point which the Western bloc at Unesco had conceded in its acceptance of the "free and balanced flow" compromise.

M'Bow himself apparently was not satisfied with the report. In a perfunctory foreword to the published version he described it as a first stage and said the commission's work "must be continued and taken deeper." Ironically, a motion at the 1980 General Conference called for a kind of "son of MacBride" to define the new world information order — something the original did not try to do — but was ruled out of order by M'Bow after it was approved.

The commission's conclusions were cast as 82 specific recommendations, most of which dealt directly or indirectly with some aspect of communication development, as defined either by the old development-as-growth idea or the new development-as-independence approach. They were grouped under five general headings: strengthening independence and self-reliance (reasonable); social consequences and new tasks (ambiguous and worrisome in its suggestions of media responsibility); professional integrity and standards (no calls for licensing); democratization of communication (also ambiguous), and fostering international cooperation (also reasonable). The two areas that drew most comment from Western journalists were the recommendation to give preference to noncommercial broadcasting (to which Abel took exception) and one not to request special protection (and presumably licensing) for journalists.

Most of the recommendations were vague suggestions to give special attention to communication development and equally vague prescriptions for adapting the resources of information-rich Western nations to the needs of the Third World without sacrificing indigenous cultures and traditions. The rhetoric was different in 1980, but at a technical level the problems and needs of communication development were little changed from those in the village of Balgat in 1950. The report, however, did help to shift the new world information order debate away from the politically explosive questions of government and media responsibilities and toward the one area of common agreement, the need to work toward the common goal of a "balanced" flow of information around the world by increasing the Third World's capacity to produce and share information. The United States had a specific idea of how that could be done, even if the MacBride Commission did not.

IPDC

The MacBride Commission report was not submitted to the 1980 General Conference for ratification. Instead, most of the specific recommendations were incorporated, scattershot fashion, into other resolutions. Most of the interest in communication development, which had become the major thrust of the new world information order debate, was on a resolution establishing a new organization within Unesco to focus and expand development activities.

The idea of a "mechanism," the word used to avoid the suggestion of yet another layer of bureaucracy dealing with old problems, had been proposed by the United States at the 1978 General Conference. In proposing a new mechanism the United States delegation had hoped to defuse some of the anti-Western rhetoric by offering the technical assistance that most Third World countries wanted and needed but could get only in the West. The offers of assistance and especially the idea that became the International Program for the Development of Communication, however, were not well planned. The offer of advanced communication satellite technology to aid Third World rural development, for example, was put together the night before it was announced in Paris. And John Reinhardt, who was responsible for international communication policy during the Carter Administration as head of the then U.S. International Communication Agency, had little authority over or influence with other relevant government agencies.

IPDC was accepted, although not in exactly the form Reinhardt had envisioned. The General Conference resolution was suitably vague, specifying only that the program was "to increase cooperation and assistance for the development of communication infrastructures and to reduce the gap between various countries in the communication field." M'Bow, addressing the first meeting of the IPDC's 35-nation Intergovernmental Council in June 1981, identified three tasks for the council that represented the link between IPDC itself and the Unesco General Conference: determining projects to receive IPDC support; mobilizing resources, mostly financial, to carry them out; and devising rules under which the program could operate.

Even the advocates of a moderate interpretation of a new global order wanted something besides more handouts and certainly more than a wholesale dumping of obsolete Western communication equipment under the guise of technology transfer. For reasons that ranged from national pride to experience with earlier development assistance efforts, Third World representatives in IPDC wanted a decisive voice in the new programs to tackle the old problems of national development.

Organizing IPDC included matters of philosophy as well as procedure, and the Western nations succeeded in getting several key points accepted. One was to operate by consensus, which meant that the Western delegations could insist on compromises it could accept and would not be outvoted routinely by a majority of council members. A second was to accept financial support from all sources. That was a code phrase for participation by private mass media organizations, such as the World Press Freedom Committee and the International Press Institute, and inclusion of bilateral, government-to-government projects in support of IPDC objectives.

On another issue the United States was not as successful. IPDC originally was proposed as a clearinghouse for matching communication development needs and resources. That meant donor countries could pick and choose projects that they found acceptable from both pragmatic as well as ideological considerations. The word "clearinghouse," however, soon became a codeword and was rejected because it meant IPDC itself would not have the direct authority to allocate funds. The spirit of both the new world information order and new world economic order from which it derived demanded that information and economic resources be transferred from the North to the South as a matter of justice and that control of these resources be in the hands of the recipient Third World countries. The prospect of contributions supporting a school for journalists in Cuba or a news agency for the Palestine Liberation Organization, both of which were among the early project suggestions, in fact was enough for most Western delegations to reject the idea of turning over blank checks without any control of contributions. The United States said it would not contribute at all, although it promised to expand its bilateral development assistance in programs parallel to those of IPDC.

Most of the Western countries also had substantial communication development activities already built into bilateral aid programs and were not willing to shift those funds to IPDC. Former colonial powers typically focused their aid projects in former colonies; the Scandinavian nations, Germany, and Austria had extensive communication development packages that often supported moderate socialist regimes. The United States claimed it provided several million dollars a year in communication development. Some of the development support was built into USIA exchange and educational programs, but most was incorporated into USAID projects concerned directly with health, family planning, education, and agriculture.

In fact, from its beginning IPDC did accept funds with various strings attached. Most involved the pledging of money for specific projects or "in kind" contributions of technology, expertise, or training. The Soviet Union and German Democratic Republic made substantial pledges, but in local currency that could not be spent outside their countries.

When the IPDC Governing Council met for the first time in Acapulco in January 1982, it had before it a very large stack of project proposals, a very small stack of financial guarantees, and no clear criteria for matching the two. An early and reasonable decision was to emphasize regional and global projects and to give special attention to Africa, the least developed part of the Third World. In addition, priority was to be given to national planning for communications development; creation of infrastructures; institutional arrangements to facilitate news and cultural exchange; training in various aspects of development; enhancement of "development communications" in support of education, agriculture, health, and rural development; and increased access to the latest technologies, such as satellites and data banks.

The trouble, of course, was that this omitted nothing that smacked of national development. On the surface this plan of priorities did not sound much different from the outline of Schramm's book. "Planning" had been a key element of the Unesco litany for decades and did not seem to threaten press liberty. Nor did training, another old favorite, or "development communications," which had been the basis of American programs for two decades. When the project proposals were examined it was not so much the mechanisms to improve Third World communications as much as their goals that had changed. "Infrastructures" and "institutional arrangements" referred to organizations, such as the Pan-African News Agency, which was still a political prisoner of its sponsoring Organization of African Unity, and the Asian News Network, which later argued that it should be the single point of news flow between Asia and the rest of the world.

Still, the more exaggerated ideas had disappeared, and IPDC was a tangible expression of the Third World's continuing needs and the West's public commitment to do something about them. Compared with the rhetoric of the debate that had occupied Unesco a decade earlier, IPDC was a model of restraint and moderation.

More than 50 projects were proposed, about half of which benefited only one country. A review committee finally selected 19 projects for IPDC's freshman year. The 15 regional projects emphasized exchange of news and other programming as well as the development of mechanisms to facilitate intraregional flows. The three global projects all dealt with telecommunications. Only one national project, a broadcast training facility in Zimbabwe, was approved, but with bilateral funding from the Netherlands.

The list of approved projects carried a lifetime cost estimate of about $7 million, but IPDC allocated only $741,000 of its own meager funds to get them underway. Another $169,000 was approved to aid in the development of future projects. Total pledges amounted to about $6 million, but a majority of it was designated for specific projects, coordinated bilateral funding, or soft currency. In its important precedent-setting first year the organization had not set a course that its original supporters had envisioned, but on the other hand, it did show flexibility and pragmatism — traits the West encouraged.

Almost a year later the IPDC Governing Council met in Paris for a second round of project evaluation and funding. Eleven of the original projects were extended on a modest scale. The Pan African News Agency, which was the favorite of many of the Third World delegates and had been in the planning stage for more than a decade, got the largest allocation — $125,000 — even though it still had not produced a word of copy.

Seven new global and regional projects were approved. One that did not find favor among the Western delegates was $45,000 to the Organization of African Unity for the development of a "National Liberation Movement press." The United States did not object, however, because no regular Unesco funds were involved. One project that did have strong American support — $15,000 worth — was research on kenaf, a botanic relative of marijuana. A hardy shrub which can be grown rapidly in most parts of the world, from kenaf a good quality of newsprint can be produced. The kenaf project represented the kind of pragmatic project that the West wanted to promote. And it was proposed originally by the International Federation of Newspaper Publishers

(FIEJ), with strong support from the American Newspaper Publishers Association. This, according to William G. Harley, head of the American delegation, helped establish the principle of private sector involvement in IPDC, a point the organization had accepted reluctantly.

For the first time, except for the one token project in Zimbabwe approved the year before, the IPDC Intergovernmental Council voted funding for national projects. Fifteen got some money from IPDC and three others were to be funded through bilateral programs. Six other national projects were endorsed with the recommendation that non-IPDC funds be sought. Among the national projects the highest priority went to the development of national mass media and news agencies. Media development projects were approved in Gabon, Guinea, Guinea Bissau, Senegal, and Rwanda. Programs to establish or expand national news agencies were established in Cameroon, Senegal, Tanzania, Tunisia, Rwanda, and Togo.

The United States, which by prior agreement took over France's seat on the eight-nation executive bureau, earned a modest degree of respect by pledging an additional $100,000 to IPDC objectives through USAID bilateral assistance and $350,000 from USIA. The latter was in the form of a funds-in-trust grant with IPDC acting as fiscal agent. That brought the total American commitment to IPDC to almost a half-million dollars, although, of course, the money remained under American control.

Even after several years of operation, it was difficult to predict whether IPDC would work. A policy of supplying seed money only to a wide range of projects meant that none got the support it needed. Even well-funded projects like the Pan African News Agency, which finally got on the air after 10 years of talking, had a bad track record and little chance of success because the political structures on which they depended were themselves in disarray. Others, such as the assistance for national media and news agencies, could be expected to produce modest results at best because funding was at no more than token level. In most projects there was too much money for conferences and consultants and meetings and too little for communications hardware and hiring and training the people to get it into operation.

In fact, the list of projects that IPDC funded was not much different from the kind of activities that had defined communication development aid in the earlier generation. The United States had never funded a national news agency, but other countries had and they had been a priority for Unesco even before Schramm's book endorsed them. Regional exchange mechanisms, too, were nothing new; in the 1960s regional cooperation and integration was a major goal of American foreign aid. What better way to promote it than with a regional news or TV exchange?

Curiously, none of the discussions in or about IPDC paid much attention to the checkered history of communication development programs. Beyond a widely held but untested assumption that the first generation of assistance had failed, there was no apparent interest in examining what the earlier cadres of changes agents had tried, what they had accomplished, and where they had failed. It was a pity, because the new legions of change agents had to spend a lot of time reinventing old wheels and rediscovering old truths.

In the end, communication development in the 1980s looked a lot like it did in the 1960s. It was still using mass media to extend the reach of change agents, still educating people to be "modern," and still transferring Western technology. It could have learned from those who had tried the same things two decades earlier.

The Record of Communication Development

DEVELOPMENT IN ACTION

The Voice of Zaire operates from a modern miniskyscraper, built with French aid, at the edge of Kinshasa. In the newsroom for the radio service, located in a modest corner of the facility, serious young men sit at tables, editing and re-editing stories that appear slowly on a teletype printer from the News Agency of Zaire (AZaP). In the center of the room is a single manual typewriter and one telephone. The spartan facility produces news for the 30 million people of a country one-quarter the size of the United States. For many the radio is their only link to a world beyond their village or urban slum.

The Voice of Zaire building, only a few years old but already deteriorating, is typical of projects organized under the old style of communication development. Most emphasized high-tech communication facilities that would, in theory, allow the nation to accomplish in a few years what Western countries had done in centuries. In practice, projects seldom met their construction timetables or technical objectives and modern facilities began to decay, sometimes before the paint was dry.

The problem was more than spare parts and maintenance, more than the incongruity of the Voice of Zaire's glossy skyscraper, known locally as the white elephant, at the edge of a crowded city lacking adequate housing, medical facilities, and schools. The problem, the critics of communication development argued, was that modern, high-tech communication facilities merely reinforced the existing dependence of the Third World on the West. The new world information order was supposed to change that.

To officials of the Voice of Zaire, however, that criticism was irrelevant. They needed a facility that would allow them to reach the vast areas of the country, and Schramm and just about everyone else had argued that radio was the single medium that could circumvent obstacles of illiteracy and lack of roads. Throughout the Third World politicians could argue against the transplanting of glittering Western technology, but when it came to putting a development plan into action there was only one place to go. That was to the West for the best and most modern technology they could buy or beg.

Central to the style of communication development that reigned for more than a decade before it was challenged by the new global order debate was massive transfer of Western technology. Mass media themselves were created with the idea of promoting a litany of advancements, usually but not always in the countryside: literacy, better agriculture, improved health and sanitation, birth control. Telecommunication systems, too, were built or expanded, and all the efforts were supposed to be tied together as the core of a nation's leap toward modernization.

In retrospect, building a new facility to promote development was the easy part. The real problem in the early days of communication development assistance projects was weaving a communication project into a larger cloth of development. Getting all the other pieces into place and getting everything moving on time and in the right direction; that was the hard part.

The only way to do it, Schramm argued, was to integrate communication into a broader context of national planning and to give communication the attention it deserved. Without that, the magic multiplier could not work.

COMMUNICATION PLANNING

The Voice of Zaire's white elephant presumably was the product of some plan that specified how radio was to fit into a broader scheme of the nation's economic, political, and social development. But with the eccentric Mobutu dictating virtually every aspect of Zaire's national life, we cannot be sure. The importance of communication planning, like the basic tenets of the Lerner-Schramm theory of development, seemed so obvious that calling attention to it was like pointing out that water is wet. But emphasizing the obvious does not mean that it will be heeded. And something that seems simple in principle can get horribly difficult in practice.

The importance of communication planning that Schramm stressed in 1964 was repeated in all the literature since then. Whether supporting the original simple vision of rapid political and economic growth or radical alternatives, writers as diverse as Schramm himself and Cees Hamelink, a Dutch leader of the neo-Marxist school, called on developing nations to decide first what they want to accomplish in communication, then develop a realistic plan to reach their goals.

Schramm even attributed the failure of communication development to a lack of commitment to it and argued that the best guarantee of that commitment was "a well-thought-out plan that integrates the development of mass communication into the general pattern of social and economic development." Twenty years later, Hamelink argued that authentic development independent of the West could come about when "a country starts with the principle of self-reliance and selects elements that are conducive to long-range cultural autonomy." From either the traditional or radical perspective, development meant starting with a good plan.

For Unesco itself, communication planning assumed the proportions of a crusade both in the heyday of the early optimistic idea of communication development and after. In the mid-1970s Unesco began to issue a series of monographs on national communication policies. They covered countries as diverse as Ireland and India, but focused mostly on the Third World.

All of the monographs chronicled basic laws and detailed the complexities of media systems, but none could identify a comprehensive national plan for communication development. What are the goals of our national development? What part does communication development play? How are we going to reach the goals? How do we now if we are making progress? One could find few answers to such basic questions in the monographs or in a second Unesco series devoted specifically to the communication planning.

The first monographs were written from a journalistic perspective, the latter series from the theoretical perspective of the economist and business school professor and were filled with models and technical language. Even the second monograph in the series published in 1981 could cite only one pertinent case study based on contemporary theory, a long-range communication system planning survey in Afghanistan.

The survey, carried out by Unesco and the International Telecommunications Union with money provided by the Federal Republic of Germany, produced, as most such projects did, a report, but little else. Some of the gaps between the assumptions and what Alan Hancock, a

Unesco official who wrote the study, called "reality" are illustrative of the hazards of the communication planner's craft:

- ASSUMPTION: It is possible to draw up a long-term (10–15 years) communication plan. Reality: The possibility has been proven; there is, however, the problem of getting bogged down in the present.
- ASSUMPTION: Decision-making is based on rational, logical analysis: on cost-benefit studies, for example. REALITY: Decisions on important and basic matters are made on arbitrary or political consideration.
- ASSUMPTION: A coherent communication policy exists and can be culled from official documents. REALITY: An explicit, coherent communication policy did not seem to exist; the task of trying to cull it directly from documents was an impossible one.
- ASSUMPTION: The host country has a high level of interest in the communication planning exercise and attaches importance to it. REALITY: This cannot be assumed. (Hancock 1981, 104–105.)

The report was not widely distributed or acted on, "principally owing to political events in Afghanistan," as Hancock discreetly put it.

Unfortunately, the Afghanistan experience was not a fluke, even though most efforts to develop a comprehensive plan were not interrupted by a military invasion. Still, after the MacBride Commission surveyed the whole spectrum of international communication issues nearly two decades after Schramm's influential book appeared, its first recommendation dealt with planning:

[We recommend that] communication no longer be regarded merely as an incidental service and its development left to chance. Recognition of its potential warrants the formulation by all nations, and particularly developing nations, of comprehensive communication policies linked to overall social, cultural, economic and political goals. Such policies should be based on inter-ministerial and inter-disciplinary consultations with broad public participation. (International Commission for the Study of Communication Problems 1980, 254–255)

The MacBride report's conclusion was a vague prescription that offered little new inspiration to a Third World government or practical guidance to its bureaucrats. That was not surprising given the divergent views within the commission — and within the Third World itself in the 1980s — over the definition of development and the contribution of communication to it. What was dismaying, however, was the lack of learning from the two decades of experience with communication development. If more clearly written, the MacBride Commission's recommendations could have been included in Schramm's 1964 book.

To find out something about how communication development principles were applied in the early days we need to go beyond the pleas for planning and vagaries of planning documents. The biggest part of development programs was focused on rural development, and here we can see how the ambitious and optimistic vision of rapid social and economic change fared against the realities of Third World poverty, illiteracy, and inertia.

RURAL DEVELOPMENT

The gap between the vision of a typical national development plan and the reality of an isolated Third World Village is immense. It is not surprising, therefore, that efforts to use information to promote rural development formed the core of communication development programs or that the record of accomplishment was mixed at best. Even projects generated under the rubric of the radical goal of "authentic" non-Western development more often than not addressed old problems with old techniques covered with a gloss of new rhetoric.

The typical rural development project, whether organized in the 1980s under the banner of the new world information order, described in the 1964 Schramm book or even undertaken in the 1930s in the American dustbowl, began with a serious problem and a worthy objective of alleviating it: reduce the birth rate, improve crop production through better agricultural techniques, promote adoption of a health practice. The project usually involved a test phase in a relatively limited location. For the traditional communication researcher, isolated villages were ideal because they could be used for various kinds of experimental manipulations and evaluations.

During the test itself, information explaining and advocating the change was introduced. Usually the information campaign centered on an authority figure or "change agent," such as an extension worker or specialist from the capital, who explained the innovation and encouraged a few adventuresome villagers to adopt it. With luck the benefits of the change were apparent to others who then, in increasing numbers, began to accept it as well. Finally, the practice became an integral part of village life and the change agent moved on to other villages or introduced other innovations.

The promise of mass media was that, as Lerner and Schramm

predicted, they could be the great multipliers. What one agricultural agent could do in a single village, radio and later television could do in a hundred or a thousand villages simultaneously. Some projects even envisioned great campaigns of modernization reaching even the remotest villages at the same moment through the miracle of new communication technology.

It did not take long, however, for promoters of rural development to identify a catalog of things that could go wrong, even in authoritarian systems. Centralized media campaigns often ignored local sensitivities or conditions; innovations sometimes produced unintended and unforeseen changes in the complex social fabric of the community that offset the advantages of the innovation; people in the villages frequently did not share national development officials' goals. In many cases, the campaigns were more successful than their originators intended. Like the fairy tale sorcerer's apprentice who set off forces he could not control, development programs often sparked hopes for a better life that governments could not fulfill. Lerner's "revolution of rising expectations" gave way to a revolution of rising frustrations.

India is a good example of these varied rural development efforts. The country was a leader in efforts to use communication to promote rapid change; it received special attention from the West because of its size, political importance, and commitment to democracy. Indeed, a bibliography of projects aimed at a range of rural development goals from family planning to agriculture alone would fill several volumes.

In 1956, well before Schramm's book appeared, India with the help of Unesco began an experimental project of rural radio forums. The idea, borrowed from Canadian experience in World War II, involved special radio programs directed at rural villages in which groups of listeners were organized to discuss the programs and then to apply the information to their own circumstances. Correspondence with the radio station was encouraged and supplementary printed materials were provided.

The experiment in 145 villages was successful enough that the Indian government expanded the program nationally. Eventually about 12,000 forums were established, although the goal was to create more than twice that number. All sorts of problems arose when the program went national: less financing, less training, less supervision, less enthusiasm. As Schramm put it later, "The pilot project was undertaken with dedication, and in a blaze of enthusiasm. The expansion was not. The radio rural forum proved to be not a good enough idea to run itself."

That was characteristic of many such projects. They did not reach a self-sustaining takeoff point. Without constant attention they tended, like the Indian rural forum project, to wither away with no permanent impact. India, however, continued its development interest and unlike some other Third World countries, emphasized the use of domestically produced materials rather than the import of hardware from the West.

In 1975–1976, a decade after Schramm's book, India undertook an ambitious experiment that reflected the leap in technology that had occurred during the first generation of communication development. This time the medium was television, but the goals were the same: improve education, agriculture, health, family planning, and political participation in some of the most remote, poorest areas of the country. Domestically produced TV sets were put into more than 2,000 villages where residents had little regular contact with any outside source of information. The sets were designed to receive signals directly from a satellite borrowed from the United States, where it had been used for rural development experiments in Appalachia and Alaska.

During the day the satellite broadcast programs for an hour and a half in four languages to school children; at night, two and a half hours of programming were transmitted for adults. On the average about 100 students watched each set; about the same number of adults clustered around each set for the evening programs.

The project, called SITE for Satellite Instructional Television Experiment, was as well planned as any comparable project and better researched than most. Results, as usual, were equivocal. School children in selected villages did show more interest in science, the major subject of the daytime programming, but very little overall achievement. Among the adults as well, changes in knowledge of and attitudes toward new ideas in health, agriculture, and family planning were modest and often inconsistent. A decade later no one was sure whether these changes in individuals had had any real impact on the nation as a whole.

Still, the program was considered successful enough for the Indian government to plan its own satellite system that included telecommunications and weather forecasting as well as nationwide TV broadcasts. Unlike the direct broadcast system used in SITE, the permanent INSAT (Indian Satellite) satellites broadcast mostly to large-scale earth stations from which signals were retransmitted by conventional means. The first INSAT was launched in 1982, but failed after three months. A second satellite was successful and led India into the space age.

By most criteria the Indian experience in rural development would be judged a success. SITE was an experiment, but INSAT was a big step — despite satellite failures — toward the creation of a modern, multipurpose, national communication system that could serve a range of national needs, but particularly rural development. Not many Third World countries in the 1980s had gone that far, but most seemed ready to follow India's example of trying to use the new technology to leapfrog over old problems. Even her failures could be instructive to others.

Schramm argued that sharing the common experience of communication development failures as well as successes could smooth the turbulence of the early efforts, but recent syntheses identified the same obstacles and generally offered the same solutions as he did 20 years ago. Communication and rural development programmers seemed committed to a constant reinvention of the wheel. Consider a recent Unesco summary.

Juan E. Diaz Bordenave examined what he called 10 fairly typical major development projects in all parts of the Third World from the late 1940s to the mid-1970s. Most stressed the use of radio to improve rural life, although the scope, sponsorship, and objectives of the projects varied. The projects ranged from the rural radio forums in India and adult literacy programs in Senegal to family planning in Iran and civic education in Tanzania.

All the projects seemed to take into account, in varying degrees, the advice Schramm offered in his 1964 book. Evaluation procedures varied, but most of the projects seemed to accomplish something, although usually less than their objectives called for. Still, Diaz Bordenave could find few common threads and little to recommend to rural development specialists. The problem, he decided finally, was a lack of adequate theory.

Diaz Bordenave wrote at the time that the old approach to rural development was already under attack, and his cautious recommendations were consistent with what was becoming the popular alternative. It is hard to estimate how much of the decline of the Lerner-Schramm emphasis on economic and political growth was a function of the concomitant disenchantment with the appropriateness of Western liberal democracy to the Third World and how much of it was attributable to the failure of early development projects to live up to their advance billing. Rural development was far more complex than many early program planners had thought, and the kind of contact with modernity that Lerner attributed to the road in Balgat and mass media throughout the Third World often led to frustration and unrest, not to a better life.

What good is a modest increase in knowledge or production skills if they cannot be put to use or, worse, if they benefit mostly the social stratum that already has a leg up on a better life? Even Schramm loyalists began to ask the question. Of course the Marxist alternative identified a radical solution, but moderates also began to look at factors outside of the individual. These included the political, technical, and economic constraints on innovation, the lack of equity in distribution of the fruits of development, and the social costs of disruption of traditional ways compared to the usually modest improvements.

Thus the path was prepared for a new definition of rural development, the result of the appeal of the radical alternative and the failure of the once-dominant, moderate theory to live up to its early, exaggerated promise.

Of course rural development is an extraordinarily complex task, whether the inspiration is ideology or pragmatism. It is not surprising that simple and often vacuous recommendations offered very little guidance to people in the field wrestling with the day-to-day problems of bureaucratic inertia and popular resistance, as well as inadequate resources and direction.

Nor is it surprising that enthusiasm for rural development projects diminished in the late 1970s and early 1980s. It was difficult enough to do the kinds of things that development specialists had recommended for 20 years, and new calls for "total" development plans and integration of rural development with other aspects of national development only made the job harder. If that were not enough, the failure of even comprehensive and carefully thought out plans to demonstrate their value and an absence of promising alternatives, particularly in a world economy turned upside down by OPEC, was enough to dampen the enthusiasm of even the most committed supporter of rural development.

Perhaps other aspects of communication development, especially those more subject to orderly planning and growth, offered more hope for the 1980s.

TELECOMMUNICATIONS

In the early years of communication development, telecommunications got surprisingly little attention. It was probably the result of a bias toward *mass* media in the 1950s and 1960s. Journalists use telecommunication facilities routinely in their job but fail to appreciate the value of the system until it fails. Economists and businessmen do better: They tend to think of telecommunications in terms of cost/benefit ratios and return on investment. By both criteria, telecommunication appeared to be a key to economic and social growth, but until recently was frequently ignored in communication development plans.

That, too, is surprising. Telecommunication networks are the cardiovascular system of any mass communication network, as well as of long-distance interpersonal communication. The same channels, whether heavy copper lines looped from pole to pole, microwave signals, or pulses bounced off satellites 23,000 miles above the equator, carry news agency dispatches and pictures as well as telex messages and telephone conversations between two people. Modern digital circuits carry all such messages at the same time as a stream of tiny packets of 0s and 1s, without distinguishing among text, voice, picture, or news dispatches, business messages, or gossip between friends.

The telecommunication gap is not always apparent to the casual Western visitor to the Third World. For the average citizen in the Third World, however, a simple telephone can be as exotic as a space satellite. And part of a problem Westerners can grasp only with difficulty: in most Third World rural villages and urban slums there is no way for individuals to communicate with other individuals except face-to-face. There are no permanent addresses, no mail delivery, no access to telegram or telephone networks. The only way to get a message of birth, death, or marriage to a relative in a neighboring village or the capital is to go there. Even in the information age, many in the Third World are as isolated from separated family as were early immigrants to the Americas who sailed from the old country with no hope of maintaining family ties.

Ithiel de Sola Pool, whose long career spanned a wide range of communication-related interests, underscored the importance of tele-communications to rural development in studies of Egyptian villages and calculated a direct cost to benefit ratio of 40 to 1 that rose to 85 to 1 when indirect social benefits were added in. A telephone speeded and smoothed local bureaucracy, made commerce more efficient, and reduced the disruption and impact of emergencies. These were expected. But Pool also found that peasants spent a large part of their time and limited money on transportation. How else to contact family members?

For travel to neighboring villages, almost half relied on animals or walked. Even for travel to district towns or Cairo or Alexandria, half to two-thirds used taxis, not mass transit. In villages where telephones were available for emergency use — usually a message would be dictated to someone for later delivery — emergency calls averaged about one a day. As a result there was great demand for access to a system that was always overloaded and often on the brink of collapse.

Next to radios and television sets, telecommunications may be the one aspect of a modern communication system for which there is the most public demand. A rapid burst of growth in telecommunication seems to come at what the traditional theories of economic development call the "takeoff point," where growth accelerates and becomes self-sustaining. In Brazil, for example, the decade of the 1960s and early 1970s saw an annual growth in excess of 10 percent in both the economy and telecommunication systems. In 15 years, the number of telephones in the Brazilian system went from 20 to over 60 per thousand population, a figure that compares with several industrialized Western nations.

Third World countries without the resources of Brazil's then rapidly expanding economy were not as fortunate. Many of them could not find the resources to expand an inadequate existing system or to replace it with one appropriate to the space age. Investment in telecommunication facilities averaged about 0.3 percent of GDP (gross domestic product) in the Third World, compared with 0.6 percent in the United States. The failure to emphasize telecommunications investment was unfortunate because of the rapid and big payoff in economic and social benefits. Returns from an expanded telecommunication network can be used to fund further expansion, making the initial investment self-sustaining and generating seed money for future growth. In Brazil, new subscribers paid in advance, thus providing a major part of the initial cost.

Telecommunication systems are ideal for the kind of integrated planning that has been promoted as the lynchpin of effective communication development. By necessity, systems are monopolies and are operated directly by government or public authorities. Even deregulated systems are subject to government oversight and technical standards; for virtually all Third World systems, every aspect of the system — technical, financial, and political — is the result of a public decision.

Despite evidence of speedy and generous return on investment, many Third World governments hesitated to put the kind of money into telecommunications that they invested in broadcasting or news agencies. Frequently, the charges for routine circuits and especially the specialized services needed for news organizations were set deliberately above the actual cost to the national telecommunications agency.

Even when circuits were available, they could be too expensive for news media. The complaint of high telecommunications costs came through the reports submitted to the MacBride Commission again and again. The cost of telecommunication was the single biggest obstacle to a wider flow of news *between* Third World countries and, except for the handful of city-states or tiny countries where all media are located in the capital, *within* developing countries as well. Telecommunications assumed a more appropriate place in the center of development schemes in the 1970s, when architects of the new national and regional news exchanges realized that the biggest obstacle to increased news flow was often the lack of cheap, reliable circuits between and within countries. Fifty years ago, when messages traveled over heavy copper wire, there was a reason why Botswana could not speak directly to Kenya; in the space age there were only excuses.

Unlike telecommunication, which was often ignored in early development schemes, mass media were at their core. It was radio that Lerner emphasized, and Scramm's vision of rapid economic growth was built around the traditional *mass* media. He, like Lerner, had a bias for radio, but identified a function for newspapers and television as well.

The questions about the political purpose of mass media and the definitions of news that divided the traditional Western and radical versions of development in the 1980s seldom arose in the earlier decades. Attention was mostly fixed on rural development goals, which were not controversial. If American development programmers were uneasy about too close an embrace between government and media — a concern that was almost never expressed — they could comfort themselves with Lerner's promise that democracy came late in the development cycle. In fact from the beginning, Third World governments used mass media for very political ends and the early media development programs, which Western aid agencies supported, contained some of the ideas that later formed the new world information order.

NEWSPAPERS

Third World countries that achieved independence after World War II and into the 1960s and 1970s typically had newspapers patterned after those in the colonial homeland. The newspaper tradition was strongest in the British colonies where generations of British journalists had planted versions of the *Times* in such disparate places as India, Singapore, and Zambia. Some of the strongest Third World newspapers today trace their roots to the curious breed of journalist who extended British imperial influence in a way that proved more lasting than that of her imperial armed forces. A similar journalistic tradition was found in Latin America, where newspapers' mentors in the north provided an influential model for the development of a commercial press, usually tied to a conservative national power structure, but often a force of opposition and reform as well.

In many countries where European-style governments that were left by departing colonial powers collapsed in the first decade of independence, takeover of newspapers followed. Governments gave different reasons for taking control of newspapers: the inability to survive without subsidy, the importance of installing native staff and control, and even in nonradical regimes the need to create a new style of journalism to support national development objectives.

The phrase *national integration* was sometimes used rather than *national development*. It usually meant an effort to mold a sense of national identity and commitment transcending the ancient tribal, linguistic, and religious antagonisms that resurfaced in many Third World countries once the colonial power left. As the list of civil wars, revolutions, and counterrevolutions in the Third World grew longer and longer, the cultural fissures seemed to get wider.

Could mass media heal them? Probably not, but under the banner of national integration, many Third World leaders who presented themselves as symbols of the new nationalism justified their dominance of the media and the creation of what was later called "protocol news." In Kenya, President Daniel Arap Moi maintained his own presidential press unit at the Voice of Kenya. It is not surprising that his day's activity was the lead story on virtually every radio and television newscast, sometimes taking up half the total time. The two submissive newspapers in Nairobi followed suit.

Even in Mexico, where the press is generally independent and critical, the president as a symbol of the nation along with the flag and church is almost beyond rebuke. Of course, the executive dominates the news in most countries, but there is a difference between the skeptical treatment of public officials in the Western press tradition and the adulation heaped on leaders who have seized the press under the banner of national integration and defined news as that which promotes their political fortunes.

While the seeds of a radical definition of development were being sown in capital cities, it was in rural development projects that newspapers were put to use in support of the old theory of development. Objectives were occasionally political but mostly the familiar goals of literacy and social and economic improvement.

Africa, which had the least developed traditional press system, was heavily involved in experiments in the 1960s and 1970s. Some of the experiments survive. A Unesco survey of 11 African countries in 1971 concluded that rural papers could support basic development objectives, particularly literacy. Most of the early rural papers were mimeographed sheets that appeared irregularly. Most of the papers in the Unesco survey were monthlies; a few appeared weekly.

A Dutch development experiment in Kenya in the mid-1970s extended the original concept by equipping a mobile van with the hardware required to produce a simple offset paper and moving it to a village where local residents were encouraged to become reporters and editors and were trained to produce the newspaper. When the paper became self-sustaining technically and socially, the van was reequipped and moved to another village.

None of the papers was ever self-sustaining financially or intended to be. Social objectives, besides literacy itself, included education, practical information on health, economic and social conditions, encouragement of the reading habit, participation of readers in development, and the development of links between villagers and central governments.

Rural papers were not designed as alternatives to more conventional newspapers, which seldom reached isolated villages anyway.

Those that survived functioned mostly in the tradition of the extension agent with some overtones of the political character of many of the mainline papers published in the national capital. Newspapers in the Third World, despite the efforts to adapt the medium to rural development, remained mostly part of the information environment of the urban elite and part of the control apparatus of the regime in power.

BROADCASTING

Radio, from the beginning of the development effort, was touted as the most important and most powerful medium for Third World growth. It still is. At the time Schramm wrote, the bulky, battery-operated set in the middle of an unidentified Asian village that was pictured on the dust cover of his popular book was already obsolete. He acknowledged the potential influence of the new transistor but did not foresee how close the 1980s would come to Unesco's goal of a universally available five-dollar radio.

In virtually any Third World marketplace or village center, the traditional chatter of barter and gossip is a counterpoint to the tinny sound of a pocket radio. Usually the radios are tuned to different stations, generating a curious blend of indigenous music, talk in several languages, and the inevitable Western pop music. "No village seems so remote," Emile G. McAnany noted in a survey of communication and rural development, "that radio, at least, does not reach it."

The advantages of radio in promoting national development of either the traditional or revisionist kind are so obvious that they hardly seem worth stating. But as a reminder, they should be. In countries where roads dwindle into trails at the edge of the capital city, radio may be the only means of reaching outlying areas regularly. Newspapers can get distributed only where efficient physical movement is possible, but radio cuts across almost all barriers of geography and terrain. Radio is also cheap. Most receivers do not require electricity or elaborate maintenance. If not yet universally available, radios have become the most ubiquitous of all mass media and the least vulnerable to government control because most receivers pick up signals from outside the country as well.

Radio is relatively inexpensive to put on the air. The techniques for producing programs and getting them out over a transmitter are comparatively simple; the tools are portable. Finally and most importantly, radio can be tailored to the most exotic language or unusual target audience as long as someone is there to speak. Of all the mass media, radio has the greatest potential for easy and inexpensive adaptation to the needs and interests of Third World audiences without intruding on their cultural traditions.

It is not surprising, therefore, that radio has shown the greatest growth in the last 20 years or that it is still considered the cutting edge in efforts to use mass media to promote national development. For Lerner and Schramm, radio was about as close to a perfect medium for multiplying development efforts as they could find. Schramm put it this way:

> Radio can do almost too much. Therefore, it is asked to do too much. When it is broadcasting to the farmers, it is not serving the city people. When it is broadcasting to the schools, it is usually not serving the adult population. When it is broadcasting the classical culture of the country, it is likely to lose some or much of its audience to the commercial station broadcasting light entertainment from across the border. So what should it do? (Schramm 1964, 226)

The answer then and now is "just about everything." But that meant that radio was often used, scattershot fashion, to promote a range of technical and political development goals. One hour for rural village forums, then a lesson for school children, next an interlude of music and, almost always, good doses of information, usually political.

Radio was already in place when Third World countries began systematic efforts to use mass media to promote rapid social and economic development. That could be both a blessing and a curse: a blessing because the hardware was in place and functioning, but a curse when governments wanted to harness an entrenched system to development programs. Most of the developing countries had a radio system and operating philosophy as part of their colonial heritage, but as Katz and Wedell noted in a survey of Third World broadcasting, radio springs from a variety of motives: ". . . the extension of empire, the making of profit, the rallying of independence forces and missionary activity."

Most countries followed one of three models. In Latin America and a few other countries, such as the Philippines, radio was privately owned and commercial. That meant an emphasis on popular entertainment programming, consumer advertising, and hostility toward efforts to mobilize the medium for development purposes. The former British colonies had a BBC-like system that emphasized independence of government, quality programming, and a sense of noble purpose. In the Francophone colonies, the tradition of high culture and political control continued.

Few of the original systems, whatever their origin, explicitly linked radio to national development, but most Third World governments soon learned the value of control. In a coup, seizure of the radio station was as important as seizure of the palace. Except in Latin America, and not always there, radio became a key element of the government, promoting politics as much as economics, personalities of national leaders as much as rural development.

Despite their emphasis on radio, few Third World governments ever defined a specific role for the medium. Even in the mid-1970s, Katz and Wedell found few Third World national systems that had detailed, explicit statements of radio's objectives in national programs promoting economic, social, or cultural growth. Like Topsy and television, radio just grew and grew.

Television, in contrast to radio, was widely regarded as the wrong medium for national development. It was mostly a service for the urban elite. Sets were expensive, not easily maintained, and required electricity. Signals from urban transmitters seldom reached beyond the suburbs, and operation of even a modest TV system drained scarce national resources for the benefit of a few. Most important, prgramming was so expensive to produce that virtually all Third World TV systems were dependent on foreign programming to fill even a short evening schedule.

Even though architects of the early ideas of mass media's contribution to national development acknowledged that television could be useful, most counseled against spending scarce national resources on it. However, pressures from elites accustomed to the entertainment fare in London and New York and political leaders who saw the medium both as a symbol of modernity and a powerful tool for promoting national integration (and their own fortunes) overcame the hesitations of the development planners, and the medium grew with explosive speed and power throughout the Third World.

Nothing in the call for a new world information order, which at its heart tried to justify the use of all mass media to support political objectives in the name of national development, aroused such passions as the charge of cultural imperialism via television. The new medium, powerful beyond anything that had come before it to raise expectations and demands, seemed capable of leaping the gap between the old and the new faster and more efficiently than all other media combined. In retrospect it is unfortunate but not surprising that so much attention was paid to the medium. Nor is it surprising that TV became the symbol of what so many advocates of the radical definition of development decried later. TV, inevitably, it seemed, was the embodiment of consumption, leisure, and materialism, all of the evils of Western-style development that the new order was supposed to avoid.

Few nations resisted the temptation to introduce what they saw as a two-edged sword. On one hand, if a picture could be worth a thousand words, imagine the potential power of television to multiply national development efforts. All the factors that made radio a tool for rapid change were magnified when pictures were added to sound.

But on the other hand, the insatiable appetite of television for programming meant that almost no single country could keep even a simple single-channel system on the air with its own programs. For Third World countries as a whole, Katz and Wedell found that imported programming ranged from 30 to 75 percent, averaging about 55 percent. Most of the imported programming still comes from the United States, with Britain a distant but important second. Third World countries represented a tiny part of the $500 million annual foreign sales of American programs, but U.S. imports continue to dominate the TV schedules of most developing countries.

A kind of sameness fills TV screens just about everywhere. Third World programming sandwiched between flashy imports differs from that in the West mostly by a lack of slickness; its content is strikingly similar even when tied to promotion of economic or social development. Elihu Katz tells naive travelers what to expect:

> Wherever they go, they will find that news occupies 10% of television time, with an added 10% for current affairs and documentaries. Series and serials share about 20% ... children's programs, light entertainment and feature films ... 10% ... sports and adult education ... somewhat less than 10% ... religion, music of all kinds and plays each ... 2–5% of television time. And there is about a 30% chance of seeing *Kojak* some evening of the week at 9 PM. (Nordenstreng and Schiller 1979, 65)

By the late 1980s, "Dallas" and "The Muppets" had replaced "Kojak" as both the world's most popular TV programs and the symbols, depending on one's point of view, of either American cultural imperialism or the irresistibility of America's market-oriented, mass-appeal television. Even Disney cartoons and the highly acclaimed "Sesame Street" were accused of contributing to a confluence of objectives serving the interests of the American government, mass media, and multinational corporations.

Why did the same mix seem to show up on TV screens around the world? Not because there was no choice, but because program buyers chose it. In fact, in many countries in the 1970s, American and British imports decreased modestly and were replaced not with national programming promoting development, but with imitations of Western programs from growing Third World production centers. With some differences. Latin Americans got heavy doses of prime time soap operas from Mexico, Argentina, and Brazil. In the Middle East, Egypt emerged as an important producer of sirupy musicals, and Hong Kong's violent kung fu films became almost as familiar as American cop shows. Studies in the early 1980s documented a slow but significant decline in Western programming and concomitant increase from Third World regional centers, but such changes had little influence on the debates over the appropriateness of television as a component of national development.

The ambivalence of the Third World toward television is evident in the medium's short history in the developing countries. In a majority of countries, television was introduced for reasons unrelated to development. In most cases the motivation was pressure from urban elites and, in a surprising number of cases, simple business reasons or national vanity. Television was introduced to Iran by the Iranian distributor of Pepsi Cola, who also owned the franchise for RCA television sets; Indonesia introduced its system in 1962 when it hosted the Asian Games. President Gustavo Rojas established TV in Colombia in 1953 to mark the first anniversary of his dictatorship.

Color TV was introduced to Thailand to coincide with the Miss Thailand beauty contest and to India in 1983 when India hosted the Asian Games. Israel introduced color to wean viewers away from the color transmissions from Jordan. Even Unesco, which now leads the fight for a new global order devoid of Anglo-American dominance, was instrumental in the introduction of television — to be sure, educational television — to Peru and Senegal.

Of all the artifacts of the debate over the purpose of mass media as an engine of development, television still represents best the gap between the consumer- and leisure-oriented Western societies and the Third World. Slum dwellers in Cairo watch programs they cannot possibly understand from the unreadable subtitles that are supposed to substitute for the original English dialogue. Even less can they comprehend the culture represented — or caricatured — by the glossy but superficial stories designed to attract the minimum 30 percent share of American audiences. In a bizarre way, though, this kind of program represents the one common denominator for people in many parts of the Third World because the poor in Cairo, in the shanty towns ringing Caracas, and in the makeshift squatter villages in Lagos often watch the same programs with, one must assume, the same sense of fascination and puzzlement.

REVIEWING THE RECORD

Well after the original idea of communication development came under attack, its major architects had occasion to comment on what had been accomplished under the banner of mass media as the great multiplier of modernization. Clearly, the optimism of the 1950s and early 1960s was overstated. The Third World had not evolved smoothly into stable democracies and the record of social and economic growth was mixed. Only in the area of electronic media growth itself was there apparent success, and now even that was attacked as an arm of imperialism, not a milestone of progress. What had gone wrong?

More than Schramm, Lerner remained adamant in defense of his old and (to some) discredited idea. The problem, he wrote in a 1978 paper, was the inability of Third World governments to accommodate the revolution of rising expectations that mass media had sparked. The result was a revolution of rising frustrations that had led to the common feature of Third World governments in the 1970s and 1980s: military takeover. Dictatorships are unstable, he wrote hopefully, as he called for a new generation of development communicators who could moderate rising expectations and sustain a realistic understanding of the possibilities and limits of development in their countries. Only democracy, he still maintained, could accommodate the rapid social change that marked the twentieth century.

Schramm offered his perspective on the first generation of communication development in one of the supplementary reports commissioned by the MacBride Commission. He prepared by rereading *Mass Media and National Development*. The experience was humbling.

Although the recommendations he had made in 1964 still seemed worthwhile, Schramm admitted that the old vision of mass media as the engines of rapid social and economic growth was out of date. Schramm offered several reasons for the failure of his once unchallenged theory: the stresses from trying to compress centuries of Western development into decades; the evolution of an agricultural economy as an intermediate step to industrialization in the West; land and natural resources that were plentiful in the West but scarce in much of the developing world.

Schramm more than Lerner acknowledged that development goals had changed to emphasize self-reliance and preservation of traditional values and that "small media" might be more important than the grand schemes for rapid social transformation built around massive national mass media systems. But neither of the two intellectual fathers of hundreds of development projects and probably thousands of communication development practitioners, even in their latter-day apologies, addressed directly the radical critique of their work. They did not play a strong card.

If the once dominant idea of communication's role in national development had simply strengthened an exploitive system of Third World dependence, then the shifting from development aimed at democracy and economic growth with mass media as the multiplier to one based on equity and self-reliance with small media and appropriate technology as means ought to be reflected in the projects undertaken under the banner of radical national development. Enough countries had, in fact, built Marxist-inspired societies that a record of alternative development was available, but little examined.

Occasionally delegates from these countries got up at conferences to tell how they had used communication to create a society of equity, self-sufficiency, and authentic Third World reality. But mostly, like the intellectual critics of the Lerner-Schramm approach, they preferred to criticize those they accused of responsibility for their plight. It was — and is — easier to attack the discredited idea of how mass media could aid traditional development than to defend the record of the alternative. We cannot let them get off that easily.

5

Communication Development for a New Order

IMPLEMENTING THE NEW WORLD INFORMATION ORDER

One of the projects approved by the new International Program for the Development of Communication (IPDC) in 1983 was a national news agency for Liberia, a country with fewer than two million people, one radio station, and two newspapers. The government of West Germany agreed to contribute four million marks and technical assistance to the project.

QUESTION: What is the difference between the Liberian news agency and the Voice of Zaire's white elephant?

(a) They were paid for with different currencies.
(b) The Liberian project was inspired by the new vision of communication development; the Voice of Zaire was not.
(c) Liberia was much smaller than Zaire and, therefore, did not need a skyscraper broadcasting house.
(d) There was no difference.

ANSWER: No points for the obvious responses, and even the choice between (b) and (d) is not clear cut.

Roberto Savio, the founder of Inter Press Service, a global news agency dedicated to the new world order, recognized that the theory of communication development under the banner of the NWIO sounded a lot like it did for two decades under the inspiration of the

Lerner-Schramm theory: transfer Western technology and ideas to the Third World to speed the process of industrialization and political maturation. Savio told a congressional committee that the project would merely create "a cathedral of high technology in an information desert, with the result in practice that nothing has changed in Liberia, except for a new technological and professional dependence on Germany."

Savio at least recognized that it took more than a difference of motive to change the direction of communication development. Radical purists such as Hamelink, who argued that true Third World development could be furthered only by disengagement from the West, seemed to see developing nations as naively as Marx envisioned primitive communism. While it was true, as Schramm had noted, that traditional Third World societies often did stress cooperation and caring, they were just as often characterized by rigidity, lethargy, and the constant threat of war, disease, and the weather. Traditional societies typically lived on the edge of disaster. Modern communications technology was not necessarily a cure for Third World problems, but neither was it a cause.

Hamelink, who would probably choose answer (d) and argue against both projects, represented a romantic view of the Third World that was almost Kiplingesque in its yearning for an imagined purity, uncontaminated by the ills that were the inevitable product of contact with Western industrial capitalism. His view, while popular as a debating point in the arguments over Western responsibility for aiding Third World development programs, represented a minority position.

After attributing most Third World problems to Western colonialism and decrying the threat to authentic Third World values from inappropriate Western technology — a theme of nearly all speeches in the new world information order debate of Unesco — spokesmen for the radical model of development then often proceeded to demand an increase in communication development assistance. That, of course, meant primarily assistance for projects such as the Voice of Zaire facility or the Liberian news agency.

It was a curious logic that both demanded a transfer of resources as a matter of recompense for colonialism and condemned those resources as a threat to authentic Third World development. The syllogism went something like this: All technology carries inherent social values. The values of modern communications technology are incompatible with authentic Third World development. Therefore, we demand that transfer of technology be increased. Was the proper response an increase in assistance or severing the programs already in place? Even when the West played its strong card by promising greater assistance in return for a dropping of some of the most objectionable elements of the new world information order, no one could be sure what was in the bargain.

In fact, most of the development projects created under the rubric of the new definition of development looked much like those generated under the old definition. Choice (b) probably best represents the style of communication development that grew out of the new world information order debate in the 1970s, even though realists such as Savio could argue that the difference was more rhetorical than real.

Some useful differences, however, did emerge. In the 1980s, the emphasis in hardware was more on structures for the exchange of information and less on broadcasting, which was largely in place and growing rapidly. Rural development also seemed to diminish in importance while telecommunications, which had not been central to early development schemes, took on new prominence. The old call for planning for communication development also took on a new burst of energy, but recorded no more success than it had in the previous decades.

NEWS AGENCIES

News agencies were to the 1980s what television was to the 1970s and radio to the 1960s — a priority for communication planners and politicians, a magic machine to overcome the still growing information gap between the North and the Third World. In the 1980s, however, the goals of communication development were more political than economic, and national news agencies, regional exchanges, and alternative world agencies were seen as the structure on which a new global order supporting a new kind of national development could be built.

The stress on new structures reflected both the shift of communication development goals from economic growth to the use of mass media to mobilize a national population in support of political objectives and at the same time an effort to redress the failure of the existing, mostly Western, global information system to provide information to support such goals. The priority assigned to national agencies and regional exchanges by IPDC should not have surprised Western journalists. Unesco had actively supported the development of national agencies in its own long-standing but little publicized communication development programs, and 20 years earlier Schramm had noted that "most developing countries would say flatly that, if they do not already have a national [news] agency, they must have one as soon as possible."

At the time Schramm was writing, most Third World countries in Asia and Africa were beginning or about to begin their history as independent nations, and as Schramm had predicted, a news agency came soon after a flag and United Nations seat. Unesco figures from

1971–1972 identified 90 national agencies and noted that all Asian nations but five from the eastern Mediterranean to the Pacific had their own news agencies. The proliferation of Third World countries, however, outran their ability to organize news services.

As late as 1979, the pool of Non-Aligned News Agencies counted 35 countries still without news agencies, 18 in Africa and most of the others new microstates in Oceania. While IPDC and the Non-Aligned Movement both pressed to reduce the number of countries without a national agency, more than 100 Third World countries already had one. Some were large and professional; others were little more than government offices that distributed packets of material gleaned from the Western news agencies and puffery from the regime in power. Why did Liberia and the handful of other Third World nations need their own news agencies, especially when they tied the countries more firmly to the existing global information system?

At the technical level, a news agency was a convenient mechanism for the distribution of information to the country's usually poverty-stricken newspapers and broadcasting authorities. It could also provide information within the government, a significant task in countries that had to rely on their own media for much of the public intelligence that was exchanged routinely by telephone, telex and government cables in the industrialized countries.

Beyond that, the agency served as a convenient single point of contact between the global news system and a government that determined what information would be allowed into the country and how it would be interpreted. The same surveillance function — censorship is a harsh word for the same thing — can be performed at various media directly, of course, but consolidation of control and coordination within a single agency promoted efficiency and increased the chances that various domestic sources of information would speak with consistent voices.

The new regional exchanges, which got a strong endorsement and modest financial support from IPDC, typically comprised national news agencies, most of which were organs of their governments. The Pan African News Agency was organized under the auspices of the Organization of African Unity and committed to the principle of exchange of official information. The Non-Aligned News Agencies pool was also an organization of national agencies, although a few agencies operating independently of government did participate.

Western aid donors were willing to support the efforts to develop and strengthen national agencies, even though they were suspicious of the rhetoric that redefined national development in political terms and called for mobilization of the new media to support political development objectives. In fact, the major Western news agencies cooperated actively with the fledgling national agencies and exchanges, offering training, technology, and special concessions in exchange or sale of information. The quid pro quo for support was independent access to the developing nations so that the Western agencies could continue their own reporting, even though Western-style "bad news" was now considered dysfunctional to Third World needs and a symbol of the discredited old style of communication development.

By the mid-1980s the web of world news flow comprised a diverse network of agencies, some sculpted in the vision of the new world information order, some dedicated to the principles of press mobilization enunciated years earlier by Lenin and Mao, and others committed to the principles of independence and market forces that had created Western dominance of the whole system. Later we will look in detail at the very different pictures of the world they offered readers, listeners, and viewers; we can anticipate that by probing their organizations and guiding principles. Three types of news organizations, all dedicated to implementing differing definitions of the new world information order, emerged. They were the Third World national agencies, specialized regional and global services, and second-tier Western agencies with a special interest in cooperating with Third World partners.

PROTOTYPES OF THE NWIO

NAN

In retrospect, it was curious that Nigeria, the most populous country in Africa and one of the few blessed with oil, did not have a national news agency until so late. The News Agency of Nigeria (NAN) was founded in 1976 as a state enterprise and began operations two years later. Like most news organizations, its charter called for it to report news and opinion in a professional and objective manner. But with conditions. According to one observer, NAN "must not act as an institutional opponent to any government or interests, but where it is in the public interest to report criticism of public policy, it must do so in a restrained and objective manner." And where national sovereignty or unity was at issue, NAN had a further responsibility "to come out firmly on the side of Nigeria without prejudice to its adherence to the truth."

Although its facilities were inadequate by Western standards, reliable communications with the rest of the world were possible, thanks to OPEC money that built an elaborate national telecommunications center. Domestic communications, however, were another matter and a big problem for news gathering and distribution within the sprawling nation of nearly 100 million. Five regional domestic offices were tied to the Lagos headquarters by varied communication links. Radio-teletype and teleprinters were used to distribute news dispataches, but heavy reliance was placed on the personal delivery of mimeographed dispatches. In Lagos, whose legendary traffic jams continued virtually around the clock, even that system could be uncertain.

NAN put out regular dispatches at 11:30 AM and 3:30 PM and a late bulletin in the early evening. They contained both world news, mostly rewritten from Western agency dispatches, and staff-written domestic news stories. Economic news was carried in a separate economic service distributed at 2 PM. NAN dispatches totaled 40 to 45 short stories a day in its regular service with another 10 stories and commodity price reports in the Economic News Service.

Xinhua

It is hard to imagine a news service more different from NAN than Xinhua, from the People's Republic of China. One was mostly independent of government, a neutral if not critical observer of government, the other a component of a highly centralized and tightly controlled dictatorship. Neither was exactly what the new world information order had called for.

Xinhua was founded in 1932 as the Red China News Agency during Mao's insurgency days. After joining the Nationalists in a united front against the Japanese in 1937, the Chinese Communist Party renamed its new news agency the New China News Agency, a name that continued during the Communists' renewed struggles after World War II and after their seizure of the country in 1950.

Xinhua, part of an elaborate control and indoctrination apparatus that was a key element of Mao's style of communism, made no claims of neutrality or independence. At the agency's twentieth anniversary celebration in 1952, the former director of the national Propaganda Department described the agency as "the weapon of class struggle . . . the Party's eyes and tongue."

China was not alone in mixing journalism and politics, of course, although in few countries were the ties so close. At one point, in the 1960s, Xinhua personnel were considered interchangeable with officials of the Ministries of Foreign Affairs and Foreign Trade. One former minister of foreign affairs had been a Xinhua correspondent, and four of the six directors and deputy directors of Xinhua before the Cultural Revolution held concurrent positions in major "friendship associations." In August 1982, Xinhua formally became a component part of the state council as the state organ for unified news release, a move roughly akin to making the Associated Press part of the President's Cabinet and the only legal source of news.

Even with China's new openness, little was known about Xinhua's organization and activities. It maintained correspondents in 85 countries and had extensive exchange agreements with major Western news organizations, as well as regional exchanges like the Asian News Network. It was not active in the Non-Aligned New Agencies pool, however, and seldom tried to exert influence in the new world information order debates.

Xinhua transmitted about 150,000 words a day in English, French, Spanish, Arabic, and Russian to news organizations outside China. From its own correspondents and files of other agencies, Xinhua put together several dispatches for distribution within China. It was not the only source of foreign news in China — the *People's Daily* had its own small stable of foreign correspondents — but Xinhua was close to a monopoly. It sent daily 40,000 to 50,000 words to national newspapers and broadcasters, another 30,000 to 40,000 words to provincial and municipal papers, and 10,000 to 20,000 words to smaller, local newspapers.

Tanjug

Tanjug, like the country it serves, defied a simple classification. Yugoslavia is part of central Europe but different enough from its neighbors that the State Department referred to the desk that dealt with it as "Eastern Europe and Yugoslavia." It was a leader of the Non-Aligned Movement but not a developing Third World country. History and geography made it a crossroads between East and West as well as between capitalism and socialism. Most of all, World War II left it as a fragile coalition of very different and historically hostile religions, languages, and peoples, a common curse of the Third World.

Tanjug itself was also something of an anomaly. According to a monograph prepared for the MacBride Commission, it was "neither a state institution nor a private or corporate one. It is a professional news agency serving and belonging to the whole of Yugoslav society, and run in keeping with the principles of workers' self-management." By criteria of size and scope of operation, Tanjug was in the same class as the larger second-tier Western agencies. It maintained 46 fulltime foreign correspondents and served 103 countries. Its total staff of nearly 900 employees included some 130 domestic correspondents in all of Yugoslavia's six republics and two autonomous provinces. A general domestic service, operating 24 hours a day, transmitted 75,000 to 120,000 words daily to Yugoslav newspapers and broadcasters.

Tanjug transmitted newscasts abroad in English, French, Spanish, Russian, German, and Serbo-Croatian, mostly by shortwave radioteletype. The English and French files were general services sent worldwide; the others operated regionally for one to six hours a day. The Serbo-Croation service was intended for Yugoslavs abroad. Tanjug also distributed internationally by mail features in six languages, a special economic service (EKOS), that looked like a junior Reuters Economic Service, and news photos.

Shihata

Shihata, News Agency of Tanzania — the name is Swahili for the English title — had little in common with Tanjug except a commitment to the ideology of a new world information order. It was weak as a domestic service and invisible in the global news flow. It was precisely the kind of undernourished national service that IPDC was supposed to help. IPDC, in fact, did allocate limited, mostly cosmetic, financial assistance, but not enough to make much difference.

Shihata was founded in 1976, the same year as NAN in West Africa, but Tanzania missed Nigeria's oil bonanza and remained one of the most media-poor countries in a media-poor continent. When a Unesco consulting team visited Shihata in 1978, the agency had an editorial staff of 99. Its biggest problem was a lack of equipment and telecommunication facilities. Of 20 regional offices on the African mainland only one had a road-worthy vehicle. The agency director's plan for development, endorsed by the Unesco team, called for more vehicles, especially Land Rovers and bicycles.

Shihata received foreign news from Reuters, AFP, and Tass. It was supposed to be the sole receiver and distributor of foreign news in the country, but Radio Tanzania and the country's two daily papers also received foreign transmissions. Shihata's Home Service consisted of a daily bulletin issued in the language received, mostly English but with an occasional Swahili story. The bulletin was distributed twice a day in hard copy and via teleprinter. News stories were occasionally telexed to Zambia and Mozambique, but the agency maintained no regular exchanges.

The agency's finances were tied to the fortunes of the country, which were bad and still declining. Upgrading of technical facilities, the top priority, was hampered by a chronic lack of foreign exchange. In December 1982 IPDC authorized $40,000 for Shihata, but that amount would not go far toward upgrading an inadequate system that lacked basic transport and equipment.

IPDC, whose grants were supposed to represent a consensus of communication development needs in the 1980s, originally made regional exchanges and a couple of global projects its top priority, rather than the impoverished existing or planned national agencies. Even before its checks were mailed, however, two organizations had begun to practice the kind of journalism mandated by the new world information order. They were the two most important examples of the new communication development precisely because they were far removed from the "theoretical" discussions of the new world information order. Every day they had to prepare a news file that could be accepted or rejected by news organizations around the world; every day they had to cope with the gap between the high rhetoric of the Unesco statements and the shrill rhetoric of warring neighbors. The two new global services, the Non-Aligned News Agencies pool and Inter Press Service, interpreted the new world information order very differently.

NANA Pool

The idea of establishing a world information system controlled by and operated for the non-aligned countries (a Non-Aligned News Agency Pool) went back to the origin of the Non-Aligned Movement itself when Yugoslavia's Tito, Egypt's Nasser, and India's Nehru first met in 1955 in Indonesia to envision a world power bloc composed of nations aligned neither with the United States nor the Soviet Union. It was not until the non-aligned summit conference in 1973 in Algeria, however, that a concrete recommendation for action was approved.

The initiative for the pool came from Tanjug, which began relaying news from 10 other non-aligned national news agencies in its own shortwave radio-teletype transmissions in January 1975. A formal constitution for the pool and guidelines for participants were approved at a meeting of information ministers and news agency directors in New Delhi the following year. India and Yugoslavia shared the responsibility for running the pool in its early days, but during the emergency declared by Prime Minister Indira Gandhi in 1975, leadership shifted to Belgrade, where it remained.

The pool, like so much of the rhetoric of the Non-Aligned Movement and even Unesco itself, was based on an assumption of good will and unity of world view. The pool constitution called for the exchange of news "on the basis of mutual respect" and "full respect for equality and democratic principles." Article 5 of the constitution also defined the purpose of the pool as "promoting cooperation and strengthening the unity of member countries ... and the decolonisation of information." All very close to the Unesco rhetoric.

The 85 members of the pool were invited to send, by whatever means they had available, up to 500 words a day to Tanjug headquarters in Belgrade. There a selection of items was made by Tanjug editors assigned to the pool. The items were translated into English, Spanish, and French as necessary and sent around the world on Tanjug's powerful radio-teletype network. All pool members were encouraged to use the file and to retransmit it in their own dispatches. In practice, a few agencies, particularly Inter Press Service and the agencies of India and Cuba, were the main supplementary carriers.

An early study of the pool found that two member organizations,

Yugoslavia and Egypt, contributed 29 percent of all news items and that these two plus 14 more accounted for 88 percent of the total. Of the 41 news agencies that claimed to be participants in the pool, only 26 showed up at all in the 11 or 12 days included in the study. It also concluded that "pool members see the medium to be useful for voicing grievances and stating positions on critical confrontation issues." The study could have added that the file was often plagued by turgid prose, shrill rhetoric, and the kind of puffery that passed for news in the new world information order.

It is easy to criticize the NANA pool. Even after a decade, it was still invisible in the world's press. But the pool survived and that was no small accomplishment in a decade that saw a large part of the Third World savaged by the quadrupling of oil prices and most of it caught up in economic and social turmoil. It was hard to imagine the pool ever trying to replace the Western agencies or even seriously competing with them. It did, however, in a very small way, increase the flow of information and provide valuable lessons about the problems of operating an international news system that no amount of advice from the Western agencies could provide.

IPS

Inter Press Service shared with the NANA pool a commitment to a new journalism, but little else. Where the pool was an exchange of government news agencies, IPS dispatches were written by journalists independent of government; where the pool emphasized mostly "good news" as defined by government-controlled national agencies, IPS reporters dealt regularly and openly with problems of Third World development.

The organization was founded in 1964 by an energetic Italian, Roberto Savio, who still runs it. It was a nonprofit organization registered and headquartered in Italy. A floor in an inconspicuous villa not far from the basilica of St. Mary Major in Rome was the nerve center for a large communication system — the sixth largest in the world, according to IPS — that, unlike the NANA pool, relied heavily on satellite distribution.

In addition to a Spanish-language service that carried 42,000 words a day and a much smaller English-language file of 24,000 words a day, IPS served as a carrier for a wide range of other services, including the pool, the Latin American regional exchange ASIN, several specialized Third World-oriented feature agencies, and even national agencies. Unlike virtually all the other alternative news agencies, IPS had an extensive global communication structure that permitted fast, reliable, regular collection and dissemination of information from its network of bureaus and correspondents in more than 60 countries to more than 400 newspapers, broadcasting operations, and other agencies. Some Western professional media organizations, notably the World Press Freedom Committee, complained of a systematic anti-American bias in IPS dispatches. While it was unusual to find stories openly critical of leftist governments or flattering to rightist regimes, the coverage of a particular country seemed to reflect mostly the news judgment of the individual reporter there.

According to an IPS statement prepared for a Unesco conference, IPS emphasized "coverage of development issues of global concern, including the role of women, environment, science and technology, information and communications, human settlements, natural resources, agriculture, health, population, education, transnational corporations, etc." Not much related to Third World development was left for the category of "etc." While for the most part IPS used a Western reporting style and news values, it claimed to treat news "as a social right, not merely a commercial commodity." National foreign aid agencies in several West European countries thought enough of the service to fund local-language files for domestic distribution, and an American affiliate, Interlink News Service, attracted an impressive list of corporate and media customers, but little visibility, and died in 1986.

The Western agencies were also involved in these communication development activities to a surprising degree, considering their hostility to what many of the new services were committed to. For the Big Four global agencies, exchange or sales agreements with national agencies sometimes got them independent access to the country; usually it got them the right to mine the agencies' dispatches for nuggets of information to pass on to their own customers. Some of the smaller Western agencies went further and got involved in development programs. The German agency, DPA, was one of them.

DPA

Deutsche Presse Agentur, like so much of the modern Federal Republic of Germany, was a product of the postwar occupation period. It was established in 1949 by newspaper publishers and broadcasters by combining the three news services that had been established independently in the British, French, and American zones of occupation. Original cooperative arrangements with Reuters and AFP were allowed to disintegrate, but UPI continued to be DPA's major foreign partner. It was owned by German publishers and Land-level (state) broadcasters in the Federal Republic and West Berlin.

DPA's editorial and administrative offices were in Hamburg; its photo service operated from Frankfurt. Like AFP and the two American world agencies, DPA was essentially a domestic service with international reporting and distribution as a secondary activity. A national service of 45,000 words a day was edited in Hamburg for distribution to clients in Germany; eight regional domestic services produced another 75,000 words a day.

Foreign services included a German-language European service, an English overseas service distributed by radio-teletype, an Arabic service sent to Cairo and distributed from there by the Middle East News Agency, and a Spanish service for Latin America. Features and background information were distributed by mail. DPA distributed photos in Germany and provided pictures for UPI's international telephoto network.

DPA probably had the largest international operation of any of the second-tier Western agencies. According to the MacBride Commission monograph in the mid-1970s, it had 144 subscribers in 78 countries and maintained 105 fulltime foreign correspondents among its 800-person staff. Correspondents or stringers were stationed in 80 countries. DPA also operated a film service, making it a junior competitor with the newsfilm companies as well as the news agencies. Film was distributed in 37 countries, mostly in Europe and Latin America.

The German agency claimed exchange agreements or working relationships with some 45 foreign agencies. The two most important were the "full-service" agreements with MENA in Cairo and ORBE in Santiago, which provided for retransmission of regional files. Comparable agreements for cooperation and exchange with TAP (Tunisia) and KUNA (Kuwait) extended DPA's influence in the Arab world.

Kyodo

Like DPA, Kyodo, from Japan, was a product of the post-World War II period. And like DPA, Kyodo was heir to a history that extended almost as far as that of Reuter and AFP. At the end of World War II, Domei, the huge national Japanese agency with 6,000 employees, voluntarily disbanded. Most of its employees moved to two new agencies, Kyodo and Jiji Press. Kyodo became a general news service whereas Jiji, from its beginning, emphasized financial information. Today it is almost entirely technical economic information, not unlike the Reuters Economic Service.

Kyodo was a cooperative owned by Japanese newspapers and NHK, the Japan Broadcasting Corporation. It also serviced Japan's commercial broadcasters and several nonmember newspapers. Kyodo operated 53 domestic bureaus and had a fulltime staff of 1,900, including 900 correspondents. Kyodo put out 220,000 Japanese letters a day and 35,000 words in English. It maintained 37 foreign bureaus, including six in the

United States, and exchanges or working arrangements with 39 other agencies and 30 foreign photo services.

The new national and regional organizations, with whatever cooperation the Western services could be shamed or coerced into giving, were touted as the cornerstone of the new communication development, but journalism was only part of the "total" development that the new information order called for. And to achieve total development, Third World countries were admonished to pursue the old goal of coordinated planning with communication as its core.

The refrain was familiar, of course, but the new world information order debate gave the issue of planning a new urgency. Could mass media, which had failed to promote rapid economic and political growth, perhaps because they had never really been mobilized properly, now become the driving engine of a new march toward liberation and solidarity? Probably not, but the question became an important part of the new interest in development.

DEVELOPMENT PLANNING REVISITED

Developing countries that tried to braid the pieces of the new model of communication development into a coherent national plan had both an easier job and a tougher job than those that had tried the same thing 20 years earlier. It was easier because communication technology had developed so rapidly, was more plentiful, and was cheaper. The job was harder, however, because communications systems were more developed and reform meant uprooting existing facilities and bureaucracies, not simply filling a void. Building or expanding systems with Western technology was easier, but insulating them against Western content was just about impossible. Short of a real revolution, mobilizing a national communication system to meet the requirements of the new global communication order was something akin to moving a cemetery. It was a slow, delicate operation and one never knew where skeletons would be uncovered.

In a few countries, efforts were made to undertake the kind of systematic examination of communications that the MacBride Commission report urged and, in even fewer, to implement an integrated program of communication development that touched all of the components of the existing systems.

Comprehensive communication development was difficult enough when a country began with a clean slate, as when India introduced its SITE experiment with educational television or when Indonesia designed a new satellite-based telecommunication system. When it had to restructure existing bureaucracies and systems, the problems were even greater. Latin American countries typically had the latter problem and in most cases faced opposition from powerful commercial broadcasters and newspaper owners as well.

But Latin American countries also had advantages. On the whole they had a higher level of economic development than countries in other parts of the Third World, and any development program cost money. They also had highly developed mass media systems that rivaled those in some Western countries. A lucky few countries also had oil. If comprehensive communication development can work anywhere, it should work there. Three countries tried.

Peru

After the coup of 1968 that brought General Juan Velasco Alvarado to power, the government began a long process of restructuring broadcasting, telecommunications, and the press. The Peruvian telecommunication system was then owned mostly by ITT; broadcasting outlets were controlled by nationals but concentrated in the hands of four families. Most radio and TV stations were commercial and devoted more than one-third of their air time to commercials. Two-thirds of all TV programming was imported, most of it dreary but popular soap operas from other Latin American countries and the usual run of adventure shows from the United States. Newspapers, too, were concentrated in the hands of a few conglomerates that also exerted influence in economics and politics.

The new military government established a Ministry of Transport and Communication with responsibility for planning and implementing policies on broadcasting, the press, and telecommunications. Most changes were couched in the rhetoric of the new world information order, although many were set into motion before the Unesco debate politicized communication development issues.

A press law passed in 1969 outlined newspapers' responsibility for "respect for the law, truth and morality, the demands of national security and defense and the safeguard of personal and family honor and privacy." The government also became majority owner of 95 percent of the country's TV stations and 20 percent of the radio stations. The amount of advertising was reduced and some efforts were made to restructure programming, but the twin goals of rapid expansion and conversion of the broadcast system into a force for the development of a true national identity ran into the perils of politics and the world economy.

In 1971, a telecommunications law nationalized the system and required it to operate consistently with "public necessity, utility, and security, and of preferred national interest." However, the biggest changes in the 1971 law affected broadcasting. All stations were to be placed in "workers' communities," members of which were supposed to share in management of the stations and receive 25 percent of their profits. The law also reduced the amount of advertising and specified that 60 percent of programming was to be of national origin, emphasizing Peruvian cultural and educational material.

Changes in the law also had a direct effect on newspapers. Ownership and control of major newspapers were transferred to various workers' and professional groups. One paper, for example, was given to rural organizations, another to educational groups, a third to labor organizations.

These efforts to restructure the country's mass media were supported by many intellectuals and some journalists atuned to the new model of communication development who saw them as an application of the principles of the new global order and an escape from cultural dependency. Others, notably the former media owners and business leaders, took a different view. Meanwhile, economic problems and the traditional Latin American plagues of corruption and inefficiency eroded enthusiasm for the effort to mobilize the media in support of national development.

After General Bermudenz Morales became leader of the military junta in 1975, he maintained state control over broadcasting but prepared to turn the newspapers back to their private owners. His reasons? The populist groups were incapable of managing the papers, journalistic quality had declined, and the failure of the Peruvian economy undercut the populist reforms. After civilian government returned to Peru in 1980, the new president, Fernando Belaunde Terry, returned all papers to their former owners but maintained traditional government influence by new tax laws, control over import of equipment and newsprint, and substantial government advertising. Firm control over broadcasting and telecommunications was continued as well, although programming continued to emphasize low-brow entertainment surrounded by advertising.

Venezuela

Less radical approaches to communication development were tried by Venezuela and Mexico which, with Peru, shared a common tradition of communication policies imported mostly from the United States. In both countries, broadcasting was privately owned and oriented toward entertainment with some generally ineffective oversight by government bodies.

Until the mid-1970s, the three North American commercial networks owned significant minority interests in the three largest Venezuelan networks which, in turn, received up to 40 percent of their advertising revenues directly from government agencies or public corporations. Two-thirds of all programming was imported. As in the United States, weak public or noncommercial educational stations existed but attracted few viewers.

Public discussion about communication policy, or the lack of one, emerged in 1960s at the time that the old Lerner-Schramm theory of mass media as the engines of economic and political growth came under criticism in other parts of the world. Led by the advocates of the cultural dependency school, the debate embraced a wide range of possible public policies. At one end of the spectrum was a call for an expansion of the public system and enforcement of the existing regulations of commercial stations.

To the cultural imperialism school, however, the commercial system itself was the problem. It called for a true nationalization of broadcasting and its mobilization in a campaign of radical restructuring of the country. Unlike Peru, however, Venezuela's democratic traditions were strong and a revolution or coup was unlikely. Without a radical change in government, reform was the best that advocates of a new information order could hope for.

In 1974, the national government appointed a commission to study policy options for Venezuela. The report, which sparked strong opposition from the commercial broadcasters and other parts of the private sector, called for a restructuring of the broadcast system into one like the BBC. It recommended a three-program public radio network aimed at different audiences and two national TV networks also appealing to distinct up-scale and down-scale socioeconomic class viewers.

The commission also called for more domestic production, limited commercials, public financial support of broadcasting, and integration of broadcasting with other elements of national development.

The report appeared when Venezuela, an enthusiastic member of OPEC, was riding the crest of a wave of new wealth and influence in Latin America. Its president, Carlos Andres Perez, who nationalized 21 foreign oil companies in 1976, and his successor, Luis Hererra Campins, embraced the rhetoric of the new world information and economic orders. On the day of his inauguration in 1974, Perez appointed the first cabinet-level minister of information.

Social communication, the preferred Latin American term for mass media, was included for the first time in the fifth national five-year plan covering the years 1976 through 1980 and given prominence in the plan for the succeeding five years. As most such plans do, these documents spelled out philosophy more than specific actions, but their effects were visible on Venezuelan TV screens. Regulations enacted by the Ministry of Information and Tourism banned advertising of tobacco and alcohol on radio and TV and all use of children in television commercials and required the playing of the national anthem three times a day. Half of the music on radio was required to be by Venezuelan artists.

The most controversial requirement, which went into effect at the end of 1982, classified all TV programs by a four-letter rating system, much like the code of the U.S. Motion Picture Association, and prescribed the times they could be broadcast. The section that created the most fuss was the limitation of the popular *telenovelas* to 60 episodes and a maximum running period of three months. They were also limited to broadcasts of one hour at a time with at least one hour between different series.

The plan also committed Venezuela to active participation in international communication affairs and to support of the new world information order. It participated in the OPEC News Agency and the Non-Aligned News Agencies pool. The five-year plan called for an ambitious expansion of domestic broadcasting in the mid-1980s and the establishment of a Voice of Venezuela for overseas audiences. What it did not anticipate was the collapse of the world petroleum market or the mushrooming of Venezuela's foreign debt, both of which cast a pall over the country's communication development scheme.

By the end of 1982, the government's public broadcasting system had been extended to some rural areas and minor changes were visible in the still dominant private broadcasting system. But economics and political hesitancy had postponed and probably killed the grand national plan.

Mexico

In many ways, Mexico's brief experience with communication development was similar. Its broadcast system also was heavily influenced by the United States and belatedly mobilized in support of new world information order objectives. Despite early laws against foreign ownership, by 1938 the National Broadcasting Company had 14 stations affiliated with its radio network. By 1945 the Columbia Broadcasting System had an 18-station network; a third network, backed by French capital, had 20 affiliates. North American corporations, however, did not get into television.

Mexico became the world's twelfth country to have a television service when President Miguel Aleman, still today one of the nation's biggest media owners, decided to authorize a commercial system modeled after that in the United States. Three competing commercial stations, all founded in the early 1950s, eventually merged into a uniquely Mexican broadcasting structure: TELEVISA, which grew into a full-blown communications conglomorate with 45 participating companies. It included two corporations that sell videotapes and live programming to the United States and other countries. The Spanish International Network (SIN) in the United States was a TELEVISA affiliate. The parent company also owned cable franchises throughout Mexico and was a major exporter of programs to other Latin American countries.

The Mexican government, like that of Venezuela, got into broadcasting first through a weak public educational system and later, in 1972, with its own network that in 1977 became a self-supporting commercial system. In 1972 a presidential decree also created Television Rural Mexicana, which grew in five years to 120 outlets. The national system is essentially a private, commercial, multichannel, noncompetitive network coexisting with a large and diverse government system.

The Mexican government could get its message disseminated widely through its own system and a unique system of access to TELEVISA. A federal law passed in 1960 outlined both technical and philosophical broadcast requirements. It defined broadcasting's responsibilities to "affirm respect for moral principles, human dignity, and family relationships . . . prevent negative disturbances for the harmonious development of children and youth . . . contribute to the raising of the cultural level of the people and conserving the national characteristics, customs of the nation, traditions, exalting the values of the Mexican nationality; and fortify democratic convictions, national unity, and international friendship and cooperation."

There was not much to guide the day-to-day operations of radio and broadcast stations, especially when their schedules were heavy with the *telenovelas*, Grade B movies, and pale imitations of North American adventure programs. The government influence, however, came from another section of the 1960 law, which gave the government the right to use 30 minutes a day of air time on every station, presumably to promote the principles of the basic law.

In 1968 a law was passed levying a tax on all public service industries. For broadcasting, the tax was to equal 25 percent of net income. After vigorous protests by the private broadcast organizations, an agreement was reached that allowed the broadcasters the option of making 12.5 percent of their air time available to the government in lieu of payment. The tax was considered paid if the time was made available; the government did not actually have to use it. In fact, it and other government activities resembled a slick public relations operation more than the blatant control of mass media that occurred in many other

Third World countries. For the most part, the oligarchy of broadcasting, press, and government coexisted comfortably.

During this period other regulations began to reshape the content of broadcasting, although most changes had little effect on the ownership or basic structure of the industry. Advertising was controlled, minimum requirements for live broadcasting were established, and "corruption" of the language was prohibited. Even by North American standards, the requirements were not severe. Television advertising was limited to 18 percent of air time, about the same level as on prime time commercial channels in the United States. For radio, it was 40 percent.

As Mexico's oil revenues and her political ambitions began to grow, the idea of a communication development plan modeled after Unesco statements took form. Communication development took a sharply different direction under President Jose Lopez Portillo when the 1976–1982 Basic Government Plan defined for the first time, albeit superficially, a "right to information," a concept that had been heard with increasing frequency at Unesco. The Mexican plan contained several of the popular codewords such as "democratizing communi-cation," "overcoming the exclusive commercial conception of the media," and information "as an instrument of political and social development."

Not much happened with this new right of communication until the summer of 1979, when the legislature announced that public hearings would be held to discuss laws to specify how this right would be protected. Since the national legislature generally followed the sugges-tions of the executive, some legislation seemed likely. Hearings, not based on any specific proposals, were held through most of 1980. Meanwhile, the government commissioned a group of specialists to draft a proposal. The group worked inconspicuously under the director of planning of the General Coordinating Agency for Social Communication, an office directly under the president.

Interest in the topic declined until a Mexican magazine published what it claimed was an abstract of a 6,500-page, 30-volume draft of a right-to-information law. According to the magazine, the law contained much of the rhetoric of the new global communication order. Its purpose was to "encourage the democratization of the social communication at all levels of operation," "to defend and fortify the national culture and to promote the national integration of the country's different regions." New government institutions would be created to protect the right to "accurate, objective, complete, pluralistic and comprehensible" inform-ation; the right to "respond, amplify, rectify, and answer" media would also be recognized. The law would also guarantee access to information and require publication of certain messages deemed important by the government.

Not surprisingly, the country's powerful private media opposed the proposal and even the leading government officials made little effort to defend it or campaign for public support despite enthusiasm for public control of broadcasting in the public hearings. Meanwhile, Mexico fell victim to the disarray of the oil cartel, and Lopez Portillo left office with his grand plans for rapid economic development and world influence in ruins.

At the IPDC meeting in Acapulco in January 1982, Luis Javier Solana, the director of the General Coordinating Agency for Social Communications, spoke bravely of his country's support for the principles of a new information order supporting a new definition of development:

> Mexico is convinced that social communication should be more democratic, more pluralistic and more participative. . . . It is our responsibility to formulate, implement and sustain initiatives [that would make the media] effective instruments for liberty, justice and the development of our people. . . .

Within a few weeks, however, Solana was removed from office and the government's commitment to national development under the banner of the new world information order disappeared. His replacement was Francisco Galindo Ochoa, a man remembered as one "who in the days of Diaz Ordaz [president from 1964 to 1970] ran the money from the public relations office of the president, which he headed, to newspapermen who then published whatever he wanted." Galindo Ochoa proceeded to fire 120 employees in his department and to cancel 32 of 33 projects they were responsible for, including some international news agency cooperatives within Latin America. He also canceled all government advertising in the magazine that had first disclosed the government's plan. The huge study that was supposed to be a blueprint for Mexico's development was not made public.

If anything, advocates of the new information order, even the moderates in Venezuela and Mexico who wanted to bring some degree of order to a chaotic situation and some public purpose to media that seemed committed only to making money while bowing to the power establishment, learned the difficulties of translating noble sentiments into practical programs. They had to measure their progress in centimeters, not kilometers, but presumably could look forward to a distant time when some semblance of order and purpose might be possible. The proponents of the radical dream of revolutionizing, not reforming, the global system to support the still undefined new global economic and information orders lacked even that consolation.

RADICAL DEVELOPMENT RECONSIDERED

As the 1980s passed mid-decade, the operative word among advocates of harnessing mass media to a Marxist vision of the future was disarray. The new world information order, they argued, had been hijacked by the West with its enticements of glittering technology and meant nothing. Worse, according to Schiller, was that capitalism, once on the ropes from the combined punches of its own exhaustion, socialist opposition, and OPEC, suddenly leaped back to life with information as the new medium of wealth and the multinationals reinvigorated. Those who had hoped the inspiration of the new global orders would lead to a new era of development based on disengagement from the existing world information system were disappointed. The information age seemed to embrace the Third World even more firmly in its technology, global systems, and values. Had the new vision of communication development failed as much as the model articulated by Lerner and Schramm a generation earlier?

Maybe, but some things had changed. Third World countries were cobbling together the mechanisms they claimed they needed and learning firsthand the requirements of editing newsfiles minimally acceptable to audiences inside and outside their own countries. They were learning the futility of filling their media with the puffery that passed for news in many government-run news systems and the impossibility of maintaining a government monopoly on information. A few countries were beginning to assess realistically what kind of national communication systems they wanted and how they could move, however slowly and hesitantly, toward them.

Those who survived the rhetoric of Unesco were, for the most part, pragmatic men and women who recognized that development — however it was defined — was a slow, grueling struggle that could not be shortcircuited by an elixir of communication. If Third World countries mobilized under the banner of the Lerner-Schramm theory of communication and development had not grown in a decade or two into politically stable, economically vibrant democracies, well, no more successful were those countries committed to the use of mass media to create a radical socialist regime based on the new global orders.

Was China's apparent success the product of enlightened use of communication or the strong arm of a brutal regime? Had Tanzania and Cuba, totally dependent on outside aid for economic survival, moved closer toward sovereignty? Had any Third World country achieved an equitable distribution of resources? Had the few countries favored with oil used their treasure to create a better life for their citizens or merely added to the woes of the many without easily exploitable resources?

The loudest advocates of development as disengagement from the West had little to show for their modest experiments. Under pressure they could defend Cuba and China but usually preferred to overlook what was happening there. Cuba, of course, was economically dependent on the Soviet Union and paid for its lifeline by supporting Soviet policies with troops, U.N. votes, and rhetoric on demand. China even seemed to discard the very radical policies that enthralled her Western defenders in favor of a modernization that was built on individual incentives and Western industrialization.

Worst of all, there was Tanzania. Tanzania seemed to embody all of the humane ideals of the new world information order. President Julius Nyerere, a poet and philosopher, commanded respect throughout the world. His country received more foreign aid per capita than any other developing nation, mostly from the Nordic countries. But under his leadership, output per worker declined by half while government bureaucracy doubled in a decade, half of nationalized companies went bankrupt, and a food exporting nation became an importer and a begger before the World Bank. Amnesty International accused the government of imprisonment and torture of political prisoners. After Nyerere's retirement in 1985, the new government even agreed to International Monetary Fund conditions for a loan and officially discarded his policy for building an authentic African socialism. Was this radical national development in action?

A Finnish communication specialist in 1984, reflecting on two and a half years at the Tanzania School of Journalism, concluded that the intent to build a new order was there. Nyerere had committed his country to democratization of communication, horizontal communication, and authentic development, all of the buzzwords of radical development. He had nationalized the existing media and had created new institutions in the image of the new world information order. The commitment to an alternative future was there, and the infrastructure was more or less in place.

But clearly, the experiment had not worked, and the future looked bleaker than the gloomy present. She attributed most of the problem to lingering "colonial tendencies" that militated against embracing the new world information order. Journalists were especially guilty. In fact, a graduate student's thesis had spotted the problem. All but one of 15 journalists interviewed accepted the Western idea of press freedom and felt it did not exist in Tanzania. They thought it should.

Marxists do not like statistics. They make their argument with definitions and dialectic logic. But defenders of the radical definition of development such as Hamelink, Schiller and Masmoudi, need more than Unesco resolutions and their rhetoric to make a case. They need evidence that countries committed to a radical vision of development have fared better than those committed to the traditional goals of political stability and economic growth. It is not easy to find out what happened to Third World countries, whatever their political leanings. The issues of communication development in the 1990s are important enough, however, that we must begin to sort out what happened in the turbulent years of the 1970s and early 1980s and what contribution communication made to the change that engulfed every part of the Third World.

6

The State of Third World Media

THE PROBLEM OF SIMPLE QUESTIONS

According to Unesco figures, there were 39,000 TV sets in Algeria in 1978. Three years later, according to the *World Radio TV Handbook*, the number was 256,000. For the same year, 1981, the BBC estimated the number of TV sets at 900,000. Another estimate put the total at 975,000 in 1980.

The number of TV sets in Algeria obviously did not jump from 39,000 to 975,000 in two years. But if 320,000 sets were licensed (a European Broadcasting Union figure), the total number must have been more than 256,000. Maybe it *was* 975,000.

As we saw in the previous chapter, neither advocates of the use of mass media to promote economic and political growth nor those who defined development as a disengagement from the West could point to dramatic success of development projects, with or without mass media as magic multiplier or catalyst. As we will see later, it was impossible to demonstrate that an investment of X-dollars in a broadcasting system led to a reduction of Y-percent in illiteracy or an increase of Z-units in GNP. Development goals such as "democratic communication" or "cultural sovereignty" defied definition, let alone measurement.

Occasionally the problem was too many numbers, as in the count of TV sets in Algeria, but usually it was too few. Despite efforts of organizations such as Unesco, the missing data columns in the international yearbooks made any definitive assessment of the state of the Third World just about impossible. Still the question of results of the first decades of conscious efforts to use mass media to promote two radically different definitions of development is important enough for the 1980s and beyond that we cannot throw up our hands and return to the old arguments.

THE 1960s IN REVIEW

For the 1975 Honolulu conference, Schramm dug through the available numbers, mostly from Unesco yearbooks, to look at the 10-year period from 1963 to 1973. The patterns he found then were a taste of what would happen in the next decade as well: modest gains in print media along with spectacular growth in broadcasting; some increase in the physical quality of life in the Third World but with most gains swallowed by population growth; not much progress in building democracy. At the conference itself there was growing suspicion that mass media by themselves lacked the power to drive development that Lerner and Schramm had ascribed to them.

For the Third World as a whole — three-quarters of the world's population as varied in development as in politics and culture — daily newspaper circulation increased from 33 to 45 million copies while the number of radio receivers jumped from 46 million to 145 million. Television, unknown in most developing countries even in the mid-1960s, grew from fewer than a million sets in 1963 to 28 million sets a decade later. Were mass media themselves at the self-sustaining takeoff point of growth where they could begin to do the work Lerner and Schramm assigned to them?

Hardly. The gross numbers hid several important parts of the picture. When totals were divided by population, the growth was less impressive and the gap between West and Third World became clear. Third World newspaper circulation barely increased at all, from 15 to 16 copies per thousand people. Worse, even though the percent of illiteracy in all regions of the Third World decreased, the total number of illiterate adults increased by 65 million.

Electronic media did outpace the population growth, the first rumblings of an explosion that reached even the remotest corners of the Third World a decade later. Between 1963 and 1973, radios increased from 21 to 53 per thousand population; TV sets grew from three to ten per thousand people.

Consider what these figures mean. Even if these scarce media were evenly distributed throughout the Third World and equally accessible, one person would have to share a radio with about 20 others, a TV set with almost 100 people, and a newspaper with 60. And, of course, the media were not evenly distributed.

Most of the mass media in the Third World were — and still are — in Latin America. Africa and Asia continue to be the most media poor. Even in the early 1970s, Africans on the average had to share each copy of a newspaper with 71 people, each TV set with 250. Asia, because of the influence of China in regional figures, was as poor as Africa in TV sets and poorer in radios.

Third World gains also obscured the disparity between the developing countries and the developed West. We do not have comparable data for 1960, but figures from 1970, when the West was well into the communication explosion that precipitated the new world information order debate, show the dimensions of the large and expanding gap. In 1970 the Third World, with 71 percent of the world's population, had 27 percent of all radio transmitters and only 15 percent of all radio receivers. Less than 5 percent of the world's TV transmitters and only 17 percent of TV receivers were in the Third World. While the average person in the Third World consumed 0.9 kilograms of newsprint a year, his or her counterpart in the developed world consumed 17.8 kilograms.

Schramm found some basis for optimism in 1975, mostly the rapid growth of broadcasting that outpaced other areas of development and population growth as well. His hope was that new communication technologies would allow Third World countries to leapfrog some of the stages of communication development. That optimism was tempered with the recognition that Third World countries, because of continuing population growth, would have to run faster than the West just to keep up, that the gap was likely to get bigger, not smaller, and that the dominance of the information-rich West would continue into the next decades.

THE 1970s IN OVERVIEW

By the early 1980s, more and better data were available and the patterns that Schramm noted a decade earlier came into clear focus. But not without gaps and contradictions in the evidence. For our exploration of the 1970s we collected numbers from different sources, mostly Unesco, World Bank and, for estimates of radio and TV receivers, the BBC. To fill in the holes we estimated the missing data by dividing the roster of 126 Third World countries for which minimal figures were available into 10 groups based on per capita income and used the average of the decile group as an estimate for any missing national figure on literacy, life expectancy, etc. The numbers are only estimates, of course, but probably as accurate and certainly more complete than any other available summaries. Unless otherwise noted, they are used in this discussion.

According to Unesco estimates, Third World population grew from

2.6 billion in 1970 to 3.2 billion in 1980, an increase of 25 percent. The result was that the modest gains of development had to be divided among more people and, as had happened in the 1960s, absolute gains were often lost among the larger population. Still, as was befitting the information age, mass media ran against this tide in two ways. The first was that radio and television continued to expand at an exponential rate in the Third World. Beyond that was the encouraging sign that the developing countries' share of all media increased.

According to BBC estimates, the total number of radio receivers in the Third World increased from 100 million in 1970 to 227 million in 1980. The Third World's share of all radios increased from 15 to 19 percent. For television, the growth was spectacular: 22 million TV sets in 1970 to 69 million, an increase in the Third World's share of all sets from 8 to 13 percent.

The snapshot of newspaper change is less clear because Unesco summaries are not always comparable. They do report, however, that total newspaper circulation in the Third World in 1979 was 450 million copies per day, 17 percent of the world's total. In total numbers of newspapers, however, the Third World showed remarkable strength. In 1965, Unesco counted 2,622 dailies in the Third World; its estimates for 1979 included 3,580 Third World daily papers, an increase of 35 percent. Even more surprising: in 1979, 43 percent of all of the world's daily papers were in the Third World.

What did these numbers mean for the families that Lerner and Schramm had described more than 20 years earlier? Their lives certainly were changed, and mass media played a big part in the change. A few closeups are available. In 1982, Dharem Yadav returned to two rural Indian villages that he had studied 18 years earlier for his dissertation at Michigan State under Rogers. The villages were part of an early rural development program designed particularly to increase agricultural production. One was selected because it was relatively "progressive," the other because it was not.

Yadav found that most people in the villages had indeed changed; they had developed "a propensity to innovate, to excel, to achieve and to believe in economic rationality and personal efficiency." Mass media played an important role in people's daily lives "by providing them with a larger and more diverse universe of social, cultural and political discourse."

Family radio ownership increased in the more progressive village from 33 to 98 percent, from 20 to 89 percent in the less progressive village. More than 90 percent of the people listened frequently in both villages. Even TV viewing, unknown in 1964, was widespread. One-third and one-half of residents of the less progressive and more progressive villages, respectively, watched frequently, and 9 and 17 percent of the families owned their own sets. Regular newspaper readership in the less progressive village increased from 33 to 74 percent; in the other it rose from 41 to 61 percent. Magazine readership also increased; only attendance at movies declined. Some of the earlier disparity between the two villages had disappeared.

By virtually all the criteria of development, life had improved in these two Indian villages, but there were costs. Peasant families were spending more of their still scarce resources on things like soft drinks, fancy cooking and dinnerware, and tape recorders. The new, better life was defined mostly by materialist consumption. And not everyone shared. Traditional occupations of those without land — weaving, shoemaking, carpentry, toolmaking — had virtually disappeared when it became cheaper and easier to buy ready-made substitutes in the city. Yadav does not speculate, but the tradesmen and tinkerers of the two villages probably migrated to the city where they joined the growing mass of India's urban poor.

This is basically an optimistic closeup of the changes that had taken place in millions of villages throughout the Third World under the banner of the old idea of national development. When we enlarge the picture, however, to include the displaced craftsmen as well as the newly prosperous farmers, the countries where basic development programs foundered, and the millions of new-born, the picture dims.

Between 1970 and 1980, per capita gross national product grew by 30 to 40 percent in both the developing and developed countries. But the gap between rich and poor — chasm is a better world — remained. Per capita GNP among the rich nations was $7,803 in 1980, only $743 in the Third World. It is GNP, of course, that allows people to buy radios, TV sets, and newspapers, and their governments and sometimes private corporations to build broadcasting facilities and printing plants. And wealth also makes possible education, health care programs, and public works projects. Even those who advocated disengagement from the West as an alternative vision of development had to acknowledge that an increase in wealth was the foundation for any progress.

Most measures of social change in the Third World reflected some good news, some bad. Adult literacy for the Third World as a whole reached 59 percent by 1980. This represented a steady if unspectacular growth over the preceding two decades, when adult literacy was 44 percent in 1960 and 52 percent in 1970. In 1980, however, there were more than 800 million illiterate adults in the developing countries, about 75 million more than Schramm had counted a decade earlier.

The immediate problem of the increasing pool of illiterate adults was overshadowed by a longer-range concern. Only 51 percent of school-age children were in school, less than the proportion of literate adults. Unless adult literacy programs could make up the difference or school-age children were learning to read and write informally, the number of illiterate children becoming illiterate adults would continue to swell the numbers of this unfortunate group.

The same good news–bad news picture emerges from health statistics, which represent the kind of social goals that communication development was supposed to promote. The number of physicians in the Third World doubled in the decade of the 1970s from 659,000 to 1.3 million, twice the increase in the developed countries. Each physician in the developed world, however, served an average of 430 people; in the developing nations each doctor served an average of 2,612 people. In the North, one hospital bed was available for every 100 people; in the Third World, each bed had to serve 579 people.

The human side of these discrepancies can be seen in two simple comparisons. In the Third World, of every 1,000 infants born alive at the end of the 1970s, 107 would die before reaching their first birthday, compared to 20 in the developed nations. A baby born in the developing countries of Asia, Africa, the Middle East, or Latin America could expect to live to age 58. A baby born in the developed world could expect to live 14 years longer, to age 72.

Critics of early communication development, such as Schiller and Beltran, would probably dismiss this evidence as irrelevant. Of course, even the harshest critics acknowledged that increased wealth was a requisite for any kind of development, but they would argue that even the meager resources within each country of the Third World ought to be shared equitably and, more to the point, that the more generous resources of the developed countries ought to be dispersed around the globe as a matter of justice, not politics.

The key words of the alternative model of development were *equity, appropriateness,* and *independence.* By equity they meant that development should emphasize sharing of the nation's resources, however limited they were. The notion of appropriateness was linked to the preservation of traditional cultures and values and particularly to the integration of new and mostly Western technology into traditional practices so as to avoid the political upheavals and social disruptions that had characterized so much of the first two decades of Third World independence. Finally, independence meant the ability of nations to control their own destinies or simply to exert cultural sovereignty as well as political sovereignty.

It is difficult to know whether Third World countries as a whole and specifically whether textbook models of alternative development such as China, Cuba, and Tanzania were making progress toward their alternative vision of development. Data on distribution of wealth are still hard to come by, but recent estimates of a small number of countries suggest that the differences between developed and developing countries remain significant. With data from the World Bank on 20 developing countries and 12 developed countries (all part of the mostly capitalist West), one study found, not surprisingly, that that distribution of wealth was more skewed in the developing nations, regardless of political system, than in the West. However, some useful comparisons between neighboring Third World countries can be made. In Tanzania, for example, the wealthiest 20 percent of households received half (50%) of disposable income in 1969, while the poorest quintile received less than 6 percent. In neighboring Kenya in 1974, where the government actively promoted capitalism, the richest 20 percent of the families received 60 percent of the total income, while the poorest 20 percent received slightly less than 3 percent. When other factors in Tanzania's record are considered — the highest per capita foreign aid in the world, shift from food-exporter to food-importer, social disruption from forced uprooting of rural life — the modest numerical improvements over Kenya's capitalist development are not impressive.

The gulf between rich and poor nations is greatest when we look at the indicators of development that measure education, health, and social conditions. Do differences in these development goals differ by social and economic system? In some cases the answer is yes. Between the two giants of the Third World there were big differences. China had a per capita GNP, for example, of $290 compared with $240 in India. China spent five times as much on military per capita as India ($26 vs $5) and three times as much on education ($15 vs $5). Literacy in China was 66 percent but only 36 percent in India. And the Physical Quality of Life Index (PQLI) that combines infant mortality, life expectancy, and literacy was 76 for China but only 44 for India.

Cuba, which was one of the other models of alternative development, did even better by these standards: a per capita GNP of $1,410, expenditures of $82 and $49 on education and military, nearly universal literacy (96 percent) and 93 on the PQLI scale. Of course, Latin America was the most developed of all of the Third World regions and Cuba rated about the same as nearby Costa Rica, whose political and economic system was very different and among the most "developed" countries in Latin America at the time of the Castro revolution.

In Africa, Kenya and Tanzania both rated a 53 on the PQLI index, while Tanzania had a higher level of literacy (66 vs 48 percent) but lower per capita GNP ($260 vs $420). Tanzania spent less than Kenya on both education ($12 per capita vs $17) and its military ($10 vs $12).

These figures support the common-sense conclusion that Third

World countries that have opted for an essentially socialist, non-Western development enjoyed a higher level of social standards and greater sharing in the benefits of educational and health programs, especially by the people who comprise the mass of the Third World population. On the other side of the argument is the generally lower level of economic development and, more important, the high price of loss of personal freedom.

"Democracy" is a development objective no one would reject, but a definition is elusive. In Western terms, many of those Third World countries that have attained impressive victories in the fight against illiteracy and disease have done so at a great price. There is no index of socialist democracy, but the annual ratings of civil and political liberties made by Freedom House are a good measure of democracy as defined in the West. Freedom House rates each country from 1 to 7 on the two scales and summarizes the ratings by labeling each country as "free," "partly free" or "not free." It will come as no surprise that countries like China, Cuba, and Tanzania are in the "not free" category.

Of course, advocates of a vision of the future based on the radical model of communication development might want to reverse most of the "free" and "not free" classifications. Nevertheless, both sides could agree that mass media development in the Third World in the 1970s favored those countries and regions that were generally "free" by traditional Western definitions. Many of these same nations and regions also showed the greatest economic development, although they generally were less successful in improving the quality of life of their citizens.

One aspect of the alternative goals of communication development that is amenable to measurement was what Rogers and others called "horizontal communication." In its more political interpretations, *horizontal communication* was often cited to support the new regional news exchange mechanisms or, even more vaguely, people-to-people communication independent of the one-way structure of mass media or government control. The simplest mechanisms for this kind of communication are so familiar in the West that they are often taken for granted: mail, telegrams, and telephones. Telecommunication was especially important because it became the centerpiece of the new development efforts in the 1980s backed, as we will see, by solid evidence that it did promote economic growth.

The gap between developed and developing countries in this often overlooked element of communication development can be illustrated by calling to mind the situation in many Third World countries where there is no mail delivery, only rental boxes in a central post office, and often no access to mail outside of the capital. Phone service is limited to those willing to stand in line at a PTT office. Many people in the Third World still cannot send or receive mail, telephone calls, or telegrams.

It is not surprising that the greatest growth of horizontal communication was in telephones. Per capita availability of telephones increased by about 50 percent in Africa and Latin America between 1970 and 1978 and by more than 100 percent in the Middle East and Asia. These are encouraging figures, of course, until we recall that, as is true of every communication indicator we have examined, what we take for granted in the West is still a luxury in most of the world. In Africa, for example, in 1978, there was about one telephone for every 100 people. And in the neighboring Middle East, where telephone availability increased rapidly, there were only eight phones for every 100 people.

REGIONAL COMPARISONS

So far, we have looked at the three-quarters of the world's total population that form the Third World as a whole, with only occasional glimpses of regions and individual countries. We cannot examine the state of mass media in all of the states represented in the data, but we can look at regional differences, keeping in mind that any geographic clustering puts together disparate nations.

In this exercise in map making, we will divide the Third World into four regional categories. Africa includes all of the continent except South Africa. The northern tier of Arab countries is included in the continent rather than in the group of Middle East countries. The Middle East group includes Turkey, plus the nations of the eastern Mediterranean (except Israel) across the Persian Gulf through Iran. Pakistan is classified as an Asian country along with all the other nations and territories of that vast region except for Australia, New Zealand, and Japan. We have put all of the countries from Mexico south through Central and Latin America into the category of Latin America, along with all of the islands of the Caribbean.

Africa
The greatest fallacy about Africa, according to John Barton, whose experience as a journalist and trainer of journalists in Africa is without equal, "perpetrated by Africans themselves quite as much as by White Westerners or Yellow Easterners, is that Africa is one great homogeneous whole, almost one country with one pattern and one inevitable destiny."

Within a continent that stretches 5,000 miles from the Mediterranean to Capetown and more than 4,000 miles from the Cape Verde Islands to the Horn of Africa, there are 400 million people grouped into 50 countries, almost all of which are formally independent of colonial control. Within that patchwork quilt of political boundaries, mostly the

legacy of irrational colonial patterns, are 1,000 distinct and mutually
unintelligible languages. Or is it 2,000? Or 600? Sources vary; none
claims to be definitive.

One characteristic all African countries share is a lack of reliable
information. Are there 39,000 TV sets in Algeria? Or 900,000? Estimates,
most of which are guesses based on varying degrees of expertise, can
vary by as much as that, and sometimes even more. Beyond the common
frustration of missing and contradictory statistics, African nations and
people share little.

The African press is equally diverse. Barton concluded that the only
common denominator was the hand of official control. The same could
be said for broadcasting. As he put it, as political freedom came to Africa,
press freedom disappeared. And with that disappearance came a decline
of what had been a modest press system linked, of course, to the colonial
system rather than to African independence.

David Lamb, the Los Angeles *Times* correspondent in Africa in the
late 1970s, reported that the number of newspapers in Africa declined by
half from 1960 to the end of the 1970s. And he quotes Barton that the
question of newspapers in Africa's future is whether they will survive at
all. Barton himself counted 156 dailies in Africa at the beginning of 1977,
down from a Unesco count of 220 in 1964. Lamb reported that six black
African countries had no newspapers at all. The Unesco minimum
criterion for what it regards as an "adequate" communication system is
100 copies per 1,000 people. Africa in the 1980s at barely one-tenth of
that minimum remained the most newspaper-poor part of the Third
World.

The picture of broadcasting in Third World Africa, however, was
brighter. In retrospect, Schramm's predictions about the effect of
transistors on the Third World were conservative. Consider these data
from annual BBC estimates of radio and television receivers.

In 1965 there were 9.4 million radios in Third World Africa: by 1980
the number had jumped to 40 million and to 60 million four years later.
The number of radios increased much faster than population, from
34 per thousand people in 1965 to 100 radios per thousand in 1980 and
129 per thousand in 1984. In about 1970, Africa reached the Unesco
minimum of 50 radios per thousand; a decade later the number of radios
per thousand had doubled.

Television was mostly unknown in Africa in the 1960s, when most
countries achieved independence, and several still have none, although
in some cases receivers can pick up signals from neighboring countries.
Almost without exception, advisers on mass media development have
argued against a rapid expansion of TV. It is expensive, serves only a tiny
urban elite, and opens the nation to foreign cultural influence because so

many programs must be imported. But the pressure to build a TV system is more than most governments can withstand. TV is a symbol of modernity and an irresistible medium for African leaders.

In 1965, BBC estimates put the total number of TV sets in Third World Africa at about 500,000, only two receivers for every 1,000 people. By 1980 the total number of sets had grown to more than six million. Only four years later, it was 14 million. By 1984 the number of sets had grown to 29 per thousand.

Although no figures are available to support the assertion, television by most accounts is even more unevenly dispersed than radio. In most cases only the national capital has a signal and it does not reach outside the metropolitan area. TV, beyond the means of all but a few, is inevitably a window to a foreign world which most viewers, even those few who can afford it, can never hope to achieve. Yet the pressure for more transmitters and more receivers grows, and the accelerating growth of the 1970s is not likely to slow.

What we have defined as horizontal communication — mail, telegram, and telephone — began the 1970s at the lowest point among the four Third World regions and grew only modestly. The continent in 1970 averaged only eight telephones per 1,000 people, a figure which grew 117 percent in the next eight years. Mail, both international and domestic, and telegrams expanded rapidly from a low base at the beginning of the decade.

Middle East

No region of the Third World changed as much in the 1970s as the 15 countries that encompass the Middle East. If there is any example of the new world economic order in action, defined in practice as the transfer of wealth from the West to the Third World, it is in the handful of countries in the Middle East that were fortunate enough to be located over massive oil reserves. In the wealthiest of the newly rich OPEC countries, any kind of economic development seemed possible.

The Arab region of the Middle East probably underwent more change in the past two decades than any other part of the Third World. The result was that several of the OPEC nations are among the richest in the world in terms of per capita income or GNP and that their media systems grew from primitive or nonexistent to the most sophisticated in the world in only a decade.

William Rugh, a Foreign Service officer with extensive experience in the region, described Arab media as politically patronized, fragmented, geographically concentrated in a few urban centers, and low in credibility and prestige. Direct oral communication among family, friends, and traditional opinion leaders was still of great importance despite rapid growth of mass communication.

Rugh put Middle East press systems into a three-category typology. The "mobilization press" (Algeria, Egypt, Iraq, Libya, Sudan, Syria, and South Yemen) was that new breed of media which became legitimate in the 1970s: an agent of the regime used actively to promote national economic, social, and political development. The "loyalist press" (Bahrain, Jordan, Qatar, Saudi Arabia, Tunisia, and the United Arab Emirates) had more in common with traditional authoritarianism. While generally privately owned, the loyalist press was passive and supportive of the government; government pressure rather than direct ownership was used to prevent the press from becoming an active challenge to authority. Finally, there was the "diverse press" (Lebanon, Morocco, and Kuwait), which was akin to the Western concept of journalism: privately owned for the most part, challenging the government on occasion, reflecting some diversity in public debate.

As is true in Africa as well, broadcasting was a government monopoly in virtually all countries of the Middle East and in most was mobilized to promote development efforts.

Despite the rapid infusion of petro-dollars into the Middle East, the area as a whole showed less than spectacular newspaper growth in the 1970s. In the 15 countries we have included in the region, the number of daily newspapers increased from 489 in 1965 to 607 in 1977. Circulation increased only from 4.5 to 4.8 million, but the average circulation per thousand population dropped from 45 copies to 37. These estimates put the Middle East slightly ahead of Africa in newspaper availability, but not by much.

It is in broadcasting, however, where the greatest growth in Middle East media came. According to BBC estimates, the number of radios increased from 6.4 million in 1965 to 10 million in 1970 and to 32 million in 1984. Radio receivers per thousand people increased from 82 in 1965 to 221 in 1984. Television sets, of course, were still rare in 1982, but the number grew rapidly. In 1965 the total was less than half a million sets in the entire 15-country region; by 1970 the number had increased to about 900,000. By 1980 the total had increased tenfold to 8.8 million, and four years later, it was almost 14 million. Sets per thousand increased from six in 1965 to 894 in 1984.

The same spectacular but uneven growth in broadcasting in the Middle East was also shown in telephones. From a 1970 figure of 37 telephones per 1,000 people — slightly behind Latin America but ahead of the other Third World regions — the figure doubled in the next eight years to 75 phones per 1,000 people, the highest of any Third World region. Mail figures were uneven and the number of domestic telegrams increased, but international telegram traffic decreased.

Asia

The third of the globe we have included in "Asia" is so large and diverse that one hesitates to treat it as a single entity. It includes more than half of the world's population and more than 70 percent of the Third World. China alone contains more than a fifth of the world's population; India, with an estimated 700 million population, accounts for 15 percent of the world total.

Asia, as we have defined it, stretches from Afghanistan to the tiny island nation of Tuvalu (population 7,000). Languages, cultures, and histories are as varied as the nations themselves; a majority of the world's Muslims live in Asia and the world's third-largest English-speaking country (the Philippines) is Asian. India alone uses 16 official languages and half the world's alphabets. Colonial powers that have exerted varying long-range influence include Britain, France, the Netherlands, Spain, the United States, and Japan. Asia is a distinct regional entity only geographically and, even then, dispersed over distances that have prevented the kind of common experience that gives the Middle East, Latin America, and even parts of Africa the appearance and occasionally the sense of unity.

One often thinks of Asia in terms of the hardware that has produced the communication revolution in the West and the gathering momentum of radio and television growth we have seen in Africa and the Middle East. But this "Made in Asia" symbol is limited mostly to Japan, which is excluded from Third World Asia, and a few small pockets of growth like Hong Kong, South Korea, and Singapore. In fact Asia, with or without China, is the most media-poor part of the Third World.

According to Unesco estimates, the number of daily newspapers in Third World Asia (excluding China) grew from 916 in 1965 to 1,431 in 1977. Total circulation grew from 34 million to only 36 million. Even without China, however, these numbers are misleading because of the huge population against which they must be measured. Circulation per thousand averaged 19 copies per thousand people in 1965 and declined to 16 per thousand in 1977.

In broadcasting, the differences between Asia as a whole and other developing regions were more dramatic. In 1965, for all Asian Third World countries (including China and India) there were 22 million radios or 14 radios per thousand population. By 1970 the total number of radios had increased to 48 million; by 1980 it was 153 million and 230 million four years later. But these averaged out to only 14 radios per thousand people in 1965, 27 per thousand in 1970, 70 per thousand in 1980, and 96 per thousand in 1984. This is the saturation the Middle East had in 1965 and the level Africa reached in the early 1970s.

Television was even less developed. From a total of 500,000 sets in

1965, the number of sets in Third World Asian countries grew to 1.9 million in 1970, to 19 million in 1980, and to 49 million four years later. This remarkable growth — the fastest in any part of the world — however, increased the per thousand figures from only 0.3 in 1965 to nine per thousand in 1980 and 20 in 1984. The 20 per thousand figure is less than Latin America counted in 1965 and about the level reached in Africa and the Middle East in the mid-1970s.

China, of course, dominates any regional calculation because it accounts for nearly half of the total Third World Asian population. And China, despite rapid growth in the past decade, was still behind most of the rest of the Third World in broadcasting development. According to BBC estimates, China's 90 million radios in 1984 averaged only 88 per thousand population, and her 20 million TV receivers represented only 20 sets per thousand population.

Another major contributor to the surprisingly low figures for Asia was India. Despite its tradition of democracy and press vigor, India had fewer radio and TV sets than China. In 1984, the BBC estimates put the total number of radios at 45 million and TV sets at 2 million. These represented only 63 radios per thousand population and only three TV receivers per thousand. Against the population and media poverty of these two countries, the several small but relatively well-developed Asian countries such as Taiwan, Singapore, and South Korea, carried little weight in regional totals.

Horizontal communication estimates showed Asia below the Middle East and Latin America and only slightly ahead of Africa. Mail and telegram traffic increased modestly in the decade. One bright note: telephones grew faster in Asia than in any of the three other regions. From 14 units per 1,000 people in 1970, the figure increased 100 percent to 28 per 1,000 in 1978. While three times as high as the figure for Africa, the 28 per 1,000 figure was less than half that of Latin America and the Middle East.

Latin America

Of all of the major regions of the Third World, Latin America was the first to be conquered by European colonial powers and the first to be liberated. Unlike so much of Africa, the Middle East, and Asia, most Latin American countries achieved political independence in the first half of the nineteenth century. The cultural and religious influence of Spain and Portugal remained, of course, and the United States replaced the colonial powers as the dominant political influence. Some would argue that the American influence, exercised occasionally by military force although more by political and economic force, constituted a new style of imperial control. It was no coincidence that much of the theory and rhetoric of economic and cultural imperialism developed in Latin America. It was easy to find support in many parts of the region for the old lament about Mexico: so far from God and so close to the United States.

Latin America is often considered the most culturally homogeneous of the Third World regions, but even that generalization is misleading. "Latin America" includes more than the continental land mass from the Rio Grande to the Strait of Magellan. When we include the Caribbean, the number of independent nations involved almost doubles and the historical and cultural generalizations fall apart. Here are countries that speak French, English with both American and British accents, and even Dutch. Here are islands that are still part of European and North American motherlands and independent nations less than a decade old. Some are models of parliamentary democracy; others succumbed to dictatorship. Most favor some form of capitalism; a few opted for moderate to radical socialism.

The one thing that separates Latin America from the other Third World regions is the high level of media development, a product of private ownership, even in broadcasting, and U.S. influence. Though some countries, particularly in the Caribbean, are exceptions, almost all Latin American nations have newspapers and radio and TV receivers at levels that are close to those in many Western nations.

The media in most Latin American countries function in authoritarian regimes: they are usually independent of government ownership but subject to considerable government influence that ebbs and flows with the character of government. Many saw in the 1980s a movement away from military dictatorship and toward elected civilian government and, presumably, greater press independence. Some of that influence is open and direct, but much of it in Latin America is indirect and subtle. It includes pressures such as control of imported newsprint, occasional bribes, and the too common threat of physical violence by unknown forces against independent and critical journalists.

A leading scholar categorized three national media systems: "free" (Venezuela, Colombia, and Costa Rica); independent but operating under various kinds of "media guidance" (Mexico, Peru, and Brazil); and the rest, which were subjected to differing levels of censorship. The Caribbean improves the count of "free" media countries significantly. Freedom House in 1982 listed nine island nations as "free nations," the biggest concentration in the Third World.

Calculations reflecting the rate of growth of Latin America in the 1970s generally showed lower growth than in other Third World regions. This, however, was partly a reflection of higher levels to begin with and partly the result of the staggering increase in population. Latin America was the one region of the Third World where newspaper growth lagged behind the population increase. In 1965, Unesco data listed 1,062 daily papers in Latin America and the Caribbean; by 1977 the number had grown only to 1,160. Total circulation in the decade of the 1970s grew from 19 million copies a day to 20 million. The average national circulation, however, was 70 copies per thousand in 1970 but only 56 copies in 1980, a drop of 20 percent.

The numbers of radio and TV sets kept ahead of population, although the increase in both total numbers and rates per thousand population were more modest in Latin America than in other regions. In 1965 Latin America counted 28 million radios, a number that grew to 129 million by 1984. The number of TV receivers grew from 6.5 million in 1962 to 50 million in 1984. In sets per thousand, those numbers changed from 123 radios per thousand in 1965 to 343 in 1984; TV sets per thousand grew from 29 in 1965 to 134 in 1984.

As we might expect, horizontal communication figures showed a similar pattern: high levels of development with steady but not spectacular growth. Mail and telegram traffic grew unevenly. The number of telephones — the highest of any Third World region in 1970 at 39 per 1,000 people — grew by 52 percent between 1970 and 1978. That less-than-spectacular growth put Latin America in second place among the four Third World regions, behind the Middle East but still considerably ahead of Asia and Africa.

This array of figures, still rough estimates but probably better than anything else available, could become mind numbing if we begin to look at individual countries. And the figures add to the confusion of the central issue of communication development in the 1980s. Did mass media contribute to economic and political growth, as advocates of the old order had argued? Did they support the new theory of development, defined as disengagement from the West and promotion of "authentic" Third World alternatives? Or did the explosion of radio and television and slow plodding growth of newspapers in the 1970s take place independently of politics and economics and contribute nothing to them? Any intelligent guide to communication development in the coming decade will need answers to these questions.

If it was difficult to count the number of TV sets in Algeria in the 1970s, consider the additional problems of deciphering the influence of those sets on economic, political, and social changes in Algeria at the same time. Cautious North American academicians might contend the task was impossible; their Marxist critics would argue it was irrelevant. But the question was at the heart of the debate over the role of mass media in national development in the 1980s, the outcome of the collision between the naive belief that mass media could accelerate the Third World's terrible ascent toward economic and political stability, and the counterclaim that mass media must be mobilized to support an authentic but ill-defined development based on disengagement from the West. After 20 years, were there still no simple answers?

MORE PROBLEMS WITH SIMPLE QUESTIONS

The central question that had inspired both the original hypothesis of communication's ability to speed economic and political development and the revisionist definition of development as authentic Third World development separated from the West was still unanswered. What was the role of mass media in all the changes in the turbulent decade of the 1970s?

If it is difficult to count the TV sets in Algeria, consider the problems of sorting out their influence on the long list of social, economic, and political factors that make up the term "development," even deciding in which order they occur. Some American social scientists would argue flatly that you cannot demonstrate such relationships outside of a controlled laboratory setting, but most would accept a looser argument that you can at least see if the numbers are consistent with one or another theory. If so, the theory is tenable; not proved, but defensible until someone comes along with better evidence or a better theory.

For Beltran, as we saw in an earlier chapter, the inherent intellectual conservatism of traditional Western social science was part of the problem because communication researchers had looked mostly at individuals and how they responded to mass media, not the political and economic system in which the mass media operated. The result, he could claim, was that researchers learned a little about trees but nothing about the forest. A premise of the revisionist model of communication and development, true to its Marxist intellectual roots, was that the political and economic system determined individual behavior. A study of how much peasants learned from rural radio forums or how exposure to American sitcoms influenced attitudes was irrelevant; Marxist assumptions were subject to interpretation but not question.

The record of Third World development played only a small part in the great debate over communication and development in the 1970s, partly because of the very different intellectual positions of the participants, partly because of the lack of adequate evidence and, in the final analysis, the irrelevance of evidence to ideological positions. The first and final points of contention cannot be resolved, but the data on communication and development-related factors discussed above allow us to address old questions with better information. And with better analytical tools as well.

TESTING CONFLICTING THEORIES

Lerner and Schramm, of course, argued that mass media could multiply development efforts and, therefore, promote rapid economic growth and stable democracy. In the 1970s, most American researchers moved away from that position to one that argued for a modest role for mass media. The shift seemed to be partly a product of the ascendancy of the alternative view of development and its concomitant emphasis on national and international economic and political systems and partly the result of testing of the Lerner-Schramm approach with better evidence and more sophisticated techniques. The argument seemed reasonable in the 1960s, but cold, hard statistics to back it up were hard to come by.

It is still a difficult job to assemble adequate, complete evidence on the state of development at either the individual or aggregate national level. Lerner's evidence was weak and excluded most developing countries because data did not exist. Schramm, especially in his papers for the Honolulu conferences, had more complete information but based his analysis on admittedly shaky analytical techniques. About the same time, political scientist Frederick W. Frey tried to synthesize several major studies that had addressed the once dominant theory of development, but ran into the recurring problem of conflicting results.

Among individuals, Frey found considerable support for the arguments advanced by Lerner and Schramm. Work by psychologists, sociologists, political scientists, and anthropologists as well as communication researchers tended to demonstrate that change did occur in roughly the pattern Lerner and his supporters expected: an elite, more open to change and more exposed to mass media, became the innovators of new ideas and practices; at a certain point their example diffused to a broader segment of the population until finally all but a few laggards had changed. Mass media seemed to facilitate this process by providing information as well as the disposition to accommodate change and often to seek it out.

At the national level, analyzing aggregate data such as percent literate, per capita income, radios per thousand population, etc., Frey found the evidence less consistent. Even if limited to the simple definition of economic growth, development seemed to have more to do with factors unrelated to mass media. Political development, which was the outcome of development in the original Lerner study, was even less clearly linked to media growth. From several large-scale studies, some based on cross-sectional data gathered at one time, others based on time-series data gathered over time, Frey could find no consistent support for, or rejection of, any link in the original Lerner theory.

With some evidence of frustration Frey concluded that the precise role of communication in development was still unclear and, fur-thermore, that the key relationships could change during various stages of the development process. He questioned whether any single theory could fit the disparate set of Third World countries.

Other analyses came up with the same conclusions — and a new twist. Individuals did seem to benefit from development programs, but the benefits did not accrue to the nation. At least there was no good evidence that growth in mass media at one point led to a measurable increase in gross national product, literacy, or quality of life later on. The new concern was that the benefits typically went mostly to people who were already leaders in wealth, power, or control over their lives. As had happened with some of the antipoverty programs in the United States in the 1960s and 1970s, the result was an "effects gap." Those with the least at the beginning of the program gained something but those already better off gained more; the result was that the development program served mostly to increase the gap between the few at the top of the national pyramid and the many at the bottom.

The failure of sophisticated analysis to come up with clear-cut support for the traditional theory about the use of mass media to support development was one reason for its decline. Certainly critics such as Beltran were reacting to the cautious method of American social science as much as to its use by conservative politicians to support the existing political and economic system. But what evidence, beyond the dialectic argument of Marxism, did advocates of alternative development have?

Not much, as it turned out. When they tried to buttress their case with statistics, proponents of development as disengagement found themselves pointing to just about the same kind of cautious conclusions found in small-scale studies. Goren Hedebro, for example, a strong supporter of Tanzania's socialist experiment, noted a health-campaign experiment in which test families, on the average, turned one negative practice into two positive ones. Comparable progress in China and Cuba was taken on faith. In all three case studies, success in communication development was attributed to mobilized media, coordinated (cen-tralized?) development planning, and open vertical and horizontal communication; but he offered no evidence of any of it.

Down the African coast, two French scholars described the intro-duction of television to Mozambique courtesy of an Italian aid project. In the initial phase the project was limited to a low-power transmitter in the capital with sets installed in neigborhood cultural centers. It was to be used by education, health, and agriculture sectors. What made this different from the thousands of projects undertaken in the name of development in the preceding two decades? According to them the program, which was mostly a test run for a national program, "questions the vertical character of the established models of communication and aims to substitute a communication system made in the name of the people by a communication system made by the people." The difference must lie in the eye of the beholder; on paper and in the field the program could have been undertaken in the 1960s under the banner of development raised by Lerner and Schramm.

In Tanzania, Mozambique, and the dozen or so other Third World countries that had consciously mobilized mass media to create a future envisioned by the radical theory of development, communication development projects looked pretty much like they did in countries still subscribing to the Lerner-Schramm argument. And whether the goal of development was economic growth of the 1960s or the "authentic" Third World development of the 1970s, the result was about the same.

DEVELOPMENT RECONSIDERED

By the early 1980s, the question of mass media's role in national development was almost as murky as it was a decade earlier and considerably more contentious. Support for either of the two contending models of development was as much a matter of faith as statistics. Were mass media (a) a spur to economic and political development; (b) a product of that development; or (c) none of the above. In the 1960s just about everyone would have answered (a), but two decades later many, frustrated by their inability to design clearly effective development programs and the intellectual failure to understand why development did or did not proceed as expected, would have selected (c).

The problem was partly that most aspects of development — personal income, literacy, life expectancy, numbers of radio and TV sets, newspaper circulation — rise and fall together, like stock prices, the length of skirts, and other factors that statisticians cite to illustrate the fallacy of equating simple correlation with causation. Sorting out the sequence in which events take place and blocking out other influences add to the problem. Still, with the data collected for this project we are ahead of most of those who tackled the problem in earlier years. We have better, more complete data collected over a 10-year period and the benefit of statistical techniques not available to those who blazed the now familiar trail.

Detailed analysis of these new and relatively complete figures reinforced the growing view that mass media have little direct influence on urbanization, literacy, or democracy, or that media growth is a product of any of them. More implicitly than explicitly, the figures supported one point made by Hedebro: Communication is at best a complement to development, not its core, with power in only a few specific areas such as education. The data, however, did identify one task for communication that others had also discovered: Telecommunications did seem, as well as statistical analysis could unravel the knot of social change, to be a factor in economic growth. Was horizontal communication — really telephones — the magic multiplier that earlier generations had attributed to mass media?

Hardly, but evidence from a variety of sources argued that telecommunication, which served everything from news agencies to government agencies, individuals talking to relatives to businesses talking to customers and suppliers, could have produced significant and wide-ranging payoffs. Such diverse sources as the MacBride Commission, the International Telecommunications Union, and the World Bank concluded, with wide-ranging evidence to support them, that telecommunication had been underrated in communication development programs and deserved more attention.

Ithiel de Sola Pool estimated a return on investment in rural telecommunications of 20 to 1 or as much as 40 to 1 if social benefits were included. He did not argue whether his study in rural Egyptian villages met the philosophical rigors of a cause-effect theory but the more practical concerns of cost/benefit ratios. If you invest X-dollars in a telecommunications system, what will be the economic and social payoff? The answer, supported by institutions such as the ITU and World Bank as well as the data we have examined in this chapter, is "quite a bit." For the men and women trying to piece together pragmatic development programs in the 1980s and 1990s without the certainty of a simple theory or comfort of ideology, this was a hopeful sign.

Ironically, just when defenders of Western-style modernity were about ready to concede that mass media were not the magic multiplier of efforts to speed economic growth and stable democracy, as they had argued for two decades, advocates of the new world information order decided that communication development was the wrong question. Instead, the debate over communication development shifted to new issues and new villains.

The new villains were the Western news media and especially the Big Four news agencies, which admittedly dominated the global flow of news but had avoided the clash between the opposing development theories. In the lexicon of the 1980s debate, they were part and parcel of the global economic system that had to be broken up before the new economic order could emerge. Even more, as information became the wealth of the postindustrial age, the distinction between the new economic order and new information order on which it was based, became blurry. The Associated Press and the BBC found themselves in the same category as AT&T, British Petroleum, and the Pentagon.

The new issues concerned how disengagement from the global system controlled by the West and its replacement by a Third World system promoting its separate development could be achieved. At the heart of the debate in the 1980s were questions of new definitions of news, new structures to promote them, and international legitimacy for a new journalism that challenged three centuries of Western history.

7

The Global News Network

THE NEW WORLD INFORMATION ORDER AND DEVELOPMENT

When architects of the new global information and economic orders gathered to debate communication development for the 1980s, they sometimes cited an unusual ally. In an obscure book published in 1942, Kent Cooper, former executive manager of the Associated Press, probably the largest news organization in the world, described coverage of the United States when news from North America was distributed worldwide by Reuters as part of its cartel agreement with the French Havas and German Wolff agencies:

> So Reuters decided what news was to be sent from America. It told the world about Indians on the war path in the West, lynchings in the South and bizarre crimes in the North. The charge for decades was that nothing creditable to America ever was sent. American businessmen criticized The Associated Press for permitting Reuters to belittle America abroad. (Cooper 1942, 12)

Don't you see, Western delegates were asked in the corridors of Unesco and at the conferences convened to grapple with the resurgent issue of world communications. Replace "America" with "Third World" and "crime" and "lynchings" with "coups and earthquakes," and you've got a good summary of Third World complaints against the Western media and news agencies in the 1970s. And you've got the argument in a nutshell why national development in the 1980s required new definitions of news and new news structures that could be mobilized to support a vision of modernity based on independence from the West rather than a mimicking of it.

Yes and no, was the reply. Yes, Western media and especially the powerful news agencies that supplied wholesale news to most Third World countries did not give enough attention to the Third World. And yes, too often their coverage was uninformed and superficial. But wait, development meant dealing with poverty and illiteracy and disease, not silencing an independent and critical press. Whatever the miseries of the thousands of Balgats and the frustrations of people who glimpsed the West through their $5 pocket radios and new TVs, the failures of development efforts were not the fault of Western news agencies which, like the messengers of ancient legend, were attacked because they were the bearers of bad news.

The arguments that shifted communication development from a mostly technical problem of discovering how to use mass media for multiplying efforts to speed economic and political development to a dispute over the purpose of mass media in a Third World independent of the West were not easy to untangle. And for some Western journalists, the rhetoric in the Unesco debate that dismissed press freedom as a figleaf for neo-imperial greed was more than they could understand or take. If that was communication development in the 1980s, they said, it might be time to walk away, a step the United States and Britain finally took to the general applause of the news media in both countries.

The evolution of communication development from the simple optimism of the late 1950s and early 1960s to the strident anti-Western rhetoric of the 1970s was as tangled as the record of change in the Third World itself. Earlier chapters have tried to sort out both the arguments and record of change, but several factors that seemed to propel communication to the center of the debate in the 1980s should be noted.

Probably most important was a need to account for the Third World's failure to leap the gap from underdevelopment to modernity. Imperialism became an all-purpose explanation. Old-fashioned imperialism of the eighteenth and nineteenth century variety, of course, was exploitive, and leaders of the Third World could with some justice attribute their sad state at independence to the legacy of that exploitation. Then when the first decades of political independence produced not a flowering of native culture and rapid growth but a rapid decay into despotism and economic stagnation instead, neo-imperialism became an easy and irresistible scapegoat.

The rhetoric of Marxism as molded to the plight of the Third World in the 1960s and 1970s offered both an explanation of the failure of development that absolved Third World leaders of responsibility for their nations' predicament and a vision of the future that justified the usurpation of traditional press independence. Most of the Third World's troubles — internal repression, economic stagnation, the revival of tribal antagonisms — were laid at the feet of the former colonial powers and their multinational corporate successors, not at the feet of miserable dictators, grandiose economic schemes, and misguided social experiments that shredded the fabric of the Third World more than any conquering army ever had. Political liberation was the first step toward a distant future that might work; the new information and economic orders became its blueprint and its blank check.

A second reason for the appeal of the radical vision of development was the love-hate relationship that had existed between the Third World and the West. Lerner had spotted the problem when he rejected a distinction between a "material" West and "spiritual" East that, in his phrase, equated spirituality with "poverty, disease, ignorance and apathy among the helpless peoples" of the Third World. The problem was that advocates of alternative development had never found a definition of modernity that was not based on economic growth via industrialization.

Schramm, in his portraits of the families in Africa and Asia, had captured something of the strong human bonds that could exist in traditional societies, but he also had pointed to their plight in his litany of benefits of development — literacy, health, full stomachs — all of which required wealth and a good dose of modern Western ideas, practices, and technology. Where was the alternative vision of Third World development? Certainly not in the grim societies of Eastern Europe that were caught even more than the West in the regimentation of an industrial economy and faceless bureaucracy but, unlike the West, denied the personal and financial rewards of initiative and creativity. Nor in the romanticized version of traditional village life that was as far from reality as Marx's vision of a communist utopia.

For all of the rhetoric that tried to define and defend a vision of the future built on an "authentic" Third World development, in the end, to be modern was to be Western and to accept the flood of Western pop culture, technology, and news from those countries whose influence remained as strong as, and perhaps stronger than, it was before political liberation.

Finally, there was the irresistible appeal of the information age itself, which threatened to bind the Third World tighter in the grip of the information-rich West while promising to speed it to whatever vision of the future inspired its leaders. As we have seen, most of the development projects organized under the rubric of the new world information order looked suspiciously like those designed a generation earlier and seemed no more likely to reach their ambitious objectives. Yet the belief remained that communication was powerful and that mass media were important tools in the construction of the new order.

In the debates over the role of mass media in communication development for the 1980s, the fury with which Western media were denounced seemed to reflect the intense but ambivalent feelings many Third World leaders had for the West and its new information power. They could decry the West yet define no alternative vision of modernity, spurn information technology as enslaving yet embrace it for their own purposes, reject old notions of the role of the mass media yet assign them the major responsibilities for the construction of a better future. Western mass media, especially the global news agencies, became the target of that frustration because they held a powerful but imperfect mirror to the world. In it the Third World could see its own failures, but seldom its successes. The rest of the world saw the same reflection and the same distortion and that, according to the architects of the new model of communication development, was why a new world information order was essential.

INDICTMENT OF WESTERN NEWS

Western journalists did not respond directly to the charge that the Third World's complaints against them were comparable to Cooper's complaint against nineteenth century Reuters. But they did argue that the Third World was subject to no worse treatment than any other part of the world, least of all the powerful institutions of the West. After all, just about every group in the West — liberals and conservatives, big business and labor, the military, minorities, and on and on — had the same complaints about the way they were covered. And the Western agencies were not the only suppliers of information; plenty of alternatives existed for Third World countries that objected to the world vision of the Big Four. If they did not like the AP or Reuters, there was always Tass. The Third World was not reassured.

From the early conferences that called for a better balance in the flow of news between West and Third World to the later debates at Unesco itself that defined Western information dominance as a deliberate act of neo-imperialism, three distinct arguments emerged. One was that the powerful Western media simply ignored the developing nations where three-quarters of the world's population lived. The second was that the meager coverage emphasized disruptive events — coups and earthquakes, according to the shorthand phrase — while ignoring the slow but real progress in development, the really important story from the Third World. The third was that the global news network, dominated by the United States, Britain, and France, either by design or confluence of political, economic, and military interests maintained a divide-and-conquer system that prevented the Third World from achieving solidarity and independence from the Western-dominated political-economic system.

Because information was now the wealth of the new information empires and because development was now defined as independence from the West, efforts in the 1980s to create the still undefined new world information order focused on information for political development rather than for health, education, and rural development. Enter Unesco's IPDC with its support for national news agencies, regional exchanges, and alternative global services dedicated to the new vision of development; exit Western agencies with their news of coups and earthquakes.

Were Third World complaints about their treatment at the hands of the big Western agencies any different from those of groups and institutions in the West itself that had felt themselves slighted for decades? Yes and no. In substance the charges were about the same — failure to pay attention except to the occasional bizarre aberration, emphasis on unimportant but sensational details, outright errors and distortions. But they were embedded within the larger complaint of neo-imperialism that implied, indeed explicitly demanded, a radical restructuring of the existing economic and political system. Few Western newsmakers, however much they were bruised by unfair or incompetent reporting, demanded that.

THE MASMOUDI INDICTMENT

The most complete catalog of Third World complaints was a lengthy statement presented to the MacBride Commission by Mustapha Masmoudi, the leading architect of a new global order that tried to harness communication to political development. Masmoudi was secretary of information in Tunisia and a member of the MacBride Commission before his appointment as Tunisia's ambassador to Unesco. He was also active in information activities of the non-aligned movement, but was recalled from his Unesco post in the early 1980s and disappeared from the debate that he had shaped.

His statement to the MacBride Commission deserves extended quotation, for both its substance and style. In empassioned prose that reflected the emotion surrounding the Unesco debate, he argued the

case against the existing global news system. Information in the modern
world, he said, was characterized by these flaws:

> A flagrant quantitative imbalance between North and South ... created
> by the disparity between the volume of news and information emanating
> from the developed world and intended for the developing countries and
> the volume of the flow in the opposite direction ... [resulting in] a
> veritable *de facto* monopoly on the part of the developed countries.
>
> A de facto hegemony and a will to dominate ... evident in the marked
> indifference of the media in the developed countries, particularly in the
> West, to the problems, concerns and aspirations of the developing
> countries.... They are exercised above all through the control of the
> information flow, wrested and wielded by the transnational agencies
> operating without let or hindrance in most developing countries and
> based in turn on the control of technology, illustrated by the communi-
> cation systems satellites, which are wholly dominated by the major
> international consortia.... By transmitting to the developing countries
> only news processed by them, that is, news which they have filtered, cut,
> and distorted, the transnational media impose their own way of seeing the
> world upon the developing countries.... Moreover, [they often] present
> these communities — when indeed they do show interest in them — in
> the most unfavorable light, stressing crises, strikes, street demonstrations,
> putsches, etc., or even holding them up to ridicule....
>
> The present-day information system enshrines a form of political,
> economic, and cultural colonialism which is reflected in the often
> tendentious interpretation of news concerning the developing countries.
> This consists in highlighting events whose significance, in certain cases, is
> limited or even non-existent; in collecting isolated facts and presenting
> them as a "whole"; in setting out facts in such a way that the conclusion to
> be drawn from them is necessarily favorable to the interests of the
> transnational system; in amplifying small-scale events so as to arouse
> justified fears; in keeping silent on situations unfavorable to the interests
> of the countries of origin of these media....
>
> Likewise, information is distorted by reference to moral, cultural, or
> political values peculiar certain states, in defiance of the values and
> concerns of other nations. The criteria governing selection are consciously
> or unconsciously based on the political and economic interests of the
> transnational system and of the countries in which this system is
> established.... Even important news may be deliberately neglected by
> the major media in favor of other information of interest only to public
> opinion in the country to which the media in question belong. Such news
> is transmitted to the client countries and is indeed practically imposed on
> them, despite the fact that readers and listeners in these countries have no
> interest therein.... (Masmoudi 1979, 172–185.)

Masmoudi's indictment covered the whole spectrum of complaints
about Western dominance of communication and the Third World's

failure to achieve rapid economic and social development with communication as the driving engine. His emphasis on the news agencies as part of
the global system that comprised governments, corporations, and armies
made news organizations the core of the problem. Western news media
became agents for extending economic and political influence, not
watchdogs on institutions of power.

EVIDENCE AND POLEMICS

To Western journalists, these charges were at best puzzling and at worst
more evidence of the hypocrisy of those who embraced the Unesco
platitudes while stifling every effort at honest, critical journalism. For
one thing, the powerful Western news agencies against which the charge
of imperialism was made did not fit the description of the multinational
corporations that were said to hold the Third World in bondage.

Of the Big Four wire services, AP, AFP, and Reuters (until its public
offering of stock in 1984) were nonprofit cooperatives, and UPI was a
"profit-making" corporation only in theory. Visnews, the largest newsfilm organization, was owned mostly by Reuters and the BBC, the
paragon of responsible (and nonprofit) journalism, while UPITN (later
WTN), the second worldwide film service jointly owned by UPI and
Britain's Independent Television News, was hardly a global organization
of the stature or power of IBM, Exxon, or Shell.

Beyond that, most of the agencies' modest resources were located in
the West. Of the Big Four, only Reuters was not essentially a domestic
service with overseas operations. For all of the agencies, international
activities were concentrated in the West — where the customers were.
Third World operations accounted for only a small part of their activities
and in all cases represented financial losses. Sales to Third World
customers — national agencies in most countries outside of Latin
America — did not begin to cover costs. Why, then, did they even bother
with the Third World?

Western agencies were interested in the Third World mostly on
behalf of their customers in the West. Sales or exchange agreements with
Third World agencies often meant better access to the country or some
coverage where they maintained no correspondent themselves. Correspondents tended to be stationed where the West retained important
interests, where governments allowed them reasonable freedom, or
where facilities, communications and otherwise, were adequate. A wag
once noted that Latin American news seemed to occur along Braniff
airline routes; he also might have added that, except for wars and
famines covered by parachute journalists, news tended to happen where
telecommunication lines and living conditions were good.

News, even though many correspondents of the agencies were natives of the areas they reported from, also reflected what critics claimed was a Western bias. A meeting of the coffee cartel, for example, was reported in terms of the cost of an American housewife's cup of coffee. Even the Unesco debates themselves were usually reported as threats to a "free press" with little indication of whose freedom was at stake.

But were these admitted sins of omission and commission justification for the sweeping attack that Masmoudi leveled against the Western media? And did they constitute evidence to justify his indictment of the entire existing global communication order? Many of the specifics in the radical indictment of the Western mass media were beyond analysis. If it was difficult to count the number of TV sets in Algeria or to sort out the links between mass media and economic development, it was impossible to define "alienating influences" or measure "de facto hegemony." Researchers tried, however, and in response to the debate on communication, the study of international news became a growth industry in the mid-1970s.

Some of the studies inspired by the world information order debate were tendentious and designed to support one side of the argument, usually Masmoudi's. Others examined only the qualities of news coverage that could be quantified reliably. The best ones began with the rigor of quantitative analysis, then fleshed out the skeleton of numbers with qualitative insights about how news media operated on a day-to-day basis. From the pages of academic journals, evidence slowly accumulated about the quantity and quality of information surging through a global network that included the powerful world agencies, a secondary level of Western agencies, dozens of regional exchanges and specialized services, and more than 100 Third World national agencies.

The largest single study was, curiously enough, a stepchild of Unesco itself. It was coordinated by the International Association for Mass Communication Research (IAMCR), one of the many semi-official, nongovernment organizations represented at Unesco, pursuant to a resolution approved at the Unesco General Conference in 1976. That was the conference in Nairobi, where early efforts to approve a declaration on the role and purpose of mass media resulted in deadlock; out of it came the MacBride Commission and, far less significantly, an invitation to the director general to study images of countries as presented in mass media.

The study, although designed in Europe, was everything radical critics of American-style research had complained of for decades: ad hoc descriptions of readily measurable aspects of foreign news. No man-in-society context but no blatant ideology either. The project was simple by design and necessity, but what it lacked in depth it made up for in breadth. No previous study had looked systematically at foreign news in so many countries.

In all, simple quantitative measures were applied to foreign news in the print and broadcast media of 29 countries and the Big Four Western news agencies. The final report was suitably circumspect in its conclusions. Mostly it contained numbers, which were surprisingly similar to those in dozens of other studies carried out at different times with different samples, definitions, and techniques.

One interpretation of the results argued that the IAMCR project and virtually every other recent assessment of foreign news coverage that the information order debate had spawned were, like the Sherlock Holmes dog that did not bark, notable for what they did not show:

> [The IAMCR study] does not show that Western media and news agencies ignore the Third World. It does not show that they single out the Third World for unfair negative coverage. It does not show that they see the Third World through a filter of cultural bias. It does not show that Third World media are hostage to Western news monopoly. It does not show that the socialist and Third World media systems which claim to represent an alternative model operate much differently than their Western counterparts. ("World of the News" Study, The, 1984, 134).

However, Kaarle Nordenstreng, the president of the Prague-based International Organization of Journalists and an original architect of the project, not surprisingly contended that the study added little to common-sense knowledge and previous research and mostly demonstrated "the scientific inadequacy and political risks involved in one-sided quantitative consideration of media content." Translation: he didn't like the way the numbers came out. Apparently Unesco didn't either, because the final report gathered dust for more than five years in the bowels of Unesco's printing plant before it was finally published in 1985.

The academic studies, which continued to appear and almost always with numbers compatible to those of the big IAMCR project, often got bogged down in the details of methodology and definition, but did help nudge the debate over the role of mass media in Third World development into new directions. One heard less and less about some of the charges in Masmoudi's manifesto that had seemed important in the early 1970s. By the 1980s, the argument was less over the real or imagined failures of the Western agencies to serve the Third World and the lack of alternatives and probably less about a Western cultural bias or unfairness.

Instead, the questions for the 1980s dealt more directly with whether new definitions of news were needed to promote Third World development and how new structures to carry the new kinds of news could be created. Just as the use of communication to promote economic and political development came under attack in the 1970s, the dominant Western style of newsmaking was the focus of attack in the 1980s. The major thrust of Third World communication development was a commitment to replace it.

The about-face from emulating Western news operations to establishing very distinct Third World systems paralleled the change in thinking about development in general. In the 1960s, development meant political and economic growth, compressing the centuries of Western development into decades; in the 1980s it was often defined as completing the emancipation from Western influence that only began with political independence. In communication as well, development in the 1960s usually meant emulation of media and media-assisted systems from the West, including their ideological assumptions about purpose and goals; two decades later the emphasis was on the use of mass media to promote a Third World "reality" that openly rejected Western concepts of press freedom and responsibility.

Yet we have seen in the record of communication development efforts evidence that projects organized under both visions of development came from similar blueprints. In all cases, communication hardware was imported from the information-rich West or copied from Western prototypes, staffed by Western-trained technocrats and plugged into a global network that was firmly in Western control. The difference between the Voice of Zaire's white elephant skyscraper and the Liberian news agency lay more in the intentions of those who conceived them than in the day-to-day activities of those who ran them. As the IAMCR study discovered, foreign news was pretty much the same whether it came from New York, Moscow, Monrovia, or Kinshasa: politics and economics, the comings and goings of national and world leaders, events in neighboring countries and a small passing parade of major world events that everyone paid attention to.

But was it all the same? The advantages of an objective look at something as subjective as the news were obvious when dealing with Masmoudi's quantifiable complaints about Western media's alleged failures to cover the Third World fairly or adequately. But the full impact of the news, like truth, beauty, and the difference between old and new development aid projects, was in the eye of the beholder. Nordenstreng had a point. The *New York Times* and *Pravda* were alike in very specific and important ways. But the similarity stopped there. Western, socialist, and Third World leaders got about the same treatment from the Western media and the powerful Western news agencies. Western newsmakers learned to live with their media, but most Third World leaders did not. The new world information order was supposed to create a global information system to extend what many Third World leaders demanded from their own media: obsequiousness in the name of national develop- ment. The proponents of a radical new global order held no hope for reform of the existing news distribution system and committed them- selves to the construction of a new one.

THE GLOBAL NEWS SYSTEM

If one could look at the flow of news around the world from some perch in space it might look something like a giant scaffold, skeleton, or cardiovascular system, all of which are metaphors that have been used to describe it. By any reckoning, the Big Four Western news agencies and Big Two newsfilm services are the heart and major arteries of that global system. They hold it together and drive it; together they provide at least half and probably three-quarters of the information that flows through it. But are they a monopoly, an alienating influence, a survival of the colonial era with a will to dominate?

Not if you look more closely at the system, especially at the smaller arteries and the capillaries where the global system connects to national systems in the Third World, usually government-controlled agencies that maintain a monopoly on all information distributed within the country. According to some interpretations of the new world information order, they should also be a monopoly for all information coming out of the country. In maybe a quarter of all Third World countries, something like that two-way monopoly already exists.

The smaller, less visible and less criticized components of the global news system form an extraordinarily complex web woven from news services of diverse practices, purposes, and technical capabilities. Some operate in the mold of the Western giants; others, with Tass and Pravda as models, are used openly to maintain the power of the state and to mobilize the population in its service; still others try to promote development by providing information not available from either the Western agencies or heavy-handed socialist alternatives. Collectively they are as important to the global news system as the visible Western agencies and more important to communication development in the 1980s. Describing the system is difficult because it changes rapidly and no depository collects statistics, official or otherwise. A mosaic of the smaller, less-known part of the world news web can be pieced together however; it can be divided usefully into three parts. We have already seen examples of all three; now we can look at how they fit into the global news network.

The first part was the second tier of Western agencies, which supplemented the work of the Big Four, usually complementing them and occasionally competing directly. These agencies included organizations of world scope, such as DPA in Germany, Kyodo from Japan, ANSA in Italy, and EFE in Spain. All operated globally, if not at the scale of the Big Four, and several of them were significant sources of news in a number of countries. All issued news in several languages and most cooperated actively with Third World national services.

The second part of alternative services was a small but growing number of regional and specialized services that were established to fill in the gaps in coverage of the Big Four. They represented a surprising range of geography and purpose. The Caribbean News Agency (CANA), for example, operated as independently of government as the Big Four and was formed, in fact, with the active cooperation of Reuters, which wanted to drop its regional Caribbean service. Reuters was also instrumental in the development of LATIN, a regional exchange founded by leading Latin American newspapers in 1970.

Virtually every geographic area in the Third World had at least one regional exchange, although the Pan African News Agency, which began operations in May 1983, after a decade of talk heavy on the rhetoric of the new world information order and short on pragmatics, was far from robust. In the Middle East, the Gulf News Agency (GNA) distributed news from six member agencies; the new Asia News Network did the same for 23 agencies in 19 Asian countries.

These regional exchanges also tied into specialized global agencies, such as the Non-Aligned News Agencies pool and Inter Press Service. The NANA pool and IPS were the most visible of the alternative services and the most important because they were created with the objectives of the new world information order in mind. But other specialized services existed as well. Probably the oldest was DEPTHnews in the Philippines. The title stood for Development, Economics Population Themes; the agency functioned as a specialized regional service since 1969. Some of the development-oriented services were based in the West. Gemini and Earthscan operated from London; Interlink Press Service tailored Inter Press and other Third World services for clients in the United States.

Finally, there were the national news agencies themselves, more than 100 in number, which functioned as gatekeepers in determining what information from the global flow got into their national media and, in some cases, deciding what internal news got into the international system as well. They were as varied as the Third World itself, however, and defied simple classification. Even the number of national agencies was unclear.

It ought to be simple to count the number of national agencies, but it was not. Some agencies existed mostly on paper, and the ones in operation had a habit of disappearing without warning. Because of the emphasis on development of national agencies by Unesco and IPDC, published information is quickly outdated. A report to the MacBride Commission based on data from the mid-1970s claimed that about 120 nations had news agencies but that 40 did not, including 24 with populations in excess of one million people. Later Leonard Sussman of Freedom House counted 104 Third World agencies, three-quarters of them operating under some form of government control.

With the emphasis on national agencies in 1980s development programs, it was a reasonable prediction that virtually all Third World countries of any significant size would have their own news agencies or something that accomplished the same task by the end of the decade, with or without outside help. Even the handful still without their own agencies in the mid-1980s, mostly newly independent mini-states in the Caribbean, Pacific, and Africa, already participated in regional exchanges or had access to one or more alternative services besides one or more of the Big Four. A Big Four monopoly controlling global information flow like an OPEC pipeline? A flood of information was a more accurate metaphor, a flood that washed up against even the most impoverished, most isolated Third World agency. And a flood that promised to become a tidal wave in the fullness of the information age.

GLOBAL NEWS FLOW

As the tally of the smaller, less visible components of the global news system showed, news flowed around the world not just through the main arteries of the Big Four. The smaller agencies, many of which were a product of the new debate over the role of mass media in national development, were also tied into the world system. As advocates of a new order argued, they took more from the Western agencies than they gave, but the flow was not entirely one way. And it was far larger than even the fattest, most internationally minded paper could begin to absorb, more diverse than defenders of the Masmoudi indictment admitted.

Both the big agencies and small services used the time-honored practice of monitoring each other and borrowing news when appropriate. More to the point, exchange agreements, cooperative arrangements, and outright sales contracts tied the world news system together to a degree that the international debate in the 1970s belied. The links were impressive.

At the time it prepared the monograph for the MacBride Commission, AFP had exchange agreements with 54 agencies; it sold its service directly to 15 agencies; in Paris it handled directly the services of an additional 20 agencies. UPI at the same time had agreements with 39 countries. Neither the AP nor Reuters monograph cited specific arrangements, but the number of countries in which their files are distributed — 150 for Reuters, 108 for AP — was an indication because in most of these countries the distribution was carried out through some kind of exchange, cooperative agreement, or sales to a national agency.

The second-tier and alternative agencies had even stronger ties with Third World national agencies, in many cases because they were established precisely to fill in the gaps left by the Big Four. Their motives were a combination of business and altruism. DPA, for example, developed special links with several Arab news agencies and worked with other German development programs to provide equipment and training. The agency distributed news in 78 countries and maintained correspondents or stringers in 80. Its service was comprehensive and fast.

Like the Big Four, the smaller agencies varied in strengths and emphasis. EFE, the Spanish agency, was strong in Latin America, while Kyodo, a cooperative of Japanese newspapers and broadcasters, not surprisingly put a majority of its resources into Asia. What was surprising was that several Third World agencies operated on scales that were almost on a par with the second-tier Western services.

Tanjug, the national agency of Yugoslavia and heart of the Non-Aligned News Agencies pool, maintained 46 fulltime foreign correspondents and distributed news in 103 countries. Its daily files totaled 75,000 to 120,000 words. The Middle East News Agency (MENA) in Egypt also operated as a significant regional service and almost a global agency, although the peace between Egypt and Israel damaged its operations and influence in several Arab countries. The Camp David agreement also nearly brought about its expulsion from the pool. MENA maintained 35 fulltime foreign correspondents and transmitted a daily file of nearly 200,000 words in eight languages to customers in 25 countries.

The alternative services were newer, more controversial and less successful. The NANA pool and IPS were prototypes of the two different approaches to alternative news structures. The pool, founded in 1975 under the tutelage of the Non-Aligned Movement, distributed contributions from member national news agencies with minimum editing to keep some equity in the rate of contribution and some balance when members used the medium to carry on verbal battles. Iran and Iraq were the main example of the latter; pool officials claimed they tried to keep complaints from IRNA (Islamic Republic News Agency in Iran) and INA (Iraqi News Agency) more or less even on the assumption that equal complaints from both sides must mean even-handed coverage. Western editors would sympathize.

Inter Press Service transmitted material from the pool and a whole range of specialized agencies as well, but maintained its own stable of correspondents and was independent of the degree and kind of government control that made even many Third World editors suspicious of the pool. IPS operated with an unabashed focus on the Third World and concentrated on problems and progress in national development.

The pool, transmitted worldwide through a network of national agencies with Yugoslavia at the core and India, Tunisia, and Cuba as regional centers, and IPS, which maintained its own extensive communication network, had the structure to get their information distributed on a reliable, regular, and timely basis. Many of the other regional exchange cooperatives lacked access to reliable communication or could not afford to maintain the kind of communication links they needed to keep an impressive spectrum of exchange agreements active. As a result, many of the extensive regional and binational exchange agreements that were supposed to form the skeleton of the new world information order existed mostly on paper. Still, the web of the world news system, even as it existed in the 1970s, was far more extensive and complex than the Unesco rhetoric implied.

AZaP (Zaire) claimed cooperative arrangements with 16 agencies besides Reuters and AFP. BERNAMA in Malaysia had bilateral relations with 16 agencies and bought a regional file from AFP which it could distribute to its own, mostly government, subscribers. Unlike the circumstances in most Third World countries, the Western agencies in Maylasia until 1984 were allowed to sell their services directly to media customers. AP, Reuter, and AFP subscribed to BERNAMA; AP, Reuter, and UPI sold directly. The Iraqi News Agency, which was assuming greater importance in the Middle East, had six foreign bureaus, correspondents in nine Arab cities, and nine others in cities as far away as Moscow, New York, Lagos, and Dacca. It also claimed various exchange, puchase, and cooperative arrangements with 33 national, regional, or international agencies.

The director of ANSA, the second-tier Italian agency, commented a decade ago that even then his agency received *daily*:

[0]n merely average equipment working only fifteen hours a day 220,000 words from the socialist countries, 110,000 from the Third World and 250,000 from the international agencies. . . . Even Hsinhua (China) sends me 35,000 words a day. (Righter 1978, 51)

ANSA also got news from its 14 bureaus in Italy staffed by 350 correspondents and from 69 foreign bureaus staffed by 47 fulltime reporters and 300 stringers. ANSA put out 300,000 words a day in five languages to foreign and domestic clients. The largest foreign file was a Spanish bulletin of 48,000 words a day. It was sent to Latin America for distribution to Spanish-speaking customers and to Sao Paulo where it was translated into Portuguese for distribution in Brazil. ANSA also transmitted 9,000 words a day in Italian to Europe and North America, a 4,500-word abridgment of the file in English to North America, 12,000 words in French to Europe, Africa, and the Middle East, 9,000 words in English to Europe, Africa, the Middle East, and Asia, a 7,000-word bulletin in Italian to ships at sea, and a printed weekly review in three languages by mail. Depending on the bulletin, ANSA news was distributed by terrestrial and satellite circuits and by radio-teletype.

Consider the numbers involved in this medium-sized, second-tier news operation at the beginning of the information age. Close to 600,000 words a day came to ANSA from other agencies alone. The main domestic file contained about one-third foreign news, or about 30,000 words a day. Even if ANSA's nearly 50 fulltime foreign correspondents were excluded, only about one word in 20 flowing into ANSA could make it to the domestic service. And of course the foreign correspondents, who were maintained at a cost often in excess of $200,000 a year, contributed a large part of the foreign news component; if they did not, ANSA could not justify their expense. It is not surprising that the director of ANSA said candidly, "It stands to reason that most of what we receive [from the foreign agencies] goes into the rubbish bin."

ANSA was part of the information-rich West, a major producer of news itself and able, through contract and exchange agreement, to get access to whatever part of the world's media menu it wanted. Many Third World agencies did not suffer the luxury of such abundance, but the ratios of information available and information selected may be similar.

Even with allowances for mechanical problems, repetition and exaggeration, it is not unrealistic to describe the amount of information available to most Third World national agencies or media as a flow rapidly becoming a tidal wave washing up against flood gates through which a trickle passed. A study in 1977 found that the Ghana News Agency received 12 different wire services, six of them regularly. Five were from Western countries, five from socialist countries and two from North Africa. In its daily domestic files GNA used, despite frequent mechanical breakdown and atmospheric interference, about one word out of 10 it received.

In 1982, the News Agency of Nigeria received copy from AFP, Tass, DPA, OPECNA (OPEC News Agency), IPS, Reuters, UPI Economic Service and, occasionally, Tanjug and the Non-Aligned News Agencies pool. It also had its own correspondents in London, Harare, and New York (mostly to cover the United Nations) with plans to post correspondents to Nairobi and Abidjan. Its daily files seldom contained more than a dozen short foreign items.

Foreign news also constituted a relatively small part of the GNA daily news file. As with most Third World national agencies, its major interest was domestic and its biggest problems were with the domestic communication system.

The main headquarters of GNA in Accra was connected by teleprinter to eight regional offices, where reporters submitted stories that became part of the main domestic service of 40,000 words a day. The daily file, a mix of domestic and international news, was transmitted via teleprinter to 23 subscribers, mostly government and national media, and to about 10 more in hard copy. Printed daily and weekly summaries went to about 1,000 subscribers.

GNA's biggest problems were mechanical. It relied on radio-teletype for incoming foreign news, presumably because of the cost of satellite circuits, and terrestrial teleprinter circuits for contact with regional offices. Telephone links served as a backup for the latter but usually went out the same time the teleprinter circuits failed. Then the agency was left with mail, which was slow and unreliable, personal contact, which was possible for nearby areas, and radio-telephone, a hybrid medium which served as the main backup when PTT circuits failed. For most of the country, the MacBride monograph noted, "... breakdowns in any or all of the conventional circuits may mean total blackouts for days at a time."

Thanks to OPEC money, Nigeria's NAN had more of the fruits of the information age than the Ghana News Agency, but problems remained, mostly in domestic operations. Five regional domestic offices were linked to the Lagos headquarters by a patchwork of communication links. Radio-teletype and teleprinters were used to distribute news dispatches, but in the capital, heavy reliance was placed on the personal delivery of mimeographed dispatches. In Lagos, where legendary traffic jams continued virtually around the clock, even that system could be uncertain.

While Ghana and Nigeria represented the bottom end of the range of Third World domestic communication capabilities, they were not necessarily atypical. Nyerere's plaintive comment about Third World efforts to reach the countryside while the West reached for the moon was more than a clever turn of phrase. In fact, the miracle of 1980s space-age communication that permitted the Western agencies to send their news files around the globe at the speed of light largely ended at the Third World country's satellite dish, if it got even that far. The cost of a satellite-delivered Western agency file was more than some Third World agencies could afford; for transmitting information to and from regional centers within the country the global satellite network was usually irrelevant, partly because of the cost of imported hardware and satellite services, but mostly because local politics kept domestic news organization from setting up the systems they needed.

The encouragement of Third World national agencies and exchanges was a part of development programs under the old model of communication development, of course — remember Schramm's prediction — and took on a greater urgency as communication development took on a new purpose and urgency in the IPDC. The questions for development in the 1980s ought to be simple: how to speed up transfer of technology, how to improve Third World indigenous capabilities, how to expand the existing global system. But in the shift from communication development as a maker of modern men and women to communication development as the core of a new global order, the questions themselves changed.

The West did respond, slowly and uncertainly, to the pleas for technical assistance. Professional groups such as the umbrella World Press Freedom Committee set up training programs, helped get hardware where it was needed, and lobbied for lower telecommunications rates. They also encouraged journalists to be independent minded and tried to get them out of jail when necessary. The United States government, though not a contributor to IPDC, modestly increased funding for communication development through the Agency for International Development and the U.S. Information Agency and promised to use some of the money that used to go to Unesco for bilateral communication development projects. The response was slow in coming, modest in execution and half-hearted in enthusiasm, but the Western media, like the mule hit by the 2 by 4, were paying attention. They did not like what they heard.

If communication development issues were only technical, only concerned with strengthening the weaker links in the global news system, the response might have been more enthusiastic. But architects of the new world information order argued that communication development required more than new news structures, independent of the

Western agencies that dominated the existing system. They contended that the obsolete idea of news as coups and earthquakes — even if research challenged the premise — had to give way to a new kind of reporting that would promote the new vision of modernity. To Western journalists skeptical of such rhetoric after two centuries of fighting to get free of government control, the new journalism sounded like old-fashioned government control painted over with fancy new rhetoric. If both sides in the debate on communication development agreed on the need to strengthen Third World mass media, the disagreement on what mass media should say was as big as ever.

8

News for Development

REDEFINING NEWS

Belgrade, Oct. 25 (Tanjug) — Presidency President Petar Stambolic, on behalf of the Presidency of Yugoslavia, has sent President of the Democratic Socialist Republic of Sri Lanka Junius Richard Jayewardene a telegram on the occasion of his being reelected President. In the telegram cordial congratulations and best wishes are expressed for success in carrying out of this responsible duty for the well-being of the friendly people of non-aligned Sri Lanka.

This example from 1982 was typical of the kind of "positive" information that many national agencies transmitted under the banner of the new world information order. Was this story news? Well, maybe. Ceremonial events do reaffirm ties between nations and express hopes and good intentions. News of such events can be justified when it includes good reporting of those values or when it simply brings another nation, however briefly, into the spotlight of public attention. Outside of Yugoslavia and Sri Lanka, however, it is hard to imagine any editor who would be interested in the story and, as written, it would be barely newsworthy there.

It was precisely because this kind of "positive news of development" (puffery?) was ignored by the West that advocates of a new global information order claimed a new definition of news was needed as much as new structures for Third World news dissemination. Despite the contention that technology itself carried ideological baggage, it was with

141

the content of Western news that much of the Third World was dissatisfied, not with the technology itself. And here there was also a split between the Third World hardliners, who in the tradition of Lenin saw mass media as a tool for political mobilization and control, and the moderates, among them many Third World journalists, who envied the power of their Western colleagues but recognized an obligation to assist the fragile institutions that one day might become strong enough to withstand the scrutiny of an independent and critical press.

How did news, which was almost universally limited to politics, economics, the activities of leaders, overseas national involvement, regional affairs, and a few blockbuster world events, go from the aloof, skeptical coverage of Western reporting to the fawning, non-news style of the Tanjug dispatch? And was it a harbinger of Third World news in the 1990s? Like everything else in the debate over the role of mass media, the issue began with a kernel of truth that was turned into a sweeping principle.

In this case the truth was the inadequacy of Western coverage of the Third World — never mind that coverage of the West was just as bad — and the lack of adequate information flow within and among Third World countries. This kernel was then used to justify the mobilization of mass media as a tool to keep a regime in power and to keep outsiders from prying into areas the government wanted to keep quiet. The use of mass media in this way was not new, of course, but the new world information order debate was supposed to give it legitimacy. The MacBride Commission report explained why.

According to the commission, the American and French revolutions established a first generation of individual political and civil rights. The Russian revolution then established a second generation of individual economic and social rights — work, housing, education, etc. Now the world was about to recognize a third generation of rights, but these were collective, the rights of *states*. And they included something called the right to communicate, which meant that a government had the right to determine what information came into the country from outside and what information from the country was sent abroad. News was what a state said it was. Enter legitimacy for a centuries-old doctrine of government control of information that most of the world's governments practiced even in the 1980s. Reenter the original draft of the Unesco mass media declaration that made governments responsible for the mass media operating under their flags.

The doctrine of the right to communicate was not presented as government monopoly of information but as a positive responsibility for mass media in solving the world's terrible ills. Masmoudi even included in his indictment of the old world information order a vague idea of how information should be considered. "Information must be understood as a social good and a cultural product, and not as a material commodity or merchandise," he wrote. "Information is not the prerogative of a few individuals or entities that command the technical and financial means enabling them to control communication; rather, it must be conceived as a social function intrinsic to the various communities, cultures, and different conceptions of civilization."

Fair enough, but this did not translate into any radically new criteria for evaluating the newsworthiness of specific events. Some better idea of what the news *ought* to be, in the eyes of those who advocated a new world information order, was contained in the 1978 Unesco declaration on mass media. That all-purpose document, as noted earlier, attempted to enumerate the contributions of the mass media to dealing with several world problems. It took a 128-word sentence to list the ways mass media could contribute to a new global order:

> In countering aggressive war, racialism, apartheid and other violations of human rights which are inter alia spawned by prejudice and ignorance, the mass media, by disseminating information on the aims, aspirations, cultures and needs of all people, contribute to eliminate ignorance and misunderstanding between peoples, to make nationals of a country sensitive to the needs and desires of others, to ensure the respect of the rights and dignity of all nations, all peoples and all individuals without distinction of race, sex, language, religion or nationality and to draw attention to the great evils which affect humanity, such as poverty, malnutrition and diseases, thereby promoting the formulation by states of policies best able to promote the reduction of international tension and the peaceful and equitable settlement of international disputes. (Declaration of Fundamental Principles ... 1979, 190)

Like everything else generated by the Unesco debate, the declaration was a mixture of generalities and ideals that had little to do with the nitty-gritty of communication development projects or the day-to-day operations of a news organization. However, two specific alternative definitions of news were advanced under the banner of the new world information order. One was "development news," which many proponents of the new approach to communication development advocated, and "protocol news" which they admitted existed but seldom openly recommended.

The origin of the term *development news* or *development journalism* is not clear, but it can be traced to development programs in the Philippines in the mid-1960s, where journalists were encouraged to improve their reporting of development and particularly reporting of economics. It clearly also had ties to the kind of information distributed in rural development projects, including the agricultural extension activities still very much a part of rural life in the United States.

Like so many of the terms generated in the debate on the role of mass media in national development, "development journalism" covered both fish and fowl. Some advocates argued that news for and about the Third World ought to emphasize the process of slow national change instead of unconnected events, particularly the eruptions of Third World countries that suddenly and briefly thrust them into the global news system, but left readers and viewers wondering why it happened and what it meant. Not many complaints from Western journalists there.

On the other hand, development journalism or development communication was sometimes defined as that which actively and purposefully promoted development. Here the model was not a journalist reporting the process of Third World development but someone more like the agricultural extension agent providing technical information to help an audience participate in and contribute to development. Or worse. It was a small step from the use of media to promote agriculture and literacy to their use to promote a particular ideology, political party, or national leader.

Rosemary Righter, a British journalist specializing in development issues, reflected the skepticism of most Western journalists. "The underlying assumption," she wrote, "is that development is by way of ideology, that socialism and development are coterminous." She added:

> [Development journalism's] successes alerted governments to the importance of economic and social reporting — and its potential usefulness, if systematically applied to mobilizing mass support behind government policies. Intended to enlarge the area of free debate, the concept has been taken over by governments, extended to cover all communications and integrated into an official variant of new journalism. (Righter 1978, 189)

The issue of what news should be became the skirmish line between the two opposing camps in the new world information order debate in the 1980s. Both sides acknowledged the gap between Western and Third World information resources and proclaimed a common recognition of the need to narrow it in documents as diverse as the Declaration of Talloires and the obscure statements from Unesco. Beyond that point of agreement, however, big and probably unbreachable differences remained.

The record of Third World governments in usurping independent journalism for their own purposes was enough to justify Western skepticism about the real purpose of development journalism. The most obvious misuse of media support for national development was the blatant and still common censorship of "bad news," a technique as old as the English star chamber and as new as today's shrill coverage of the Iran-Iraq war by the combatants' national news agencies. Enough dictators admitted getting their news from Western broadcasts, newspapers, and magazines while ordering their domestic media filled with the most egregious self-flattery that statements about mobilizing news media in support of a new order were appropriately suspect. And had been long before the new world information order tried to redefine the role of media in national development.

A variant of development journalism however, required the reporting of "good news" as well as an absence of "bad news," and this was new. Phil Harris, who was active in early research in news flow and sympathetic to some of the NWIO arguments, noted this common phenomenon in Third World journalism and dubbed it by the bizarre term *protocolarian* news. We can call it simply "protocol news."

PROTOCOL NEWS

In its original formulation in the Philippines, development news was defined as information which *promoted* development, and the model was agricultural extension and educational broadcasting. But the term soon came to denote information that *reflected* development as well, and this smacked of old-fashioned public relations under the guise of nation building. Development news was the opening of a fertilizer factory, the graduation of barefoot doctors, the reduction by a few percentage points of illiteracy or infant mortality.

Development news, it was argued, documented the process of development. It deserved attention, if nothing else, to demonstrate to Third World peoples themselves as well as to Western audiences that there was more to the developing nations than coups and earthquakes. As we have seen in earlier chapters, however, the definition of "development" itself evolved from participatory democracy (Lerner) and economic growth (Schramm) to the vaguely defined emancipation from Western influence and ideals that advocates of the new theories of development tried to articulate. In the new theories, media were legitimately mobilized to support development in all of its diverse components.

For many of the new leaders of Third World countries, development meant the creation of a sense of national identity from disparate and traditionally hostile tribes, the rejection of obsolete and inappropriate Western institutions and values, a new supertribalism, and mixing the old and new, East and West, socialism and capitalism — but usually more of the former. The president or junta chief, usually self-appointed for life, became the symbol of the new nation. His comings and goings assumed new symbol of the new nation. His comings and goings assumed new symbolic importance. By definition, the protocol activities of the national leader promoted national development, were evidence of it and, therefore, by definition, newsworthy.

Of course there was nothing new about the use of mass media to promote the fortunes of dictators. What was new was the degree to which it filled the TV screens and news pages of many Third World media and the legitimacy it attained as a component of national development.

Protocol news was the congratulatory telegram from the president of Yugoslavia to the president of Sri Lanka, harmless but of little interest in Belgrade and Colombo and of none elsewhere. Protocol news was the appearance of President Daniel Arap Moi as the lead story on Kenyan television day after day, with uncritical coverage put together by his own Presidential Press Unit. The endless devotion of the front pages of Zaire's thin papers to the latest cliches of "Mobutuism" was protocol news. Repetitious TV footage of dignitaries reviewing honor guards at airports, traveling to palaces in limousines, then sitting around big tables was protocol news, especially when such events were described only in the muffled rhetoric of welcoming statements, banquet toasts, and official communiques. Protocol news was very boring and almost never exportable.

Both development and protocol news lacked reader, viewer, and listener interest and almost always credibility. The ceremonial comings and goings of national leaders paled in the face of the real problems of development that were usually ignored by regimes that mobilized their media in support of the new global information order. It was easier to condemn the demon of Western imperialism than to confront problems of corruption and incompetence. And it was easier to fill a TV screen with the platitudes of solidarity and liberation than to let cameras scrutinize the life of the nation, warts and all.

The new news traveled poorly, and the national agencies functioned more successfully as checkpoints for information flowing into the country. As members of regional exchanges they were also supposed to provide information to other countries, but found little success. For news outside the country, Third World editors still turned to the Western services.

The problem was that the new information order, rich in platitude and lofty purpose, violated the Golden Rule or, more simply, logic. States in which the new right to communicate resided were not willing to do unto others as they demanded others do unto them. Governments claimed the right to determine what was said about them abroad but were not willing to concede that same authority to other governments. How could Iran exercise its right to communicate in Iraq? Would Ethiopia ever print dispatches furnished by the government of Somalia? Would any country limit its coverage of the United States to press releases from the U.S. Information Service? And if one country decided that news put out from another country — whether it was a new factory opening, a mushy diplomatic statement, or a familiar diatribe — was of no interest there, could it, as the editors of ANSA did routinely, throw it in the trashcan? Government gatekeepers, controlling the information flow into the country, were not about to abdicate their authority. Indeed, they could not; they had to choose.

Unesco conferences occasionally danced around the problem with discussions of a national right of reply, but for the most part avoided the intractable illogic by concentrating on the "theory" of the new information order. Meanwhile, journalists and government officials went about their business as usual, which meant relying on the Western news media and news agencies both for their own knowledge of the world and the thin diet of foreign news selected for domestic consumption.

Most Third World news agencies, as we have seen, were essentially domestic operations with the small chunk of foreign news in their files, supplied either by their own small stable of foreign correspondents or gleaned from Western files. The Western agencies provided the bulk of foreign news in most Third World countries for reasons that had nothing to do with imperialism, hegemony, or a will to dominate. They had the technical capacity to get information around the world fast; they covered the major events that were of wide interest; and they were usually accurate and generally free of the ideological overkill that consigned most development and protocol news to the trashcan. The Big Four claimed to be little more than information wholesalers, trying to earn a profit by giving their customers what they were willing to buy. What the customers did with the dispatches was their business.

In fact, most of the news in the global system did emanate from the Western agencies, but by the time it appeared in many Third World media, it was no longer recognizable. Tracking news through the international network was difficult, as the IAMCR study discovered. Sometimes national agencies credited dispatches simply to "agencies"; often they attributed it to themselves or removed all reference to the source. In most cases they did some editing, usually to make certain that the version they passed to domestic customers was consistent with government policy. Harris' study of the Ghana News Agency described the process with unusual candor.

Despite access to and occasional use of 12 separate news agencies, GNA relied on Reuters and AFP, mostly on Reuters. About 10 percent of the incoming copy made it into the domestic files. Agency officials felt that both European agencies were still caught up in the cold war. They did not like references to "Soviet-backed MPLA" in the Angolan war, but the problem was easy to solve. Harris told how they did it:

> While the use of political adjectives annoyed the foreign staff the problem was not insurmountable — all that was really involved was changing the adjective. One of the most common examples cited in this context was the substitution in stories about Rhodesia, South Africa, Angola, etc., of "nationalists" or "freedom fighters" for "guerrillas" or "terrorists." Another example was that stories about Ian Smith would generally be rephrased to described him as the "racist Ian Smith. . . ." [S]ubstitution would only be made if the editor believed that the "cause for which they are fighting is just — that is, in the African interest." This, in practice, meant that most stories would be amended. (Harris 1977, 236–237)

Coverage of Smith did not improve. Two years later the IAMCR study found frequent reference in the Zambian media to the "racist puppet Ian Smith" and the "sham, bogus election" for his successor. In the same study, headlines in the Algerian press reported a "Demonstration in El-Menia Against the Treason of Sadat" and a story about the "treasonous accord signed by Sadat with the Zionist enemy." So much for the mobilization of mass media in support of "the respect of the rights and dignity of all nations."

The Western agencies often had been too quick to over-simplify Third World conflict for their (mostly Western) customers with misleading labels like "pro-West" or "right wing." In response to the NWIO criticism, however, the agencies had become more careful and by far the overwhelming transformation of information into ideology was done at the national news agency level. A few words still caused problems. One man's terrorist was another man's freedom fighter; one country's insurgency was another's liberation struggle. And there was no neutral term for people who threw bombs or hijacked airplanes. However, as the study of the Ghana News Agency showed, the Western agencies provided the most useful raw material. Whatever transformation that raw product needed to fit the national outlook was easy enough to accomplish.

Still, not all efforts in the 1980s to improve Third World communication capabilities were in the mold of the Non-Aligned News Agencies pool and not all national agencies operated like the Ghana News Agency. Just as the sweeping statements about the Western agencies were wild generalization based on legitimate concerns, some of the new news organizations tried honestly to fill in the gaps in the world news flow and to find some way to contribute to a solution to the Third World's terrible and usually growing problems. In the information age even Third World communications changed rapidly. The programs of the IPDC and other communication development projects did have an effect and whatever else happened to the plans to restructure the existing global information system and its definitions of news, Third World mass media in the 1990s would not look like they did in 1970. By the early 1980s, changes were already apparent.

NEW NEWS IN PRACTICE

The biggest influence of the new world information order on communication development programs was the emphasis on creation of national news agencies, regional exchanges, and specialized global services. The first effects of the explosion of information technology in the West reached the Third World as more reliable reception of Western agencies and then as better access to the rapidly expanding inventory of alternative services. Did the new vision of communication development, with its new definitions of news and new structures for news dissemination, make any difference in the way Third World mass media operated?

On the whole, apparently not. Studies such as the IAMCR project showed the continuing influence of the Big Four, but at the same time found some evidence of the growing visibility of second-tier Western agencies, particularly in Latin America, and the use in a few countries of Inter Press Service. Definitions of what was newsworthy seemed not to have changed, although there was some slight evidence of a greater interest in development news. Those who ran the new services were beginning to recognize the reality that the Western agencies had learned years earlier: the news business was competitive — and becoming more so — and the product had to be acceptable to potential customers. If it wasn't, plenty of other services were prepared to produce one that was.

Tass had never acknowledged that fact and, consequently, was invisible in the global news system even though it maintained one of the largest information-gathering operations in the world. Would the new services do the same? Or would they expand the existing system and thereby move, however slowly, toward the goal of a free and balanced flow, which the West accepted as the only legitimate goal of a new world information order?

To answer the question we need to look at the smaller parts of the global news system that, for the most part, have escaped the scrutiny of previous research. Our investigation will be governed by what is reasonably accessible, but the result will show us what has been wrought to date under the banner of the new world information order and what communication development in the coming decade portends.

For this purpose, files of important alternative news services were obtained for the last two weeks in October 1982. The files included important examples of the three kinds of services noted earlier: second-tier Western agencies, global alternative services, and Third World national agencies. Representing the first group were the English-language international services of DPA (West Germany), which is distributed by the Washington Post–Los Angeles Times Service, and Kyodo from Japan, which is available in English on Nexis information service. Both major alternative services of global significance were included: Inter Press Service in Spanish and English from Rome, obtained through Interlink News Service, and the Non-Aligned News Agencies pool English-language service provided by Tanjug. The sample of national agencies comprised Xinhua, in English on Nexis; the domestic services of the News Agency of Nigeria and Shihata from Tanzania, both in English except for occasional Shihata stories in Swahili; and the international English-language service of Tanjug.

At the quantitive level, these news services looked a lot like the big Western agencies they were supposed to supplement or replace. News was mostly regional. Over half (61%) of IPS's Spanish-service stories originated in Latin America (and 43% of its English file); the pool file came from the Third World: Middle East (26%), Africa (23%), Asia (16%), and Latin America (13%). Virtually all of the African agencies' files came from Africa — 78 percent of NAN, 96 percent of Shihata — while 64 percent of Xinhua's stories originated in Asia, and virtually the same proportion of Tanjug's file came from Eastern Europe.

In other ways these representatives of the new world information order looked a lot like the old order. Politicians and other officials got most of the attention and most stories concerned politics and military activities, with a big dose of economics. Little attention was paid to natural disasters and accidents, but the same was true of the Western global services, of course, despite the argument of the Masmoudi statement. Virtually all the news was oriented toward recent events, usually something that happened yesterday or today. No unfolding of history, no concentration on the process of change here.

The quantitative analysis also looked at how much the new definitions of news were used and found evidence of some differences. Protocol news did not fare very well — about a quarter of the stories in Xinhua, Tanjug, and the Spanish, much less in the others — and except for Spanish IPS, development news made up 10 percent or less of the files. Several of the agencies, however, gave a surprising amount of attention to background material, either with or without a link to a specific event. Over half of the stories in IPS English, DPA, Kyodo, Tanjug fell into that category.

Just as the IAMCR study concluded that news was pretty much the same around the world, but only in some very specific, quantifiable ways. we could argue that the new services were echoes of their more powerful models and dismiss them. That would be a mistake. While *Pravda* and the *New York Times* were really more different than alike, the same was clearly also true for the second-tier Western, alternative global, and Third World national agencies. Their files, when not squeezed into categories for useful but limited quantitative analysis, showed an extraordinary range of dedication to the old and new information orders and a diversity of style and content that challenged any claim of uniformity and hegemony in the complex global news system. To see how diverse the system was, we need to zoom in for a closeup. Thursday, October 28, 1982, seemed like a good day to do it.

A DAY IN THE WORLD'S NEWS

The day in question was the kind of day researchers like to use in their studies. It was about as ordinary as one could expect: no major coups or earthquakes, no outbreak of peace or giant leap for mankind. By way of comparison, we can begin with a look at the news that Americans have access to through network television and two influential newspapers. It was an average news day.

On October 28, 1982, the three commercial networks devoted one-fourth to one-third of their news time to foreign news, depending whether a news conference by Defense Secretary Weinberger was considered international or domestic. The top story was President Reagan on the campaign trail in the West. Major international stories included reports on imprisoned Solidarity leaders, the upcoming Spanish national election, the use of Britain's official secrecy laws to prohibit discussion of an espionage case, an attack on Israeli troops in Lebanon, and the dedication of United World College in New Mexico by the Prince of Wales.

Newspapers operate on a different time cycle, so the Reagan campaign trip was not given heavy play until the next day. On that Thursday, the *Washington Post* lead story was international: "U.S. planning to rebuild armed forces of Lebanon." Two other foreign stories were on the front page: "China's population passes 1 billion in latest census" and "South African court probes secret police." Eleven major international stories on inside pages included these: (Letter from Lebanon) "In tense Bekaa, tanks churn up fertile soil, dust stunts grapes"; "Spanish vote today expected to put Socialist in power"; "Canada sees new plunge in GNP in '82"; "Look at life from stone bracelets to beaded aprons," about a new exhibit at the Smithsonian Institution's African Art Museum.

The common assumption that American papers present a uniformly gray picture of the world is as false as many of the charges in the NWIO debate about Western media in general. The only story that made the front pages of both the *Washington Post* and *New York Times* was China's census. The *Times'* lead story was a speech by President Brezhnev's attacking the United States and promising to meet any nuclear buildup. A column of excerpts from the speech was included. Two international stories besides the lead and China's census made the front page: Argentina's willingness to cut spending and the Spanish elections. Major inside international stories included a long feature about the growing influence of Western pop culture in China, "Caribbean initiative can help U.S." on the op-ed page, "Children of immigrants feel pride in origin" in the local news section, a "Letter from the State Department" about the less personalized style of Secretary Shultz, and a review of a visiting Israeli dance company. The business section carried a lengthy story on Japan's supercomputer push.

The big Western agencies could be expected to supply the rest of the world with coverage of the handful of events with something like universal news value — the speeches by Weinberger and Brezhnev, the Spanish election, and probably Prince Charles dedicating the new college. But beneath those blips that appeared in newspapers and on TV screens around the globe, the world of the news was very different.

DPA, the West German agency, transmitted 44 stories in its English-language international service on October 28. Twenty of the 44 stories were datelined in Western Europe, but these included several routine currency and stock quotations as well as three separate stories on the Spanish election. Only one story came from North America, a detailed summary of Weinberger's press conference, and none was reported from Latin America. Middle East datelines, most from Beirut and Jerusalem, accounted for 11 stories. Four stories were reported from Africa, all from Nairobi, and four came from Asia. Three stories were reported from Eastern Europe, and one came from the United Nations, reporting the deaths three Irish soldiers assigned to the UN force in Lebanon.

Datelines can be misleading, as several stories from Western Europe had some direct tie to the Third World. Consider these lead paragraphs:

Frankfurt — Family planning in the Third World can only be successful if it is initiated by local authorities, delegates of a conference organised by the German Society for Technical Cooperation (GTZ) said here Thursday.

Bonn — West Germany's major parties called Thursday for quick and decisive action against worldwide hunger, the exploitation of resources and pollution and invited parliaments and governments around the globe to step up development aid cooperation.

These could be categorized as "development news," but development news can also apply to the West, as a story on Germany's new "ecofarms" — about 20,000 hectares devoted to chemical-free agricultural production — demonstrated. DPA also focused on the Third World in a lengthy story about discussions between Vietnam and Indonesia on problems in Cambodia, most of it based on a news conference by the foreign ministers of the two countries, and a long feature from Nairobi on deteriorating relations between Kenya and neighboring Tanzania.

Other stories from Africa included a report that the Kenyan government would prosecute 75 university students in connection with the failed coup in August and, on the bright side, a decision to try again to hold a summit meeting of the Organization of African Unity in Libya.

Protocol news got heavy play in DPA's file. Subscribers could read about Libya's Qadaffi arriving in China, Britain's Thatcher arriving in Bonn, Germany's President Carstens meeting Pope John Paul II in the Vatican, the Danish foreign minister in Beirut to discuss European Community aid to Lebanon, American envoy Morris Draper's talks in Beirut, the likely visit of the Israeli foreign minister to Zaire, and a visit by the Vietnamese foreign minister to Indonesia.

DPA's English service was crisply written and focused on the kinds of major international events that made up most of the foreign coverage of Western media. While emphasizing Western Europe and Germany more than some of its customers might like, especially if they were dependent on DPA for their window to the world, DPA resembled the major Big Four Western agencies in coverage and style. Not so with Kyodo, the agency from Japan.

Kyodo, which is characterized as a general news service in contrast with Jiji, a finance and economics service, was in fact mostly oriented toward economics and business. It carried very little news that did not originate in or concern Japan. Of the 30 stories in the October 28 file, only seven were not datelined in Japanese cities. Five of the seven were datelined in the United States, and only one — a story from Moscow about President Brezhnev wanting better relations with China — did not deal with business.

Eleven of the domestic stories also dealt with some aspects of business or finance, and five dealt specifically with relations with the United States, including tobacco import talks, cooperation on crime prevention, military cooperation, Japanese naval exercises in Hawaii, and a denial of U.S. allegations of yen manipulation.

Even political news, the single largest topic category of almost all studies of news around the world, got relatively little attention. The minister of international trade and industry criticized his rivals for president of the Liberal-Democratic party; a government report criticized big companies for slowing down their recruitment of handicapped workers; the Foreign Ministry wanted to postpone reconsideration of a nuclear ban resolution at the United Nations until Prime Minister Suzuki's successor was named; a research institute said too much spinach could be harmful; 50 Southeast Asians who studied at Japanese universities returned to renew old friendships; and doctors in Kobe removed an egg-sized tumor from a seven-year-old boy's lung.

Kyodo's news was well written — if anything in a more fluent English than DPA's — but its scope seemed narrow. Presumably the English service was largely directed to North America and Western Europe, but it seemed to ignore the kind of hard news that makes up the bread and butter coverage of the Western agencies and a large part of DPA as well. Even its coverage of Japan focused heavily on business and economics to the near-exclusion of other types of news. We had available the files of Jiji for the same period but decided to exclude them from the analysis because they were entirely business and economics, mostly reports of currency exchange figures, commodity and stock prices, and the like.

The four national agencies in the sample varied greatly in size, sophistication, and approach to news. Tanjug, from Yugoslavia, could be classed as a second-tier agency like DPA or Kyodo because it operated an extensive stable of foreign correspondents and distributed its dispatches directly and as part of the Non-Aligned News Agencies pool. Xinhua, too, was a major organization in size and scope, although it made little effort to become a major player in the global news flow system. NAN, from Nigeria, and Shihata, from Tanzania, were more modest, although NAN did maintain foreign correspondents and later became a regional distribution center for the new Pan-African News Agency.

The four represented diverse political and media systems. Three of the four countries were nominally socialist, although it would be hard to find very much on which the governments of Yugoslavia, China, and Tanzania agreed. Nigeria was openly capitalist, of course, although the government exerted considerable political and economic control of the media. At least two of the agencies — Tanjug and NAN — operated with a sense of professional independence compatible with Western journalistic values. All four were committed to a new world information order but probably could not agree among themselves on a definition of it.

Tanjug, the largest of the four agencies, transmitted 58 stories in its English-language service on October 28. As one of the more catholic national services, Tanjug included 24 stories with datelines outside of Yugoslavia. Several of the Yugoslavia-datelined stories really dealt with events outside of the country as well, such as a story based on a report in a Yugoslav newspaper about the results of a meeting between leaders of Zimbabwe and Nigeria and a long dispatch about the Spanish elections credited to the Tanjug correspondent in Madrid but carried with a Belgrade dateline.

Some of Tanjug's foreign stories represented curious news values: the Pope's statements on the Vatican's renewed dialog with China, financial troubles of Latin America, sanctions against Polish deputies who opposed the disbanding of Solidarity, Xinhua's commentary on the United Nations vote on seating Kampuchea, the Chinese census — pointing out that the figure would be about 30 million higher if residents of "parts of China that have not yet been reunified with the homeland" were included — and negotiations between the United States and Greece for renewal of military bases.

Domestic items were heavy on politics and protocol but with some attention to economics and an occasional feature. Among the latter were a story on the eightieth birthday of a Zagreb man who had fought in three revolutions (Hungary in 1919, Spain, and postwar Yugoslavia) and preliminary applications for the 1984 Winter Olympics in Sarajevo, including Costa Rica and Bolivia, which would participate for the first time.

Tanjug's style was frequently mushy, partly the result of less sophistication with English than, say, Kyodo, but also because of an emphasis on the kind of newsspeak that often passed for journalism in official statements. Consider this typical example:

> **Belgrade, October 27 (Tanjug)** — Relations and cooperation between Yugoslavia and Romania and the League of Communists of Yugoslavia (LCY) and the Romanian Communist Party are developing successfully in all fields with full mutual respect and trust, constituting an example of cooperation between two neighbouring socialist countries.
>
> This is stressed in a joint Yugoslav-Romanian statement released here Wednesday at the end of a three-day visit to Yugoslavia by Romanian President and General Secretary of the Romanian Communist Party Central Committee Nicolae Ceausescu. The visit took place at the invitation of the Presidency of Yugoslavia and the LCY Central Committee.
>
> It was pointed out that the high level of confidence and comprehensive

development of cooperation between the two countries results from the consistent implementation of the principles of independence, equality, territorial integrity and non-interference in internal affairs.

Of course, stories like this one had obvious sensitivities that could explain some of the tiptoeing around real issues and the baroque prose. On other stories, particularly the reporting of routine international events, Tanjug did better. Still, it is hard to envision an editor who could find much news value in these stories unless politics or ideology dictated it. Nor is it easy to imagine an editor preferring to work routinely with Tanjug rather than the straightforward, crisp dispatches of the big Western agencies or DPA.

Xinhua's English-language service, like the others we have looked at so far, was a "foreign" service, written in a foreign language and aimed at foreign audiences. And like the other national services it was essentially a window on China, with more than half of the stories — 33 out of 60 stories in the October 28 file — from China. Even several of the foreign datelines reported events with a strong Chinese component: Chinese women's delegation concludes visit to Zimbabwe; Chinese province and Minnesota sign agreement of friendship; China and North Korea sign protocols on scientific cooperation and long-term trade agreement; China and Yugoslavia ratify consular agreement.

Purely foreign news items were a mixture of protocol news, a few event-oriented stories whose news value was not immediately clear, and a few regular reports that seemed to fulfill the Leninist definition of news as the unfolding of history, particularly when it shows trouble in capitalist countries.

Among the first group were a story about normalization of relations between South Yemen and Oman, a summary of the Romanian-Yugoslav joint statement, and an agreement between Uganda and Rwanda to solve their refugee problems. Other stories were more difficult to characterize: the opening of the Twentieth Santiago International Fair, the Italian government's confidence vote, Draper's new mission to the Middle East, and plans for a new hotel and convention complex in Zimbabwe.

The most predictable stories were those that stressed economic and social problems in the West. Even though the rhetoric was subdued compared to what the Chinese media used a decade or two ago, the meaning was still clear.

The view of China that Xinhua offered to the world was varied, sometimes amusing, and occasionally reminiscent of earlier propaganda efforts. Sports were always newsworthy — the October 28 file included eight stories about Chinese teams participating in international competition — as were examples of protocol news. In our one-day snapshot, Colonel Qadaffi paid his respects to the remains of Chairman Mao, and in a separate story, Qadaffi and his entourage were greeted by Deng Xiaoping and feted at a banquet in the Great Hall of the People.

Development news, defined to include political as well as economic development, got regular attention, sometimes in stories that smacked of earlier days:

> **Beijing, October 28** — Zhang Hua, a 24-year-old medical student who died in an attempt to save an old peasant, is a new model for China's young people.
>
> **Beijing, October 28** — Chen Yun, political bureau standing committee member, called for doing a good job in distribution of the cabbage now being harvested around Beijing and Tianjin in order to guarantee a good winter's supply for residents of these two cities, according to Beijing Daily reports today.
>
> **Nanjing, October 28** — The Nantong fermentation factory, China's largest citric acid producer, located in Jiangsu Province, reports completion of the first stage of its expension project, doubling its annual output of the product to 4,000 tons.

NAN, from Nigeria, and Shihata, the Tanzanian agency, differed from the other services in that the files we examined were prepared for internal distribution, not overseas consumption. And, unlike the other services, English is a national language of the two countries so the international dispatches were not translations for export of a domestic service.

On October 28, NAN's main news service included a total of 39 stories. Of these, 26 were domestic news, four domestic economics, and nine foreign. The domestic news file included a range of stories that would not be out of place in most Western newsrooms: Legislator accuses ministries of overstaffing; Police arrest two robbers; Ondo commissioner for economic development resigns; Iyi-Enu Hospital celebrates 75th anniversary; Legislator calls on President Shagari to announce prices of agricultural products; Professor Achebe becomes honorary member of American art institute.

Open criticism of the president was not allowed and "bad news" was generally treated with deference. Compared with many other national services, however, NAN copy was interesting and professional. The writing was good, but occasionally suffered from a monotony of style and verbiage that could be improved by the judicious use of an editor's pencil. Examples:

Port Harcourt, Oct. 28 (NAN) — The governor of Rivers (State), Chief Melford Okilo, on Monday in Port Harcourt stressed the need for the union and management to develop a sense of partnership for the progress of the nation's economy.

Lagos, Oct. 28 (NAN) — The House of Representatives yesterday adopted the recommendations of its committee on public petitions for the improvement of the activities of public complaints commissions in the country.

Development news? Maybe, but in a very different sense than that used to justify the puffery of other national services. NAN's weak area seemed to be its foreign coverage, although the paucity of international stories may well accurately reflect a lack of demand rather than lack of resources. The scattering of foreign news in NAN's October 28 file looked like something we could expect in a small American daily: the two or three major world events, a few stories with some national or local linkage, and a bit of the bizarre. A sampling of the nine foreign datelines:

New York (from NAN's own correspondent): The president of the International Federation of Football Associations has received no official notice that Colombia will not host the 1986 World Cup.

New York (from AP): A man who pleaded guilty to six counts of murder told a judge he shot a friend "in the Christmas spirit" and killed others "to amuse myself."

Ankara (from AFP): The alleged accomplice of the man who tried to kill the Pope has been extradited from West Germany to Turkey.

Harare (from AFP): The Zimbabwean information minister accused South Africa of "information aggression."

Nairobi (from AP): The postponed OAU summit will be rescheduled.

NAN's meager foreign coverage got a modest boost from its separate daily Economic News Service. On the day of our examination, the economic service carried six foreign-dateline stories plus 13 price quotes and commodity market summaries for palm oil, coffee, cocoa, rubber, tin, and sugar. The foreign stories consisted of reports about Reagan's revocation of "most-favored-nation" status for Poland, improvement in Ivory Coast cocoa quality, Bolivia's decision not to nationalize mining, a proposed institute to improve international lending analysis, a Japanese dumping suit against South Korean cotton industry, and an AFP story about Israeli oil exploration based on the Bible.

Like the foreign coverage in virtually all media in the world, NAN's view of the world was limited in geography and perspective. One would like to think that something more important happened in the United

States than murder in the Christmas spirit or that the peoples of Asia and Latin America deserved some recognition even on a slow news day.

In Tanzania, the media were not as independent as they were in Nigeria for a combination of financial and political reasons. And Shihata, unlike NAN, was very much a part of the government's mobilization for national development.

On the day in question, Shihata distributed only 10 stories, all of them with domestic datelines. The dispatches reflected the nation's concern with ideology, socialist development, and an almost Puritan attention to the kind of selfless honesty that socialism is supposed to foster. In style as well as content, Shihata was very different from NAN:

> **Kibaha, Oct. 28** — Representatives of five friendly political parties which are attending the on-going second ordinary national conference of Chama Cha Mapinduzi CCM, today inspected development projects in the coast region where they commended Tanzania's policy of socialism and self-reliance as the only alternative to the country's development.
>
> **Dar es Salaam, Oct. 28** — The minister for home affairs, Brigadier Muhidin Kimario, today issued a stern warning against people who worked to sabotage the nation's economy and state security.

The Shihata stories, often awkwardly written, were a curious blend of Western-style crime news, pure protocol and development news, and the exhortations of government leaders trying to create a sense of national pride while dealing — not very well, in most cases — with the practical problems of modernization.

None of the national agencies made very much use of the full global flow of news. Most preferred the Western agencies for the modest foreign coverage they carried. Occasional stories from one of the national agencies or alternative services got picked up and passed through a national agency gatekeeper, but the two major alternatives created expressly to strengthen the links among Third World agencies had little visible impact.

Inter Press and the Non-Aligned pool had some things in common. Both stressed the kind of news that was usually ignored by the major Western agencies; both were committed to a redefinition of news as something other than coups and earthquakes. But beyond that, they were quite different.

Compared with the smaller national agencies, both the pool and IPS turned out a lot of copy. The pool dispatch for the day of our inspection consisted of 60 separate stories from 26 separate news agencies. If the criterion of the pool's success is the ability to edit and distribute a wide-ranging file representing geographic diversity, it can be considered a success. If however, the more rigorous criteria of comprehensive reporting and utilization are invoked, the pool fared less well. Most of the pool's reports were one or two paragraphs; few ran more than 100 words. And many were skeletal summaries that delicately balanced diplomatic codewords without any indication of what they meant or why they were being issued. You don't report the process of development in 100 words or address the complex issues of social change with happy talk.

The exception to the policy of "good news" was anti-Israel (and often anti-U.S.) rhetoric that filled an inordinate amount of the pool's dispatches. The imbalance toward the Middle East in the pool's first years of operation did not change. Twenty-five of the 60 stories were datelined in the Arab Middle East and five other stories dealt with the Middle East. The developed nations were appropriately ignored. Three stories came from Western Europe, of which only one concerned Europe, one came from the Soviet Union, and two from the United States, neither of which dealt with the United States itself.

A number of the pool stories were third-country reports: the Middle East News Agency (Egypt) reporting on Sudanese security agency claims of threats on the lives of Qadaffi opponents, Tanjug reporting Brezhnev's views on the arms race, the Press Trust of India on actions by the president of Sri Lanka, and the Malaysian prime minister's comments on the United Nations. The practice violated the information laws of some Third World countries, but the problem was less one of law than the pool's principle of letting nations speak for themselves. If the agency of one country chose not to report a particular event, the principle of information sovereignty would preclude other agencies from filling the gap. In practice, it did not work that way.

A comparison of the pool and individual national agencies showed little overlap. WAFA, the PLO agency, reported a message of congratulations that was sent to Tanzania on the second anniversary of the Tanzanian Revolutionary Party. Prensa Latina (Cuba) contributed a lengthy story on the Tanzanian party's second congress, including an address by President Nyerere. Neither event was noted by Shihata, except indirectly in a semi-feature story about the visit of foreign delegates to development projects.

WAFA, one of the biggest contributors to the pool, also reported on Qadaffi's visit to China. "During the tour," the brief dispatch said, "the leader has been briefed on the Chinese struggle against imperialism and for independence." WAFA was also one of the most vitriolic attackers of Israel and the United States, although Israel was enduring unusually harsh coverage in all parts of the world in the wake of her invasion of

Lebanon and the massacres in the Palestinean refugee camps. Still, stories ran so against the pool's dedication to the use of mass media to promote international harmony that the hypocrisy of the new world information order could not be hidden. Samples from the pool dispatch for October 28:

> **Tripoli, Oct. 27 (JANA)** — A celebration was held here on Sunday to mark the 37th anniversary of the enactment of the U.N. charter.
>
> The under-secretary of the Foreign Liaison Bureau, Mr. Abdulati Ubeidi, delivered a speech in which he referred to U.N. efforts to consolidate the foundations of world peace. He stressed the necessity of abolishing the veto right and said: "This distinction has been abused at the U.N., and the U.S. has turned the organization's most important body into an important [impotent?] instrument incapable of protecting international peace and security, which have been seriously jeopardised by Zionist wars of aggression and genocide against the Palestinian people and the entire Arab nation."
>
> **Luanda, Oct. 27 (PL)** — The chairman of the Southwest African People's Organization (SWAPO), Sam Nujoma, said that there was a plot between the United States and South Africa aimed at keeping Namibia under their colonial domination.
>
> **London, Oct. 27 (JANA)** — Seychelles President Albert Rene has strongly denounced the U.S. colonialist schemes and pointed out that the latest conspiracy against his country will not be the last. He said that the mercenaries' attempt to overthrow his regime is part of an imperialist scheme being engineered by the racist regime of South Africa against Seychelles.
>
> **Damascus, Oct. 27 (SANA)** — The villages and cities of the occupied West Bank were the scene Wednesday of violent demonstrations against the Zionist occupation and savage practices.

The pool file reflected the gulf between the rhetoric and the reality in so much of the new world information order debate. On the one hand were the pronouncements of a world order based on high moral principles, on the other, the vitriol diverting attention from the animosities within the Third World to the handy villains of Israel and, to a lesser degree, the United States and South Africa.

The pool did offer other coverage of more redeeming value. Protocol and development news got included, and a few of the stories even had some potential for placement in Western media, although one estimate that half might be suitable for Western media seemed high. The pool claimed to have placed several thousand stories since its inception, but it was hard to find evidence of its acceptability except for the occasional quoting of one agency by another, which went on through bilateral exchanges as well as through the pool.

As an alternative service oriented mostly toward development-related features, Inter Press Service claimed to emphasize the Third World. Our one-day snapshot supported that assertion. The IPS world on October 28 focused heavily on Latin America, the Middle East, and the United Nations. Of a total of 46 stories transmitted in its English-language service, 23 were staff written, nine were news briefs, and 14 were retransmissions of stories from national agencies.

The Latin American coverage included these stories:

> **Bogota, Oct. 28 (IPS)** — "Mother's milk is a public relations man's dream," said author Mike Muller in 1974. Now his words have inspired an ecological group at the University of Tolima to wage a campaign against the "immoral commercialisation of powdered milk."
>
> **Santiago, Oct. 28 (IPS)** — Human rights violations in Chile increased in the first half of this year, according to a Chilean human rights commission study reported here Thursday.
>
> **Kingston, Oct. 28 (IPS)** — The U.N. Development Programme (UNDP) expects to provide technical assistance and aid to Jamaica worth 20 million U.S. dollars over the next five years.

United Nations stories included these: Committee Against Apartheid to discuss South African loan with IMF; Chad international assistance conference set for November; Seminar on role of transnationals in South Africa and Namibia; and UNCTAD board approves framework of support for Third World economic cooperation. The last story was also reported by NAN, whose AP version emphasized that the final agreement effectively excluded Israel from participation in U.N. development programs. The IPS version, after a confused lead, noted that "the practical effect of this is that the G-77 would be able to determine whether or not China, Turkey and Israel, three non–G-77 UNCTAD members who call themselves 'developing' and wish to participate in ECDC programmes, should be allowed to do so." (Translations: G-77 or Group of 77 is the caucus of developing nations, actually now numbering more than 100; ECDC is Economic Cooperation with Developing Countries; UNCTAD is the United Nations Conference on Trade and Development.)

The three African stories reported on the expected summit of the OAU, an advance story about a course on improving urban housing in Africa organized by the United Nations Center for Human Settlements in Nairobi, and Muslim riots in Nigeria that resulted in the deaths of 15 policemen and a number of civilians.

COMMUNICATION DEVELOPMENT AND THE FUTURE

By the mid-1980s, Unesco and other agencies supporting the objectives of a new world information order remained committed to an expansion of alternative news. The pool continued to operate, mostly through the support of Tanjug, and IPS claimed to be expanding its operations. Regional exchanges proliferated. The Pan-African News Agency began operations in 1983, completing a cycle that had included the creation of new exchanges in Asia, Latin America, and the Middle East. IPDC was committed to further financial and technical support for these organizations and the fledgling national agencies. The United States said money previously spent on Unesco would be used to expand bilateral programs to improve Third World capabilities.

An irony of the debate about the role of communication in development was that as communication and economics bound the world more tightly together, interest in international affairs seemed to decline. Although percentages varied in the newspapers around the world, roughly one-quarter of the stories were foreign. In television news, the percentages were about the same or a bit lower. In the West, market pressures swung newspapers and broadcast news away from serious foreign affairs coverage to entertainment and gossip. In most Third World countries, the sense of nationalism that led to the mobilization of the media to support national development objectives was almost always directed inward.

The creation or recreation of Third World media mobilized to support a new form of development defined in terms of independence from Western influence had not taken place despite a decade of rhetoric calling for the replacement of the old, Western-dominated system. Two reasons can be cited for the failure of the new vision of communication development to take root. One was the failure of radical communication to produce the kind of results its advocates promised in countries as diverse as China, Cuba, and Tanzania. Marxists of various hues had to continue their search for a future that worked.

A second reason was that the new definition of communication development was essentially domestic. Despite the calls for international solidarity and cooperation, media that were mobilized to support political objectives invariably were caught up in internal affairs. Politicians liked protocol news because it made them the symbols of nationhood; development news was appealing because it documented the success of the regime in power. However, neither exported well. The rhetoric about information as a social right and mass media as instruments for the construction of a new world order missed the point about limitations of mass media and the men and women who controlled them.

It tried to justify what was usually a transparent use of mass media for blatantly political domestic purposes.

Jeremy Tunstall, the British sociologist who helped document the dominance of Anglo-American influence in world communication, returned to the debate in 1982 with a catalog of reasons why the media were *still* American and likely to remain so. The reasons had to do with technology, commercialism, economies of scale, the influence of the English-speaking world, and the inability of 95 percent of the world's nations to be anything but media importers. Instead of decrying this prospect, Tunstall found it more efficient, more entertaining, and safer than any of the alternatives. It was a lukewarm endorsement for the prospect of continued Western dominance in the 1990s, but a realistic assessment.

Third World leaders, too, were more cautious about the ability of mass media to reshape the world over even their own countries than they were when the Unesco debate was burning brightly. Radical development schemes were even less realistic than the promise of rapid economic and political growth that development had promised a generation earlier. The world could not be reshaped by the redistribution of existing wealth and information; the Third World's future lay in joining the West to increase the total pool of wealth and information. That meant acceptance of the Western values that led to its dominance in the first place: tolerance of diversity, encouragement of initiative, and rewarding of success in a society that accepted an open clash of ideas as the best way to define the national interest.

The American and British withdrawal from Unesco poured water on a dying fire, but it did not relieve Western governments and especially Western mass media of their unmet responsibilities to do something about the growing gap between the information-rich West and information-poor Third World. After the failure of efforts to tie radical development to new global economic and information orders and especially after the collapse of Unesco as a powerbroker in the international debate, it was easy to turn away from the intractable problems of the Third World and the inflamed rhetoric that still tried to make the West responsible for them. But if Western governments, Western mass media, and moderate Third World governments did that, they would be laying the coals for a worse conflagration. Out of the ashes of the new world information order debate in the 1970s could come a resurgence of the anger and frustration to rechallenge Western principles of press freedom and responsibility in the 1990s. Justice and self-interest demanded that the West avoid that.

9

Reassessing Communication Development

REBIRTH OF HOPE

When the United States withdrew from Unesco at the end of 1984 (and Britain and Singapore joined the exit queue), it was tempting to believe that the issues of communication development that had preoccupied the world organization for so long were dead. The certain loss of a quarter of its budget helped the institution concentrate its attention on immediate problems. These, not surprisingly, did not include the new global economic and information orders.

The American withdrawal, however, came at a time when Western influence on the Third World communication development debate was reasserting itself. The United States, it seemed, had walked away just when it was winning the fight. The analogy is oversimplified but not inaccurate. After a full decade of heated debate over the role of mass media in the developing nations, a consensus emerged that the Western model was not so bad after all. And whatever vision now inspired Third World communications developers, the hardware to lead them to it could come only from the West. The West had not played its hand skillfully but still held the trump cards.

The push for a new world information order, which a decade of debate in Unesco had not defined, failed for three reasons. One was the hollowness of the Marxist rhetoric that had shaped the issue in the first place. On first hearing, the sweeping statements about neo-imperialism sounded exhilarating and fresh, but the bits of evidence architects of the

165

new order shuffled and reshuffled under the guise of critical research began to look like a shell game. As the traditional quantitative research studies piled up, challenging one after another of the premises of the new world information order, defenders of the neo-imperialism school had to keep changing the questions. No, the Western agencies really did not ignore the Third World; they covered it badly. No, there really was no monopoly on information; the Third World was conditioned to use its own resources poorly. No, the real problem was something else. Always something else. In the end the debate was so transparently divorced from the real and serious issues of development that it became an exercise in Orwellian rhetoric even the most fervent advocates of the NWIO grew tired of.

A second and more substantive reason for the failure of the NWIO was the experience of trying to implement it. It was one thing to stand before the Unesco general conference and argue for the mobilization of mass media to support a new global order, but quite another to piece together a daily news file that was credible enough for domestic consumption and minimally palatable for international exchange. The experiences of IPDC and the various new national agencies, regional exchanges, and global services it supported were salutory. They demonstrated the gap between the rhetoric and the day-to-day problems of deadlines, mechanical failure, payrolls, and political interference.

The experiments in information exchange that the NWIO debate fostered did help expand the flow of news in a minor way, mostly within the Third World, but their real value was a sobering influence on Third World journalism. People who have to edit news stories from both Iran and Iraq or prepare copy acceptable to both Libya and Chad soon learn the value of "objectivity" that critics of Western news agencies had equated with hostility and derision. They also learn that mobilization of journalism, even when it is done under the banner of the Unesco mass media declaration, inevitably redounds to the advantage of the regime in power. Especially then. If anything, the professional values of Western journalism, particularly the independence to challenge the regime in power, emerged from the Unesco debate with greater support in the Third World than they had had a decade or two earlier.

Finally, the debate rekindled an interest in the use of communication to promote development — real development, defined as Lerner and Schramm had done in terms of economic and political growth, not the rhetoric of the NWIO. And that new concern led to the discovery of telecommunication. As we have seen, research demonstrated consistently that investment in telecommunication generated an impressive return in social and economic growth. And unlike mass media, telecommunication seemed to produce change both at the micro or individual level and at the macro or social level as well. However you looked at it, the best evidence argued in favor of special attention to tele-communication in any country's development plan.

Communication development in the 1980s and beyond seemed firmly anchored in telecommunication, and that meant incorporation of the Third World more and more into a global communication system still dominated by the West. If anything, the emergence of information as the driving force of Western economies portended a growing Western influence in the Third World, and certainly in the thickening web of global telecommunications.

For those who had argued in favor of disengagement from the West as a prerequisite to "authentic" national development, the prospects for the 1990s — Unesco adrift and foundering, Third World journalists asserting independence, the Third World itself moving into the shadow of the information age — were grim. For the Third World, however, the prospect for communication development was hopeful if not without obstacles. And for the West, the collapse of the new world information order debate represented an opportunity to reassert influence in an area of international affairs where it had faltered. But it also meant that Western governments and mass media, by default, also assumed the responsibilities for leadership in tackling problems that had grown more complex and intractable in the two decades since Lerner and Schramm first argued that mass media could speed and ease the ascent toward modernity.

THE FRUITS OF THE NWIO

By the mid-1980s the Unesco debate over the role of mass media was over, but the first products of the debate were coming to fruition. For some it was a sobering experience, but there was also reason for hope. IPDC continued to meet and to spread seed money and encouragement along the lengthening list of projects IPDC members found worthy.

IPDC's biggest problem was the same as it had been from the beginning. The list of projects it wanted to support grew, but the list of donors, small to begin with, did not. As a result, most grants were symbolic gestures that kept the projects alive but little more. Anyone present at the birth of IPDC who seriously expected the Western nations to give the advocates of the new world information order a blank check was disabused of that misconception by the time of the Paris meeting. IPDC was useful as a clearinghouse for discussions and debate — a function the organization still eschewed — but could never be a serious instrument for influencing development itself.

Other structures erected by the architects of communication development as emancipation from the West fared no better. The Non-Aligned News Agencies pool, the most visible example of journalism mobilized for radical national development, remained invisible in a world news flow that was certainly expanding quantitatively and probably improving qualitatively. Despite more aggressive editing to make it minimally palatable, the pool files remained a daily lesson of the failures of development and protocol news. A study in India in early 1983, where the government but few journalists endorsed the NWIO, documented how the flow of pool dispatches shriveled to a trickle. The Press Trust of India (PTI) picked up less than 6 percent of material received over a week. During the same period, eight major Indian papers used a total of 17 pool stories, only one of which appeared on a front page. As evidence of the pool's failure, the authors concluded that Western journalists no longer complained about the pool; they just ignored it. Third World journalists did, too.

The good news was that communication development stayed on the public agenda in the United States even after the decision to leave Unesco was announced. In fact, the brave talk about increasing development assistance that had been made at the height of the Unesco debate prompted study groups, test projects, and reports that collectively had a significant impact on the two interest groups most concerned with development, the federal government and the media themselves.

A survey of 25 federal agencies in late 1984 found that few bureaucracies knew exactly what they were doing in the field of international communications, but four agencies — Export-Import Bank, Overseas Private Investment Corp., Agency for International Development, and the U.S. Information Agency — were investing $680 million a year in communication development. At a minimum in 1983–1984, according to the government-funded study, communication development activities included at least 63 separate training and assistance programs that involved more than 1,100 Third World participants in more than 100 countries at a cost of some $422 million. The report, not surprisingly, found lack of coordination and even common purpose in most of the federal government's activities, but on the bright side also found a new interest in the area.

The new interest extended right to the top of the unwieldy bureaucracy, where the White House and National Security Council staff in March 1984, ordered an interagency committee on information and communications policy to review the issue and come up with recommendations. The report went to the White House in November. The report, as the *Chronicle of International Communication* put it, forced "the Administration to make a conscious, high level, relatively public decision on whether it can afford to continue U.S. drift and dribble responses to Third World media and telecommunications problems." In a city where power is measured by distance from the Oval Office, communication development had become an important issue for the first time.

The report framed the issue in the rhetoric of the Reagan Administration: without an American effort, Soviet influence would be strengthened; the information-based American economy needed Third World markets, and recommended both better use of existing activities and an increase in the total amount of money allocated to communication development. In an administration sacrificing all manner of domestic sacred cows to an uncontrollable debt, any talk of increasing something as friendless as foreign aid was remarkable.

The prospect of a new awareness of the importance of communication development combined with the commitment of existing and new funds to the field meant that the United States government might be able to play its very strong cards in the 1980s and 1990s more skillfully than it had in the 1960s and 1970s. And by the mid-1980s it had better support from the private media, which were important allies in countering the still prevalent argument that Third World development required the brand of journalism still practiced by the Non-Aligned News Agencies pool and many government-run news organs.

For a second conference in Talloires in 1983, the World Press Freedom Committee and the Associated Press put together a list of 300 exchange, training, and internship programs in 70 countries. No one knew so much was going on. Two new programs sponsored by the American Society of Newspaper Editors and the Alfred E. Friendly Foundation providing 22 internships/fellowships were announced. The WPFC itself increased the number of grants it had made to a total of more than 70 since the organization began supporting Third World media in 1977. In early 1985 a permanent Center for Foreign Journalists near Washington was announced. At its beginning the center was little more than an office in a Washington suburb, but it held the promise of doing something IPDC had chosen not to do — become a clearing house for all the needs and resources in communication development while sustaining a critical mass of Western private media commitment to parallel that of the U.S. government.

As interest in the United States began to lead finally to hopeful public and private commitments to communication development, the international agencies also recognized the importance of communication to broad-based economic development. Three important studies all focused on telecommunications, making it the centerpiece of a renewed interest in communication and development for the rest of the 1980s and into the 1990s.

The World Bank's 1983 study, *Telecommunications and Economic Development*, was the most cautious of the three, fitting recent research into three competing perspectives on the role of telecommunications and economic growth: (1) telecommunications does not deserve priority in development schemes because it is disruptive and ineffective; (2) demands for telecommunications service should be met and service expanded to rural areas when cost effective; (3) telecommunications deserves priority as a "prime means to achieve a wide range of social and economic goals in numerous socially oriented sectors, including the delivery of education and health services." The authors did not claim that telecommunications was a magic multiplier for the 1980s, but did come down strongly in favor of the more optimistic interpretation of telecommunication's potential. At a minimum it appeared that the study would increase the visibility of telecommunications in the World Bank and probably its commitment to telecommunications projects. That in itself promised to be significant because the bank was the major funding source for Third World telecommunications investment.

A report by the Organization for Economic Cooperation and Development (OECD) and the International Telecommunications Union (ITU) was less cautious about the importance of telecommunications to economic development. Case studies examined in the report showed cost/benefit ratios as high as 100 to 1 in a wide range of economic enterprises. A hypothetical calculation concluded that one simple satellite earth station connected to ten telephones over nine years could contribute from $4,000 to $15,000 to the gross domestic product of a relatively wealthy developing country with a minimal existing phone system. In a rural area, the return was estimated to be from $167,000 to $496,000. The authors, unlike the cautious researchers who never could satisfactorily sort out cause and effect in Lerner's and Schramm's time, argued that the direction of the arrow linking telecommunications and growth was clear — and, in fact, the opposite of what earlier research had suggested. The secretary general of the ITU, Richard E. Butler, noted the conventional wisdom that telecommunication growth followed economic development and was a luxury that a developing country could afford only after other needs were met. Now it appeared that telecommunication produced important benefits across the whole spectrum of development goals and should be at the core of development programs, not at the periphery. This was clearly a different way of thinking about development than the emphasis on one-way, vertical *mass* media of Lerner and Schramm days.

The third report added another voice to the growing chorus favoring investment in telecommunications as a key to Third World development. This one was another international commission, headed by British diplomat Sir Donald Maitland, organized by ITU. In the spirit of hard-headed realism of the 1980s, the commission recognized the importance of shifting available resources to telecommunication — such as a small tax on international calls to finance Third World development — rather than massive new investment programs. The goal, it said, should be to make basic telecommunications service available to everyone on earth by the early twenty-first century. An impossible dream? Perhaps, but no more visionary than the goal of providing five radio receivers per 100 people that Unesco had set a generation earlier, a goal that had been met and then surpassed unnoticed in the early 1980s.

Both the ITU/OECD and Maitland Commission reports offered the outlines of specific but expensive ideas for implementing their conclusions. The former argued in favor a *globdom* (for "global" and "domestic") system, comprising four satellites with global coverage linking a network of ground stations. Total cost: $1.26 billion. But a payoff of "telephone service to all the rural regions of the developing world, even the most remote, for an initial investment cost which is practically similar to that of the telephone service in the industrialized countries."

The Maitland Commission recommended the establishment of a global center for telecommunications development. Its major task would be to come up with $12 billion a year for investment needed to reach the ambitious goal the report called for. The figure seemed less dreamlike, however, when one remembered that the developing nations already invested $8 billion in telecommunications in 1983. The 50 percent increase was an ambitious goal but, given the climate of the 1980s, not impossible.

Even if all the new institutions succeeded in their ambitious plans, there was no guarantee that communication with telecommunication rather than mass media at the core would be any more successful than the overly ambitious programs of the 1960s. Certainly the Third World's climb toward modernity in the 1980s and 1990s could be no less difficult or free from turmoil than it had been in the preceding decades, but the issues were important enough that no one concerned with the fate of the Third World could afford to ignore them.

THE LESSONS OF THE FIRST GENERATION

A generation separates Balgat from today's overcrowded cities of Africa, the Middle East, Latin America, and Asia, but most of the problems in that Turkish village still confront the Third World. Some progress, painfully slow and uneven, can be counted in reducing disease and early death and in extending minimal public services. But the years after Balgat joined the modern world seemed to produce more expectations than accomplishments and, as Lerner warned, a tide of rising frustrations. Too many of those modest gains were overtaken by uncontrolled population growth, squandered on arms, or sacrificed to national vanity.

The idea Lerner's generation advocated of hitching rapid national development to the locomotive of communication failed. Despite a dramatic growth in broadcasting and a mixed record of growth in print in the 1960s and 1970s, economic growth in the Third World was uneven and its benefits poorly distributed. Gains in mass media, particularly broadcasting, can be attributed more to declining costs and popular determination to share in the West's communication riches than government policy. Social gains seemed to be as much the product of coercion (China) or private initiative (Latin America and parts of Asia) as effective integration of communication into development schemes.

Open political institutions, certainly the stable democracies envisioned by Lerner and Schramm, are rare, although India and scattered nations of Latin America, the Caribbean, and Asia stand as exceptions to a general pattern of dictatorship. It is easy to dismiss the original blueprint for compressing the centuries of Western industrialization into decades with communication as the great multiplier as naive or unrealistic, but the core of the argument is still valid. Any program of national development requires wealth to fuel it; any social change can be accommodated more easily in a democracy than in a dictatorship. Grand designs to shift the financial or information resources of the West to the Third World, as the new world economic order and information order debates demanded, are politically unrealistic and misguided. Consider how OPEC nations used their sudden wealth. If the total wealth of the world were equally distributed, everyone would be poor; if the total information of the world were equally shared, everyone would be ignorant. Third World development needs an increase in both wealth and information more than a reshuffling of that which already exists.

Neither Lerner nor Schramm anticipated the central issue of communication development in the 1980s. As we have seen, the issue was no longer defined in terms of how mass media could be used to accelerate economic growth or promote political stability, but whether communication should be mobilized to support national political objectives at the cost of journalistic and personal independence. Advocates of the old model of communication development were willing to accept a reasonable degree of government involvement in mass media, certainly in the traditional areas of health and education and perhaps more directly as an interim expedient until independent media could develop. But statements like the Unesco declaration on mass media or the still undefined new world information order called for more than that.

FAILURE OF THE RADICAL ALTERNATIVE

The principles of a free flow of information, of independent media critical of government, and of pluralist liberal democracy were denounced as irrelevant to the Third World in the 1980s or even as frauds in the West where they still held sway. In their place, advocates of a new information order called for news structures to be harnessed to the political apparatus of the state, mobilized to support national integration and development. "News" was even redefined as information that supports the state. Was the failure of communication to bridge the gap between the stable, prosperous West and the mostly unstable, poverty-stricken Third World justification for jettisoning the principles of independence that had evolved with Western political and economic development? Architects of the new global orders, of course, answered "yes," but the high-sounding promise of the radical alternative dimmed when one looked at the record of developing countries that had done more or less what the new economic and information orders called for.

It was one thing to attack the failed efforts to use mass media as the magic multiplier of development efforts but quite another to take the sometimes noble, sometimes outlandish vagaries of the new world orders and put them into practice. A dilemma that had shadowed the evolution of the radical alternative continued, however. That was the continuing search for a socialist future that worked; the present did not. No country dedicated to the principles of the development as disengagement from the existing global system had demonstrated success persuasively, and through the cracks in the facade of progress came more and disturbing evidence of failure. The new mass media were mostly weak imitations of the Western models they were supposed to replace, and worse, more the instruments of repression and deceit than enlightenment and cooperation.

Marxists on the whole do not like empirical evidence. They prefer to rest their arguments on deduction and definition and to press their attacks against the international capitalist system as though the indictment were sufficient to prove the case. They particularly do not like to submit to scrutiny the record of accomplishment under regimes committed to their principles.

However, enough countries operate under a radical model of

national development that a record has been created. The numbers presented in this survey of communication and development in the 1970s test both paradigms equally well and make a weaker case for the contribution of communication to the Marxist goals of equity and cultural independence than they do for the Lerner-Schramm goals of economic growth and political stability. Mass media demonstrated even less power to propel a developing country toward a socialist future than toward one based on capitalism.

Huge differences can be detected among Third World countries, and the socialist nations on the whole probably fared better than capitalist or mixed-economy neighbors in reducing illiteracy and early death and in providing basic social services. At the same time, however, they often paid for this impressive progress with economic stagnation and almost always with the loss of personal liberty. Programs in which communication was believed to play a significant role — China's birth control program and Cuba's mobilization of its citizenry to support economic and social development, for example — often proved to be, on closer inspection, the product of coercion, not persuasion, and certainly not a product of the kind of participatory democracy that the radical approach to nation building promised. Tanzania had exchanged its colonial dependency on Britain for economic dependency on Western aid. None had achieved "authentic" development or even defined it.

Electronic media themselves seemed to evolve independently of economic and political conditions. The cost of radio and television receivers declined steadily, of course, and the determination of people to own them, regardless of the quantity and quality of programming available, overcame the most stringent government restrictions. As a result, their numbers grew exponentially almost without regard to government policies, economic circumstances, or national development plans.

Print media, on the other hand, grew modestly and erratically, often the captive of government bureaucracies and scarce foreign exchange. Too often government plans to promote the development of mass media per se were caught in the kind of zero-sum inconsistencies that plagued other development schemes: national plans calling for expansion of newspapers at the same time that exhorbitant duties prohibited the import of printing equipment and newsprint; a public commitment to small-scale radio and local programming while expending scarce foreign currency on grandiose TV facilities and imported programming. The gap between rhetoric and reality was greatest when national media, committed to a new order based on respect and cooperation, were in fact used to shout the passions and prejudices of a mean regime.

It is easy, in retrospect, to see why the original belief in the power of mass media to speed new nations toward Western modernity eroded in the 1960s, when so many of the post-World War II certainties were challenged. The radical alternative was a product of that disillusionment as well as the growing acceptance of China and Cuba as worthy models for an emerging world of nations tied neither to the capitalist West nor socialist East. The ideology of the Third World, from its beginning as a political movement, was attuned more to socialism than capitalism, so it was reasonable to expect a distinctly Third World theory of national development to resonate with Marxist rhetoric and perspectives.

But the new model of development and new role for communication reflected as well a disenchantment with the dreary mass industrial system that the Soviet Union had become and its clumsy efforts to export it to the Third World. China, Cuba, and Tanzania, on the other hand, seemed to demonstrate the possibilities of national development better than any other country and defined their goals and pursued them independently of both the West and the Soviet Union. And these models, particularly China, practicing Mao's principle of mobilizing mass communication to support development, seemed to produce dramatic results with widespread and enthusiastic popular support. The role for mass media in these models was central and very political.

The disenchantment that pervaded the Unesco debates by the late 1970s was partly a result of a more skeptical, more critical look at the accomplishments of countries that had opted for the new model of communication and development, partly the result of the emergence of ancient and bitter hostilities between Third World countries that could not be blamed on simplistic Western imperialism, and partly the result of a decade-old debate that produced very little change in the existing world order.

At first the rhetoric of cultural imperialism and dependency, the calls for mobilization of media to create an authentic Third World development, and even the promises of increased aid to transfer the new wealth of the information age to the developing countries seemed as fresh and exciting as Schramm's book had a decade earlier.

But noble sentiments in Unesco declarations and grand schemes in national development plans do not translate easily into new mass media structures or content, as Peru, Venezuela, Mexico, and the directors of national news agencies and cooperative exchanges learned. Massive transfers of wealth, as the OPEC nations learned, do not necessarily or even very often lead to the equitable, participatory future that architects of the new order promised. In fact, the product of rapid accumulation in wealth was often instability and discontent and loss of cultural continuity, not a flowering of an authentic, non-Western society.

And most of all, for all developing nations, whether the beneficiaries of oil money or debtors to it, any definition of modernity was essentially a derivative of the Northern model: industrialization to create wealth, a complex technical infrastructure to manage it, and a competent political system to control it. Visions of a future with the benefits of industrial modernity but without its problems, a future with the power of an information-rich West but without its loss of community were, in the end, an illusion.

Those who direct the effort to define and create a new world information order in the 1990s are, for the most part, more sober than their counterparts a short generation ago. Many have had the humbling experience of running a news agency or information ministry, and most are tired of a decade's debate that produced so little change in the existing system, so little evidence of the success of either vision of national development, so few new ideas.

Communication development in the 1990s may usher in a period of realism. IPDC, on the whole, is realistic and pragmatic. so is most of the still inadequate Western response to the call for assistance in improving Third World communication capabilities. It is a mood to be encouraged.

THIRD WORLD NEEDS

Most of all, Third World countries need honesty and public accountability for what they do and do not do. Governments that use their media to maintain themselves in power while silencing critics are neither honest nor accountable. Governments that speak of mobilizing the media for peace while using them to denounce real or imagined enemies are following the well-used path of dictatorships, not blazing a trail toward a peaceful global order.

Developing nations need to acknowledge to themselves as well as to the world that most of what happens to them is of their own making. If their broadcasting systems present the worst of American commercial programming, it is because they choose it, not because there are no choices or because the choice is dictated from abroad. If their media rely on reports from the Western agencies and ignore the alternative services that are laden with development and protocol news, it is because their editors prefer the Western versions, not because they have nothing else. If audiences seek information from Western sources instead of controlled domestic media, it is because the latter have demonstrated that they are untrustworthy and boring. If national media are filled with shrill slander of convenient villains and silent on domestic problems, it is because the Unesco mass media declaration is unworkable.

Almost two decades after Schramm argued the importance of

planning, an honest, comprehensive system of allocating a nation's resources among competing needs is still lacking in most Third World countries. If mass media have only a limited role in the creation of a modern society as this and other reviews have concluded, a country may be wise to spend its scarce foreign currency on medicine, industrial machinery, or computers rather than on an elaborate broadcasting facility, newspaper production equipment, or the apparatus for a national news agency.

If a government does decide, for example, that the expansion of newspapers is an important part of a national development policy, then it ought not to allow counterveiling forces to work against that decision. It should make sure that high tariffs on imported equipment are waived, that production or procurement of inexpensive newsprint is encouraged, and that telecommunication costs are priced to benefit the newspapers. If broadcasting is to be expanded, provision needs to be made for programming and receivers as well as production facilities. And, of course, for long-term maintenance and repairs, the lack of which is responsible for turning too many grand development schemes into decaying wreckage. The ribbon-cutting ceremony is the start of a commitment, not the end of it.

In fact, many communication development efforts in the 1980s would benefit more from the clear-headed realism of a management expert than from the starry-eyed vision of those who see communication as the driving force behind a new global order. Progress comes in small steps, as those who run the NANA pool and regional exchanges can attest, and is the product of meeting deadlines, budgets, and customers' needs more than ideological purity. Open government, accountable through skeptical media to a public that can turn them out of office, remains the one proven way of maintaining honest and competent public policy. The antiseptic glare of public scrutiny is the only tested antidote to the corruption and mismanagement that have thwarted too many development efforts.

Unesco is not an appropriate forum for the concentration of development assistance activities regardless of the presence or absence of the United States and other Western nations. The bloated bureaucracy is too politicized and too incompetent to administer development programs or to advise Third World countries about how to achieve development objectives. It has demonstrated its inability to arrive at any realistic or even coherent definition of the kind of world its quarrelsome nations ought to be working toward or how mass media can contribute to such an objective.

Regional cooperative efforts are commendable, if unlikely to have a significant influence on global news flow. They can supplement the major news services and increase the anemic flow of information within geographic regions. Most important is the pragmatic lesson they teach in the realities of putting together, day by day, story by story, a news file that is minimally acceptable to diverse and mutually antagonistic customers. The editors of the Non-Aligned News Agencies pool learn more about the difficulties of mobilizing the media in support of a new world information order by dealing with Iran and Iraq on a day-to-day routine than they can listening to Unesco debates. The leaders of the new regional exchanges will learn more about the problems exporting protocol and development news by trying it than they will by discussing it at meetings of information ministers.

Third World nations should also recognize and acknowledge that talk about a "balanced flow" of information between themselves and the West is unrealistic. As long as communication innovation continues to come from a handful of Western information societies, new technology and new knowledge will continue to flow overwhelmingly in one direction, from the West to the Third World.

That flow will not be reversed by Unesco declarations or even slowed significantly by unilateral edict. It will be harder and harder to keep out unwanted information, harder and harder for governments to maintain a monopoly on the information their citizens have access to. Shortwave radio receivers get smaller and more sensitive; cassette recorders and photocopiers multiply messages quickly and efficiently, as leaders of the Iranian revolution found out. Government media that fail to deal openly and reasonably honestly with events will find themselves ignored and despised. Learning to live without a monopoly on information can be painful to sensitive Third World governments, but the effect on national development will be beneficial.

The technology of the information age in the West provides opportunities for developing nations that did not exist a generation ago. In almost all cases, the costs of developing communication infrastructures and purchasing communication hardware are declining steadily, and information, unlike older forms of wealth, does not necessarily lose value when it is shared. The Third World needs to embrace the information age, not reject it, but to do so dispassionately, taking from the cornucopia of new knowledge and technology that which is reasonable and useful, avoiding that which is merely appealing.

The task is not easy, but trying to turn one's back on the future in the name of cultural independence is as foolish as the medieval church's efforts to silence the scientists who challenged her monopoly on truth, and just as futile. Third World countries need to recognize that what is emerging is more a world culture than Western cultural imperialism. It is a culture to which they can contribute as well as derive a wide range of benefits.

WESTERN RESPONSIBILITY

Interdependence is more than a cliche of the 1980s and more than a one-way street. If Third World countries cannot escape Western influence in their future and would be foolish to try, the West also is bound more and more to the fate of the developing nations. Those with responsibilities for providing communication development assistance and those with re-sponsibilities for covering the continuing terrible ascent of Third World nations carry a heavy burden.

While they may be innocent of most of the charges leveled against them in the early days of the new world information order debate, Western media — particularly nonelite American newspapers and broadcasters — are appallingly inadequate in their coverage of Third World affairs. This is surprising when audience surveys show consis-tently high interest in international coverage and dangerous in a country where public opinion plays so powerful an influence on public policy. Neither the United States nor the Third World can afford continued public ignorance.

To a large extent, the world's media are American and will continue to be, as realistic participants in the global debate concede. While the West, and particularly the United States, continues to lead in the techniques and technology of news gathering and dissemination, it needs to demonstrate comparable innovation and leadership in finding ways to make foreign news, especially the nondisruptive, nonexceptional events in the lives of three-quarters of the world's population, interesting and comprehensible to audiences around the world. Americans should know about such things for their own sake; they need to know about them because their jobs, security, and futures may depend on them.

Better coverage can be one of the more useful products of technical assistance projects. Newspapers and broadcast organizations that es-tablish personal contacts with Third World counterparts through as-sistance and training programs can gain as much as they give; promoting Third World assistance is not a zero-sum game. Projects such as those sponsored by the Center for Foreign Journalists and the World Press Freedom Committee are commendable and need to be expanded. There are opportunities in every community to show how its fate is tied to that of peoples of the Third World. Every broadcaster and newspaper has the possibility — and the responsibility — to help its audience see beyond the incomplete and incoherent glimpse of the world it gets most of the time.

The West also has a responsibility to stand firmly against the rhetoric of the new world information order debate that would legitimize mobilization of mass media to serve the mean purposes of governments and transform the rights of individuals into the rights of governments. In this argument the West has a strong ally — journalists in the Third World.

One of the reasons that the rhetoric of the radical transformation of communication development at Unesco proceeded with such speed and ferocity was the absence of a strong, steady Western voice and the lack of a forceful defense of the Western position in favor of independent media. But the architects of the new world information order seldom represent their own media; Third World journalists, on the whole, share the professional values of their Western colleagues. They, too, want to report on their governments freely and critically. They want to be watchdogs, not lapdogs.

The power of Western journalists to report critically on governments is admired in the Third World more than most Western journalists realize. Their ability to influence public policy is envied more widely than the Unesco rhetoric acknowledges. These are powerful cards that can be played to good advantage by an enlightened understanding between media professionals and public officials.

The West, of course, is at a disadvantage is most of the international forums because it is represented by an uneasy alliance of government officials and media professionals that must argue the case for distance between government and media. No wonder Third World delegations are suspicious of the arguments for independent media when journalists and foreign service officers sit together as delegates.

Still, the discrepancy is more apparent than real and need not be an obstacle to a common front in defending the value of Western institutions. Or in expanding technical assistance to Third World countries that are farther behind the information-rich West than they were a generation ago, when development seemed to require only the establishment of a simple mass media system to set off a chain reaction of political and economic growth. At least part of the blame for the explosion of the Unesco debates over the new global economic and information orders rests with Western governments for ignoring the issue and for failing to engage the Third World vigorously in that forum. It is a mistake that should not and need not be repeated. Despite the lack of a domestic lobby and in the face of budget pressures, a coherent program of wide-ranging assistance to Third World communication development is needed for both pragmatic and altruistic reasons.

The West, represented by both government and media, needs to expand its still meager development aid programs so that Third World countries can benefit from the rapid developments of technology. On one hand, programs such as IPDC can be useful, but Western governments need to demand open accounting, honest evaluation, and realism in deciding which programs work and which ones do not. Failures can be as instructive as successes in deciding where IPDC's second generation of efforts ought to be directed.

Most of the assistance, however, will have to come from the media themselves because it is incongruous and dangerous to expect any government to support mass media overseas in ways that it cannot do at home. Efforts by the print media in the West have been modest but promising; until now, the broadcast media have participated far less. This will have to change because of the importance of broadcasting in the Third World and certainly because broadcasters have as much responsibility as print journalists for dealing with new world information order issues.

For American broadcasters, this will require recognition that the BBC is as good a model for the Third World as NBC and probably better. They need only reflect on the contribution of public broadcasting in the United States now and in the past 50 years as well as their current symbiotic relationship with government to recognize that highly commercial, heavily entertainment-oriented broadcasting is a luxury that developing countries cannot afford. Print journalists, too, must recognize that in many countries of the Third World, newspapers could not exist without some form of government subsidy. The Western agencies have learned to live with government news agencies and information ministries; the World Press Freedom Committee can, too, and should not forget that press and government in the United States are closer and more compatible bedfellows than its rhetoric sometimes implies.

The fruits of the information age — computers, satellites, printing technology, and everything else that is blurring the old distinctions among media as quickly as it is creating new media — will spill over into the Third World in the 1990s despite anyone's efforts to prevent it or to promote it. It is unlikely that this spillover will speed economic and political development in the way that architects of the old paradigm hoped or that it will help shape the vision of Third World cultural independence that advocates of the new order propose.

Instead, communication has the potential to contribute constructively if modestly to Third World development, and those in the West with the responsibility and authority to shape policy can influence constructively if modestly the size and direction of the contribution. With patience, tolerance, and understanding on both sides, the gap in understanding between the West and the Third World can be breached and the gap in wealth narrowed. Without them, the information age will breed more of the chaos and violence that have so far accompanied the Third World's terrible ascent to an uncertain future.

Sources

CHAPTER ONE: NEW ISSUES AND OLD PROBLEMS

No single work tracing the evolution of communication development from a technical issue to a political issue exists; even most of the record of the first two decades can be found only in the original documents. The first great statement was Lerner's *The Passing of Traditional Society* (1958), now out of print. Schramm's (1964) highly influential study for the United Nations Educational, Scientific and Cultural Organization (Unesco) remains the single best and most influential statement of the early view of communication and development. The Indian satellite project (INSAT) is described by Dua in Singh (1983) and Agrawal in Gerbner and Siefert (1984).

The challenge to the Lerner-Schramm argument is recorded in the two conferences sponsored by the East-West Center in Hawaii. Skepticism and hostility are apparent in the two books based on the conferences, Lerner and Schramm (1967) and Schramm and Lerner (1976). Rogers' criticism, first raised at the second Honolulu conference, was expanded and became the core of a special issue of *Communication Research* (Rogers 1976) and also printed in the *Journal of Communication* (Rogers 1978). The quote is from Rogers (1976, 129–130).

Schiller's "information imperialism" thesis is at the center of all of his extensive writings. The indictment of mass media is contained in his *Mass Communications and American Empire* (1971) and *Communication and Cultural Domination* (1976); later works dealing with information technology and data flows are *Who Knows? Information in the Age of the Fortune 500* (1981) and *Information and the Crisis Economy* (1984). The argument in favor of disengagement from the global information system is presented in Hamelink (1983).

The rise of the new world information order debate in Unesco is best described in Righter's *Whose News? Politics, the Press and the Third World* (1978). A more sympathetic view, with a good summary of the debates over the mass media declaration, is McPhail's *Electronic Colonialism* (1981). Two other general sources are Tunstall (1977) and Smith (1980). Nordenstreng's *The Mass Media Declaration of Unesco* (1984) is a strongly anti-Western interpretation. Unesco's own monograph, "Historical Background of the Mass Media Declaration," (N.D.) covers much of the same ground, but is difficult to interpret without prior knowledge of the codewords and subtleties of the debate. Official reports of the various Unesco conferences are invaluable but are difficult to understand for the same reason.

The best source for current information about the International Program for Development of Communication (IPDC) was the "Chronicle of International Communication," a newsletter published by International Communication Projects, Inc., with assistance from George Washington University Center for Telecommunications Studies. At the end of 1985 it was incorporated into the *Transnational Data News*. An evaluation of IPDC's first efforts is Block (1982) with other assessments in the same issue of *Journal of Communication*. IPDC activities are also reported regularly, usually critically, in the newsletters of the World Press Freedom Committee.

CHAPTER TWO: THE MAGIC MULTIPLIER

The description of the village of Balgat is an extended example provided by Lerner himself (1958). The quote about the psychological effects of modernization through the mass media is on page 53. The "theory" itself must be extracted from several chapters and has been interpreted in various ways. See Hedebro (1982), Stevenson (1983b and 1985c), Ghorpade et al. (1984), and Frey (in Pool, et al, 1973) for various formulations.

The background of the Schramm book (1964) is in the volume itself. The description of the South Asian village is on page 7; Schramm's enthusiastic charge to mass media is on page 271; his litany of benefits of development is on page 35. The quote from Fernand Terrou, director of the French Institute of the Press, is part of a larger essay on government's role; it is found on page 239 of Schramm's book.

Figures on communication assistance are taken from reports of the agencies cited. The World Bank number is from Pierce and Jequier (1983); the Unesco figure is from the MacBride report. Most of the American effort is directed by the U.S. Agency for International Development (USAID); current activities are summarized by Block in Singh (1983) and in various agency reports and publications. The full range of current U.S. government activities is detailed in *Communications Development* (1984). Schramm's thoughts in the 1970s were in a statement prepared for the MacBride Commission (1978). A comparable reassessment by Lerner was published by Tufts University in 1978.

The attack by Inayatullah on the "materialist West" is in the volume reporting the first East-West Center conference (Lerner and Schramm 1967, 100). Other hints of disenchantment can be found in the same source. The report of the second conference (Schramm and Lerner 1976) contains the attack by Rogers, which was later the core of a special issue of *Communication Research* (Rogers 1976) and a similar article in *Journal of Communication* (Rogers 1978). Rogers's appreciation of China is on pages 129–130 of the special issue of *Communication Research* (Rogers 1976).

CHAPTER THREE: COLLISION WITH A NEW ORDER

The quote from Tunstall is in Atwood et al. (1982), a summary of a useful conference held the previous year. Schiller's first extensive presentation of the cultural imperialism argument is his *Mass Communications and American Empire* (1971); the quote is from pages 2–3. His later works (1981, 1982, 1984) update the thesis. The attack on the First Amendment abuse is from a summary in *Channels* magazine (1982, 33).

The discussion of dependency is taken largely from Salinas and Paldan (in Nordenstreng and Schiller 1979). See also Galtung (1971) and Hanes in Stevenson and Shaw (1984). Beltran's attack on American research is in the special issue of *Communication Research* edited by Rogers. Similar views are expressed by Halloran (1978), his article in Whitney et al. (1982), and in "Ferment in the Field," a special issue of *Journal of Communication* published in 1983.

The history of the new world information order debate at Unesco is documented by Righter (1978), McPhail (1981), Nordenstreng (1984), and Gunter (1979) in the Unesco monograph, "Historical Background of the Mass Media Declaration" (N.D.). The mass media declaration itself was published in various ways by Unesco and is printed in *Journal of Communication* 29(2): 190–191 (1979) and Richstad and Anderson (1981).

The 1980 study by The International Commission for the Study of

Communication Problems (MacBride Commission) includes its own record of activities and some indication of debates. The collection of supporting documents, most published by Unesco as uncatalogued pamphlets, some never issued at all, is a diverse and valuable source of data and opposing ideas. Comments on the MacBride report, mostly critical, are in Hamelink (1980) and Stevenson (1983a). The Tunstall assessment is from Atwood et al. (1982). An outline of the report and its findings is in Singh and Gross in Gerbner and Siefert (1984).

The material on the International Program for the Development of Communication (IPDC) comes from IPDC documents, the "Chronicle of International Communication," and World Press Freedom Committee newsletters. An early assessment of the organization is in Block (1982) and in several other pieces published in the same issue of *Journal of Communication*. The early debates about IPDC are described in McPhail (1981).

CHAPTER FOUR: THE RECORD OF COMMUNICATION DEVELOPMENT

The description of the Voice of Zaire was based on personal observation in 1982. The quote from Schramm endorsing communication planning is from his 1964 book, page 210. The Hamelink quote is from his 1983 book, page 100. The Unesco monograph series on national communication policies are all titled "Communication Policies in . . . ." The evaluation of Afghanistan's communication planning (or lack of it) is in Hancock (1981, 104–105). The MacBride Commission report is cited here as "International Commission for the Study of Communication Problems (1980)"; the quote is on pages 254–255.

Studies of rural development would almost fill a bookshelf by themselves. Starting points are Rogers (1969), Rogers and Shoemaker (1971), Schramm (1964), Hedebro (1982), and McAnany (1980). The Indian experience is mentioned in these works: Diaz Bordenave (*Communication and Rural Development* 1977) and Dua (in Singh 1983).

The Pool study of telecommunications in rural Egypt is summarized in Singh (1983); the Brazilian experience is described in an article by Castelo Branco in the same volume. The lack of interest in Third World telecommunications is emphasized in the MacBride Commission report ("International Commission for the Study of Communication Problems 1980"), the ITU-OECD study (Pierce and Jequier 1983), Saunders et al. (1983), the Maitland Commission report ("The Missing Link" 1984), and Hudson (1984). The importance of telecommunications to news media is noted in Till (1983).

The comment about Arap Moi's use of news media is based on personal observation. The rural newspaper experiment is described in *Function and Organization of Print Media for Rural Development* (1981), Ansah et al. (1981), and Schramm (1964).

The Katz and Wedell (1977) book is the best starting point for a study of broadcasting. The McAnany quote is from the introduction to his 1980 study. The Schramm quote is from the 1964 book, page 226. Katz's description of TV programming in the Third World is from Nordenstreng and Schiller (1979, 65). The "cultural imperialism" thesis is argued in works by Schiller, especially his early books, Smith (1980) and Tunstall (1977). Recent examples of television flow studies are Varis (1984) and a special issue of *Communication Research* devoted to studies of television flows in Latin America (Rogers and Schement 1976).

Lerner's later view on development (1978) was published as a report by Tufts University; Schramm's essay (1978) was written for the MacBride Commission.

CHAPTER FIVE: COMMUNICATION DEVELOPMENT FOR A NEW ORDER

Savio's comments on the Liberian News Agency are taken from a statement presented to a congressional committee in 1981. Hamelink's argument for disengagement from the West is in his 1983 book.

Schramm's quote on the value of news agencies is in *Mass Media and National Development* (1964, 228). The Unesco figures are reported in *World Communications* (1975). The Non-Aligned News Agencies pool count is from documents prepared for the pool's second conference in Belgrade ("Nonaligned on Information — Documents" 1979).

Information on the News Agency of Nigeria is based on a personal visit in 1982, Document No. 13 prepared for the MacBride Commission ("Monographs I 1978") and "The Story of NAN" (N.D.). The quote on the agency's purpose is from Ugboajah (1980, 15).

Most of the information on Xinhua is taken from an unpublished master's thesis at the University of North Carolina (Chi 1983). Additional information comes from Butterfield (1982).

A visit to Tanjug in 1982 provided background on that organization. See also Document No. 15 submitted to the MacBride Commission ("Monographs III") and Ivacic (1977). Background on Shihata is from Anim and Haskovec (1978), a report of a Unesco technical advisory mission. Additional information came from press clippings supplied by Africa News in Durham, NC.

The purpose of the Non-Aligned News Agency pool is well

documented in Ivacic (1977, 1978) and his chapter in Horton (1978), Mankekar in Richstad and Anderson (1981). Yadava in his *Politics of News* (1984), and Mathur and Shrivastava (1984). The evaluation is in Pinch (1977). The personal visit to Tanjug in 1982 also provided information.

The most complete information on (and evaluation of) Inter Press Service is in Giffard (1983, 1984b). Additional information came from Hester in Lent (1979), *Towards a New World Information and Communication Order* (1981), Document 14 prepared for the MacBride Commission ("Monographs II"), and various documents provided by IPS. Background on Deutsche Presse Agentur (DPA) and Kyodo is in Document 14 prepared for the MacBride Commission.

Data on Peru are from Ortega and Romero (1977), Hamelink (1983), and Atwood and Mattos in Gerbner and Siefert (1984). The discussion of recent communication development activities in Mexico and Venezuela comes almost entirely from a study of these two countries that was carried out as part of this project. It is reported in full in an unpublished master's thesis at the University of North Carolina (Gardner 1984) and in Gardner and Stevenson (1988). Additional information comes from O'Sullivan-Ryan in Gandy et al. (1983). The statement from Javier Solana was included in the official report of the IPDC meeting. The comment about Ochoa is quoted in Gardner (1984, 75). See also the special issue of *Communication Research* devoted to media flows in Latin America (Rogers and Schement 1976) and Mateu (1985).

The Finnish communication specialist's disillusionment is in Kivikuru (1984). Other critical evaluations of Tanzania's experience are Sowell (1983b), Lamb (1982) and Johnson (1983).

CHAPTER SIX: THE STATE OF THIRD WORLD MEDIA

The figures on TV sets in Algeria are from the 1982 *Unesco Statistical Yearbook*, the *World Radio TV Handbook* (Frost 1982), and the annual BBC estimate for 1982. The 975,000 figure is from the 1985 *World Almanac*. Figures from the 1960s are extrapolated from the report of the first Honolulu conference (Lerner and Schramm 1967). Disparities between developed and developing countries are from the 1982 *Unesco Statistical Yearbook*, also contains data from the 1960s. BBC estimates are produced every year; for this project we used all the estimates from 1965 to 1984. Unesco figures are partly estimates and partly figures from periodic surveys of member states. Accuracy and completeness vary. Yadav's description of changes in an Indian village is from a paper presented to the International Communication Association in 1984.

Most figures on social indicators are from Sivard (1982) and Hansen et al. (1982). Hansen provided the Physical Quality of Life Index (PQLI) and analysis of income distribution. Freedom House figures are reported annually; those reported here are in Gastil (1982). Figures on telephones are from "The World's Telephones," an annual compilation by American Telephone & Telegraph.

Barton's book (1979) is the newest on African media. Lamb's survey of the continent (1982) includes a chapter on mass media. A new source on African broadcasting is Mytton (1983).

Rugh's book on Arab mass media (1979) is the only systematic study of the topic. Butterfield's study of China (1982) and Chi's thesis (1983) provided background on that country. Lent's 1971 survey of Asian mass media is still useful. Alisky (1981) provided the typology of Latin American mass media; Gardner's thesis (1984) includes background on Mexico and Venezuela.

Frey's reanalysis of the data on the effects of mass communication is included in Pool et al. (1973). See also Cruise O'Brien et al. (1979), McAnany (1980), McMartin (1974), Winham (1970), and McCrone and Cnudde (1967). Problems of sorting out cause and effect in nonexperimental research are in Babbie (1979) and Heise (1975).

Hedebro's useful presentation of the alternative development position is his 1982 book. The defense of television is in Mattelart and Mattelart (1982), who have written extensively supporting Marxist communication theories.

Detailed analysis of the data in this chapter is in Stevenson (1983b and 1985c) and especially in Ghorpade et al. (1984) and Ghorpade (1986). Pool's study of telecommunication development in Egypt is in Singh (1983). The World Bank's interest in telecommunication is represented by a study by employees (Saunders et al. 1983); the International Telecommunication Union study is Pierce and Jequier (1983). A summary of Third World policies in telecommunications is Stevenson in Cawkell (1986).

CHAPTER SEVEN: THE GLOBAL NEWS NETWORK

The quote by Kent Cooper, on page 12 of his 1942 book, is referred to in pieces by Schiller and Mankekar in Richstad and Anderson (1981), Boyd-Barrett (1980), and Mayobre in Atwood et al. (1982).

The Masmoudi statement was submitted to the MacBride Commission as Document No. 31. An abridged version is in *Journal of Communication* 29(2): 172–185 (1979) and is reprinted in Gerbner and Siefert (1984). Another abridgment is in Richstad and Anderson (1981).

Information on the major Western news agencies comes from Boyd-Barrett (1980); Richstad and Anderson (1981); the three monographs prepared for the MacBride Commission, Documents 13–15; and Fenby (1986).

The IAMCR study of foreign news, finally published in 1985, is Sreberny-Mohammadi et al. (1985). A summary of the results is "The 'World of the News' Study" in *Journal of Communication* 34(1): 120–142 (1984). It includes a summary of the results and two opposing interpretations by Stevenson and Nordenstreng, from which the quotes are taken. Most of the results are presented and analyzed in Stevenson and Shaw (1984), which also includes data from recent comparable studies, and in Stevenson (1985b).

The discussion of the global news system is from Boyd-Barrett (1980), Richstad and Anderson (1981), the MacBride Commission monographs on the news agencies, Document No. 11 "The World of News Agencies," and Fenby (1986). Data on the second-tier Western agencies are from these sources and from information provided by the agencies. Regional exchanges are described in Cuthbert (1981a, 1981b) — Caribbean; Ansah (1984) — Africa; Harris et al. (N.D.) — Middle East; English (1982) — Asia; Mateu (1985) — Latin America.

The Non-Aligned News Agencies pool is described in documents collected for the organization's second meeting in Belgrade ("Non-aligned on Information — Documents 1979"), Ivacic (1977, 1978), Mathur and Shrivastava (1984), Pinch (1977), and Yadava (1984). The last three include evaluations of content and use. Inter Press Service is described in Hamelink (1983), Savio (1981), Giffard (1983, 1984b), Kirat and Weaver (1985), Heyn and Uekermann (1984), and Hall (1982).

Listings of national agencies come from *World Communications* (1975), monographs submitted to the MacBride Commission, the studies of regional exchanges cited above, Harris (1977), and personal visits to NAN, AZaP, and Tanjug in 1982. The count by Sussman is in his 1982 lecture. The comment from the director of ANSA is from Righter (1978, 51). Data on its operations are from the MacBride Commission monograph. The exchange system and operation of the Ghana News Agency are in Harris (1977) and the GNA section of the MacBride Commission monograph; observations on NAN's operation are based on documents cited above and the personal visit.

CHAPTER EIGHT: NEWS FOR DEVELOPMENT

The three generations of rights are noted in the MacBride Commission's report (International Commission for the Study of Communication

Problems 1980, 187). The final declaration on mass media has been published in various formats. It is printed in *Journal of Communication* 29(2): 190–191 (1979) and Richstad and Anderson (1981).

Development news is discussed by Tartarian, Sussman and Aggarwala in Horton (1978), Aggarwala (1979), Aggarwala in Lent (1979), Atwood et al. (1982), and Martin and Chaudhary (1983). Righter's interpretation is from her 1978 book, page 189. Harris's use of "protocolarian news" is in Richstad and Anderson (1981). Studies of development and protocol news are in Ogan (1982), Ogan and Flair (1984), Chi (1983), Stevenson and Marjanovic (1984), and Stevenson (1985b).

Harris's description of editing at the Ghana News Agency is in his 1977 study, pages 236–237. The updated references from the IAMCR study are noted in Stevenson and Shaw (1984) and Cooper (1981b), and are included in the Stevenson and Shaw volume.

Samples of the news copy were obtained from the sources indicated as teleprinter rolls. Analysis of this information is included in Chi (1983), Stevenson and Marjanovic (1984), and Stevenson (1985), all of which contain quantitative assessments.

The Tunstall assessment is from Atwood et al. (1982, 133–145).

CHAPTER NINE: REASSESSING COMMUNICATION DEVELOPMENT

The report of the May 1984 meeting is taken from the newsletter of the World Press Freedom Committee. The study of the Non-Aligned News Agencies pool in India is in Mathur and Shrivastava (1984). A similar assessment is in Yadava (1984).

The study for the U.S. federal government is "Communications Development" (1984) by the Academy for Educational Development. The recommendations to the National Security Council are documented in U.S. Development Communication Assistance Programs" (1985). The comment in the *Chronicle of International Communication* is in U.S. Development Communications, Assistance Programs (1984). The private media programs are listed in Stevenson (1985a).

The World Bank study is Saunders et al. (1983). The OECD/ITU is Pierce and Jequier (1983). The Maitland Commission report is "The Missing Link; Report of the Independent Commission for World Wide Telecommunications Development" (1984).

Critical assessments of recent change are Mosher (1983) on China, Sowell (1983b) on Tanzania, and Johnson (1983) on the Third World in general. The argument of Western guilt as a scapegoat for Third World failure is the basis of Bruckner (1986).

Bibliography

Abel, Elie. 1978. "Communication for an Interdependent, Pluralistic World." Paris: Unesco. Document No. 33 submitted to the MacBride Commission.

Academy for Educational Development. 1984. *Communications Development.* Washington DC.

Adams, William C. 1982. *Television Coverage of International Affairs.* Norwood, NJ: Ablex.

Adhikarya, Ronny. 1981. *Transnational Knowledge Transfer and Utilization Process in Communication Studies*: The U.S. ASEAN Case. Paris: Unesco.

Agee, Warren K. 1979. *Drying Streams of International News: Journalism Organizations Respond to Threats to World Press Freedom.* Paper presented to the Association for Education in Journalism and Mass Communication, meeting in Houston, TX.

Aggarwala, Narinder K. 1979. What is Development News? *Journal of Communications* 29(2): 180–181.

Alajmo, Alberto Carrizosa, et al. 1977. *Communication Policies in Colombia.* Paris: Unesco.

Alexander, George. 1982. "Communication Satellites Meet High Expectations." *Los Angeles Times,* Nov. 8.

Alisky, Marvin. 1981. *Latin American Media: Guidance and Censorship.* Ames, IA: Iowa State University Press.

Altschull, J. Herbert. 1984. *Agents of Power: The Role of News Media in Human Affairs.* New York: Longman.

American Coverage of Foreign News. 1981. *Nieman Reports,* 30(3): 51–63.

American Telephone & Telegraph Co. *World's Telephones, The.* Annual. New York.

Anim, Goodwin T., and Slavoj Haskovec. 1978. "Development of the Tanzanian

News Agency (SHIHATA)." Paris: Unesco document FMR/CC/DCS/78/171 microfiche 79fr0114

Ansah, Paul. 1984. "The Pan-African News Agency (PANA) — A Preliminary Profile." Paper presented to the International Association for Mass Communication Research, meeting in Prague.

Ansah, Paul, et al. 1981. "Rural Journalism in Africa." Reports and Papers on Mass Communication, No. 88, Paris: Unesco.

Arnove, Robert F. 1975. Sociopolitcal Implications of Educational Television. *Journal of Communication* 25(2): 144–156.

Aspen Institute Program on Communications and Society. 1974. *Control of the Direct Broadcast Satellite: Values in Conflict*. Palo Alto: The Aspen Institute for Humanistic Studies.

Atwood, L. Erwin, and Nien Sheng Lin. 1980. "News for Reference: News of the Outside World in China." Paper presented to the Association for Education in Journalism and Mass Communication, meeting in Boston.

Atwood, L. Erwin, and Sharon M. Murphy, 1982. "The New World Information Order Debate: Assessments and Recommendations." Paper presented to the International Communication Association, meeting in Boston.

Atwood, L. Erwin, et al. 1982. *International Perspectives on News*. Carbondale, IL: Southern Illinois University Press.

Atwood, Rita, and Sergia Mattos. 1982. Mass Media Reform and Social Change: The Peruvian Experience. *Journal of Communication* 32(2): 33–45.

Babbie, Earl R. 1979. *The Practice of Social Research*. Belmont, CA: Wadsworth.

Babbili, Anantha Sudhaker. 1982. "Search for Order in International Telecommunications: Theoretical Exploration for Policy-Making." Paper presented to the Association for Education in Journalism and Mass Communication, meeting in Athens, OH

Bae-ho, Hahn. 1978. *Communication Policies in the Republic of Korea*. Paris: Unesco.

Barton, Frank. 1979. *The Press of Africa: Persecution and Perseverance*. London: Macmillian Press.

Becker, Lee, et al. 1981. Western Wire Services and News of the USA in the Yugoslav Press. *Gazette* 28: 105–115.

Beltran, Luis Ramiro. 1975. Research Ideologies in Conflict. *Journal of Communication* 25(2): 187–193.

Bernd, Joseph. 1966. *Mathematical Applications in Political Science*. Dallas: Southern Methodist University Press.

Bethell, Tom. 1983. The Lost Civilization of Unesco. *Policy Review* 24(1): 19–48.

Bishop, Robert L. 1985. Regional Media Export Centers: The Case of Hong Kong. *Gazette* 35(1): 61–70.

Blanchard, Margaret. 1983. The Crusade for Worldwide Freedom of Information: American Attempts to Shape World War II Peace Treaties. *Journalism Quarterly* 60(4): 583–588.

Block, Clifford H. 1982. Promising Step at Acapulco: A U.S. View. *Journal of Communication* 32(3): 60–70.

Boyd, Douglas A. 1980. "International Broadcasting in Arabic to the Middle East." Paper presented to the Association for Education in Journalism and Mass Communication, meeting in Boston.

Boyd-Barrett, Oliver, 1980. *The International News Agencies*. Beverly Hills: Sage Publications.

British Broadcasting Corporation. Various dates. "World Radio and Television Receivers." London: BBC International Broadcasting and Audience Research.

Bruckner, Pascal. 1986. *The Tears of the White Man; Compassion as Contempt*. New York: Free Press.

Bullen, Dana. 1980. *Unesco & The Media: A Report on the Developments at Belgrade*. Medford, MA: Tufts University.

Burke, Thomas J. M., and Maxwell Lehman. 1981. *Communication Technologies and Information Flow*. New York: Pergamon.

Bushkin, Arthur A., and Jane H. Yurow. 1980. "The Foundations of United States Information Policy." Paper presented to the Organization for Economic Co-operation and Development, meeting in Paris.

Butterfield, Fox. 1982. *China: Alive in the Bitter Sea*. New York: Bantam Books.

Camargo, Nelly de. 1982. "Reading and Technological Development: A New Kind of Illiteracy." Paper presented to the International Association for Mass Communication Research, meeting in Paris.

Cardona, Elizabeth de. 1975. Multinational Television. *Journal of Communication* 25(2): 122–127.

Caron, Andre H., et al. 1982. "An International Comparison of Television Programming and Audiences." Paper presented to the International Communication Association, meeting in Boston.

Cassirer, Henry R. 1977. Radio as the People's Medium. *Journal of Communication* 27(2): 154–157.

Cassirer, Henry R. 1978. "Rural Development and the Flow of Communication." Paris: Unesco. Document No. 49 submitted to the MacBride Commission.

Cawkell, A. E. [Ed.] 1986. *Handbook of Information Technology and Office Systems*. Amsterdam: North-Holland.

Ceulemans, Mieke, and Guido Fauconnier. 1979. *Mass Media: the Image, Role, and Social Conditions of Women*. Paris: Unesco.

Chander, Romesh, and Kiran Karnik. 1976. *Planning for Satellite Broadcasting: The Indian Instructional Television Experiment*. Paris: Unesco.

Cherry, Colin. 1971. *World Communication: Threat or Promise? A Socio-technical Approach*. London: John Wiley & Sons.

Chi, Jo-Lan. 1983. "Two Faces of China: A Content Analysis of Chinese Internal and External News Media." Chapel Hill: Unpublished master's thesis, School of Journalism, University of North Carolina.

Cholomondeley, Hugh N. J. 1977. CANA: An Independent News Agency Launched by the English-Speaking Carribbean Countries. *Unesco Courier.* April: 10–11.

Chu, Godwin, C., and Alfian Chu. 1980. Programming for Development in Indonesia. *Journal of Communication* 30(4): 50–54.

Clifford, Reginald A. 1983. "Television and the Education of the Periphery Nations." Paper presented to the International Communication Association, meeting in Dallas TX.

Cline, Carolyn Garrett. 1982. "The Myth of the Monolithic Media: Variations in World Coverage by U.S. Media in 1977." Paper presented to the International Communication Association, meeting in Boston.

Clippinger, John H. 1979. The Hidden Agenda. *Journal of Communication* 29(1): 197–203.

Cocca, Aldo Armando, and Jim Richstad. 1978. "The Right to Communicate." Paris: Unesco. Document No. 38 submitted to the MacBride Commission.

"Comparative Account of National Structures for Policy and Decision-Making in the Communications Field." 1978. Paris: Unesco. Document No. 28 submitted to the MacBride Commission.

Consultation on Ways to Promote the Inclusion of the Principles of the Declaration on the Mass Media. 1979. Paris: Unesco.

Contreras, Eduardo, et al. 1976. *Cross-cultural Broadcasting.* Paris: Unesco.

Cooper, Anne M. 1981a. "Friend or Foe? Egypt and Israel in the Arab Press." Paper presented to the Association for Education in Journalism and Mass Communication, meeting in East Lansing, MI.

Cooper, Anne Messerly. 1981b. "Affect of Arab News: Post-Treaty Portrayal of Egypt and Israel in the Mass Media of Three Arab Countries." Paper presented to the Association for Education in Journalism and Mass Communication, meeting in East Lansing MI.

Cooper, Kent. 1942. *Barriers Down.* New York: Farrar & Rinehart.

Costa, Alcino Louis de, et al. 1980. *News Values and Principles of Cross-cultural Communication.* Paris: Unesco.

Cowlan, Bert and Lee M. Love. 1978. *A Look at the World's Radio News.* Medford, MA: Tufts University.

Cruise O'Brien, Rita. 1977. Professionalism in Broadcasting in Developing Countries. *Journal of Communication* 27(2): 150–153.

Cruise O'Brien, Rita, et al. 1979. "Communication Indicators and Indicators of Socio-Economic Development Summary of a Study." Vol. 3, Communication and Society. Paris: Unesco.

Cuthbert, Marlene. 1980. "The Caribbean's Successful Model for a Third World News Agency." Paper presented to the Association for Education in Journalism and Mass Communication, meeting in Boston.

Cuthbert, Marlene. 1981a. The First Five Years of the Caribbean News Agency. *Gazette* 28(1): 3–15.

Cuthbert, Marlene. 1981b. "The Caribbean News Agency: Third World Model." Journalism Monographs No. 71. Columbia SC: Association for Education in Journalism and Mass Communication.

Dajani, Nabil, and John Donohue. 1973. A Content Analysis of Six Arab Dailies. *Gazette* 19: 155–170.

Dajani, Nabil H. 1975. Press for Rent. *Journal of Communication* 25(2): 165–170.

Declaration of Fundamental Principles Concerning the Contribution of the Mass Media to Strengthening Peace and International Understanding, the Promotion of Human Rights and to Countering Racialism, Apartheid and Incitement to War, The. 1979. *Journal of Communication* 29(2): 190–191.

d'Arcy, Jean. 1978. "The Right to Communicate." Paris: Unesco. Document No. 36 submitted to the MacBride Commission.

DeMott, John. 1983. "Mass Media Model for Non-Aligned Nations Movement Communication: Egypt's Middle East News Agency." Paper presented to a Northwestern University conference on communication and development, meeting in Chicago.

DeVoss, David. 1978. Southeast Asia's Intimidated Press. *Columbia Journalism Review*, March/April: 37–42.

Deskins, Lucinda E. 1982. "Unesco's Proposal to License Journalists: Protection vs. Control." Paper presented to the Association for Education in Journalism and Mass Communication, meeting in Athens, OH.

Diaz Bordenave, Juan E. 1977. *Communication and Rural Development*. Paris: Unesco.

Dikshit, Kiranmani A., et al. 1979. *Rural Radio: Programme Formats*. Paris: Unesco.

Dissanayake, Wimal. 1977. New Wine In Old Bottles: Can Folk Media Convey Modern Messages? *Journal of Communication* 27(2): 122–124.

Dizard, Wilson P. 1980. The U.S. Position: DBS and Free Flow. *Journal of Communication* 30(2): 157–168.

Dizard, Wilson P. 1982. *The Coming Information Age*. New York: Longman.

Ebo, Bosah, 1983. "Africa and the West in the New World Information Order." Paper presented to a Northwestern University conference on communication and development, meeting in Chicago.

Edelstein, Alex S. 1982. *Comparative Communication Research*. Beverly Hills: Sage Publications.

Eger, John M. 1979a. U.S. Proposal for Progress Through Negotiations. *Journal of Communication* 29(3): 124–128.

Eger, John M. 1979b. A Time of Decision. *Journal of Communication* 29(1): 204–208.

Elkamel, Farag. 1983. "The Obstinate Communicator: How Development Communication May Create and Increase Knowledge and Practice Gaps." Paper presented to a Northwestern University conference on communication and development, meeting in Chicago.

El-Oteifi, Gamal. 1978a. "Relation Between the Right to Communicate and Planning of Communication." Paris: Unesco. Document No. 35bis submitted to the MacBride Commission.

El-Oteifi, Gamal. 1978b. "Call for a New International Information Order: Preliminary Remarks." Paris: Unesco. Document No. 33bis submitted to the MacBride Commission.

English, John W. 1982. Asian News. *Gazette* 30(3): 177–187.

Fascell, Dante B. 1979. *International News: Freedom Under Attack*. Beverly Hills: Sage.

Fejes, Fred. 1980. "The 'Theory' of Media Imperialism: Some Comments." Paper presented to the Association for Education in Journalism and Mass Communication, meeting in Boston.

Fenby, Jonathan. 1982. *The State of Unesco: Background to the Information Debate*. Medford, MA: Tufts University.

Fenby, Jonathan. 1986. *The International News Services*. New York: Schocken Books.

Ferment in the Field. 1983. *Journal of Communication* 33(3). [Special Issue].

Fisher, Glen. 1979. *American Communication in a Global Society*. Norwood, NJ: Ablex.

Fjaestad, Bjorn, and P. G. Holmlov. 1976. The Journalists' View. *Journal of Communication* 26(4): 108–114.

Freese, Jan. 1979. The Dangers of Non-Regulation. *Journal of Communication* 29(3): 135–137.

Frost, J. M. 1982. *World Radio and TV Handbook*. London: Billboard, Ltd.

"Function and Organization of Print Media for Rural Development." 1981. Proceedings of a Rural Press Development Seminar sponsored by the International Federation of Newspaper Publishers. The Hague: Graphic Media Development Center.

Gajaral, Ragini. 1983. "Canadian and American Assistance for Telecommunications Development: The Case of India." Paper presented to a Northwestern University conference on communication and development, meeting in Chicago.

Galtung, Johan. 1971. A Structural Theory of Imperialism. *Journal of Peace Research* 82(2): 81–117.

Gandy, Oscar, Jr., et al. 1983. Proceedings from the Tenth Annual Telecommunications Policy Research Conference. Norwood, NJ: Ablex.

Gardner, P. Dale, Jr. 1983. "Communications in Mexico and Venezuela: The Failure of Plans Developed Through 1983." Chapel Hill: Unpublished master's thesis, School of Journalism, University of North Carolina.

Gardner, P. Dale, Jr. 1984. *Communications in Mexico and Venezuela: the Failures of Plans Developed Through 1983*. Unpublished M. A. thesis, University of North Carolina at Chapel Hill.

Gardner, P. Dale, Jr., and Robert L. Stevenson. 1988. *Communication Development in Mexico and Venezuela: Goals, Promises and Reality*. Journalism Monographs. Columbia, SC: Association for Education in Journalism and Mass Communication.

Gastil, Raymond D. 1982. *Freedom in the World: Political Rights and Civil Liberties 1982*. Westport CT: Greenwood Press.

Gauhar, Altaf. 1979. The Flow of Information: Myths and Shibboleths. *Third World Quarterly* 1(3): 53–77.

General Conference, Fourth Extraordinary Session. 1982. "Draft, Medium-Term Plan (1984–1989) Second Part." Paris: Unesco.

Gerbner, George, and Marsha Siefert, eds. 1984. *World Communications: A Handbook*. New York: Longman.

Ghorpade, Shailendra, et al. 1984. "A Re-Evaluation of the Dominant Paradigm of Communication and Development." Paper presented to the Association for Education in Journalism and Mass Communication, meeting in Gainesville, FL.

Ghorpade, Shailendra. 1986. "The Information Environment as a Catalyst for Social Change and Economic Growth: an Exploration of an Empirical Model." Unpublished Ph.D. dissertation, University of North Carolina at Chapel Hill.

Giffard, C. Anthony. 1983. "Inter Press Service: News from the Third World." Report prepared for the International Association for Mass Communication Research. Seattle: School of Communications, University of Washington.

Giffard, C. Anthony. 1984a. Developed and Developing Nations News in U.S. Wire Service Files to Asia. *Journalism Quarterly* 6(1): 14–19.

Giffard, C. Anthony. 1984b. Inter Press Service: News from the Third World. *Journal of Communication* 34(4): 41–59.

Giles, Frank. 1978. "Obstructions to the Free Flow of Information." Paris: Unesco. Document No. 52 submitted to the MacBride Commission.

Glattbach, Jack. 1982. *Media and the Developing World: Pluralism or Polarization*. Mount Kisco, NY: Seven Springs Center.

Golding, Peter and Philip Elliott. 1979. *Making the News*. New York: Longman.

Gordon, J. C. 1974. *Establishment of a National News Agency*. Paris: Unesco.

Green, Bill. 1980. "Media and the Third World." *The Washington Post*, Nov. 21.

Guback, Thomas H. 1974. Film as International Business. *Journal of Communication* 24(1): 90–101.

Gunaratne, Shelton A. 1978. The Background to the Non-aligned News Pool: Pros and Cons and Research Findings. *Gazette* 24(1): 20–35.

Gunter, Jonathan F. 1978. An Introduction to the Great Debate. *Journal of Communication* 28(4): 142–156.

Gunter, Jonathan F. 1979. *The United States and the Debate on the New World "Information Order."* Washington: Academy for Educational Development.

Hachten, William A. 1971. *Mass Communication in Africa: An Annotated Bibliography*. Madison, WI: Center for International Communication Studies, The University of Wisconsin.

Hachten, William A. 1981. *The World News Prism: Changing Media, Clashing Ideologies*. Ames, IA: The Iowa State University Press.

Hachten, William, and Anthony Johnson. 1982. "Rhodesia to Zimbabwe: Media Policy Shifts." Paper presented to the Association for Education in Journalism and Mass Communication, meeting in Athens, OH.

Hall, Payson. 1982. "National Images: A Conceptual Assessment." Paper presented to the International Communication Association, meeting in Boston.

Hall, Peter. 1982. What's All the Fuss About Inter Press? *Columbia Journalism Review* 21: 53–57 (Jan.–Feb.)

Halloran, James D. 1978. "The Context of Mass Communication Research." Paris: Unesco. Document No. 78 submitted to the MacBride Commission.

Hamelink, Cees. 1976. An Alternative to News. *Journal of Communication* 26(4): 120–123.

Hamelink, Cees. 1977. *The Corporate Village*. Rome: IDOC International.

Hamelink, Cees. 1978. "The New International Economic Order and the New International Information Order." Paris: Unesco. Document No. 34 submitted to the MacBride Commission.

Hamelink, Cees. 1979. Informatics: Third World Call for New Order. *Journal of Communication* 29(3): 144–148.

Hamelink, Cees. 1980. *Communication in the Eighties: A Reader on the "McBride (SIC) Report"*. Rome: IDOC International.

Hamelink, Cees. 1983. *Cultural Autonomy in Global Communications*. New York: Longman.

Hamilton, John M. 1986. *Main Street America and the Third World*. Cabin John, MD: Seven Locks Press.

Hamrell, Sven, and Olle Nordberg. 1981. *Development Dialogue*. Uppsala: Dag Hammarskjold Foundation.

Hancock, Alan. 1981. *Communication Planning for Development; an Operational Framework*. Paris: Unesco.

Hansen, Roger D., et al. 1982. *U.S. Foreign Policy and the Third World*. New York: Praeger.

Hanson, Jarice. 1983. "International Cooperation and Conflict in the Use of Satellites for Development." Paper presented to a Northwestern University conference on communication and development, meeting in Chicago.

Haque, S. M. Mazharul. 1983. Is U.S. Coverage of News In the Third World Unbalanced? *Journalism Quarterly* 60(3): 521–524

Harms, L. S., and Desmond Fisher. 1978. "The Right to Communicate." Paris: Unesco. Document No. 37 submitted to the MacBride Commission.

Harris, Phil. 1977. "News Dependence: The Case for a New World Information Order." Leicester: Center for Mass Communication Research (mimeo).

Harris, Phil, et al. No Date. "Flow of News in the Gulf." New Communication Order No. 3. Paris: Unesco.

Hasan, Abul. 1978. *The Book of Multilingual Countries*. Paris: Unesco.

Hedebro, Goran. 1982. *Communication and Social Change in Developing Nations*: A Critical View. Ames, IA: Iowa University Press.

Heintz, Alden. 1979. The Dangers of Regulation. *Journal of Communication* 29(5): 129–134.

Heise, David R. 1975. *Causal Analysis*. New York: Wiley.

Hemanus, Pertti. 1976. Objectivity in News Transmission. *Journal of Communication* 26(4): 102–107.

Hester, Albert. 1974. The News From Latin America Via a World News Agency. *Gazette* 20(2): 82–98.

Hester, Albert L. and Richard R. Cole. 1975. *Mass Communication in Mexico*. N.P., Association for Education in Journalism.

Heyn, Juergen, and Heinz R. Uekermann. 1984. "News Reporting from a South-North Perspective — Inter Press Service as an Alternative to the Third World News Reporting of the Associated Press." Paper presented to the International Association for Mass Communication Research, meeting in Prague.

Hirshberg, Peter. 1980. The War Over Information. *Washington Journalism Review* 2(2): 24–29.

Historical Background of the Mass Media Declaration. N.D. [New Communication Order No. 9]. Paris: Unesco.

Homet, Jr., Roland S. 1979. Communications Policy Making in Western Europe. *Journal of Communication* 29(2): 31–38.

Honig, David E. 1980. Lessons for the 1999 WARC. *Journal of Communication* 30(2): 48–58.

Hopple, Gerald W. 1982. International News Coverage in Two Elite Newspapers. *Journal of Communication* 32(1): 61–74.

Horton, Philip C. 1978. *The Third World and Press Freedom*. New York: Praeger.

Howkins, John. 1979. What is the World Administrative Radio Conference? *Journal of Communication* 29(1): 144–149.

Hudson, Heather E. 1984. *When Telephones Reach the Village: The Role of Telecommunications In Rural Development*. Norwood NJ: Ablex Publishing.

Hurley, Neil P. 1975. University Satellite for Latin America. *Journal of Communication* 25(2): 157–164.

Intergovernmental Conference for Co-operation on Activities, Needs and Programmes for Communication Development. 1980a. Basic Statistics. Paris: Unesco.

Intergovernmental Conference for Co-operation on Activities, Needs and Programmes for Communication Development. 1980b. Final Report. Paris: Unesco.

Intergovernmental Conference on Communication Policies in Africa. 1980. Final Report. Paris: Unesco.

Intergovernmental Council of the International Programme for the Development of Communication. 1981. Final Report. Paris: Unesco.

Intergovernmental Council of the International Programme for the Development of Communication. 1982. Final Report. Paris: Unesco.

International Commission for the Study of Communication Problems. 1980. *Many Voices, One World*. Paris: Unesco. [MacBride Commission Report]

Ivacic, Pero. 1977. The Non-Aligned Countries Pool Their News. *Unesco Courier*, pp. 18–20 (April).

Ivacic, Pero. 1978. The Flow of News: Tanjug, the Pool and the National Agencies. *Journal of Communication* 28(4): 157–162.

Jackson, Gordon. 1981. "TV2 — The Introduction of Television for Blacks in South Africa." Paper presented to the Association for Education in Journalism and Mass Communication, meeting in East Lansing, MI.

Jacobson. Robert E. 1979. The Hidden Issues: What Kind of Order? *Journal of Communication* 29(3): 149–155.

Jacobson, Thomas L. 1980. "Responses to the New International Information Order:

The United States." Paper presented to the Association for Education in Journalism and Mass Communication, meeting in Boston.

Jadava, Jaswant S. [Ed.]. 1984. *The Politics of News*. New Delhi: Concept Publishing Co.

Johnson, J. David. 1982. "A Test of a Model of Media Exposure and Appraisal of Two Magazines in Nigeria." Paper presented to the International Communication Association, meeting in Boston.

Johnson, Lynda D. 1981. "Magazine Use of Middle-Class English-Speaking Indians in New Dehli, India." Paper presented to the Association for Education in Journalism and Mass Communication, meeting in East Lansing, MI.

Johnson, Paul. 1983. *Modern Times: The World from the Twenties to the Eighties*. New York: Harper and Row.

Jones, J. Clement. 1980. *Mass Media Codes of Ethics and Councils*. Paris: Unesco.

Kato, Hidetoshi. 1978. *Communication Policies in Japan*. Paris: Unesco.

Katz, Elihu. 1977. Can Authentic Cultures Survive New Media? *Journal of Communication* 27(2): 113–121.

Katz, Elihu, and George Wedell. 1977. *Broadcasting in the Third World: Promise and Performance*. Cambridge, MA: Harvard University Press.

Keune, Reinhard. 1981a. *Television News in a North-South Perspective*. Bonn: Friedrich-Ebert-Stiftung.

Keune, Reinhard. 1981b. *Viertel Jahres Berichte: Probleme der Entwicklungslander*. Bonn: Friedrich-Ebert-Stiftung.

Kidron, Michael, and Ronald Segal. 1981. *The State of the World Atlas*. New York: Simon and Schuster.

Kirat, Mohamed, and David Weaver. 1985. Foreign News Coverage in Three Wire Services: A Study of AP, UPI and the Non-Aligned News Agencies Pool. *Gazette* 35(1): 31–40.

Kitanti, Kenji. 1982. "Assessment of the New World Information Order: A Content Analysis of International Affairs Coverage by the British and Japanese TV Networks." Paper presented to the Association for Education in Journalism and Mass Communication, meeting in Athens, OH.

Kivikuru, Ullamija. 1984. Beautiful Theories and Confusing Practice — Reflections on Grassroot Level Dependency in Tanzania. *The Nordicom Review* (1): 2–5.

Komatsuzaki, S., and Yash Pal. 1978. "Communications Technologies of the 1980s (III)." Paris: Unesco. Document No. 83 submitted to the MacBride Commission.

Korobejnikov, Valerij S. 1978. "Contribution of Scientific and Technological Programs to the Development of Communication." Document No. 85 submitted to the MacBride Commission.

Krauthammer, Charles. 1981. Brave News World. *The New Republic*, March 14: 21–23.

Krivosheev, M. I., and R. Z. Gazin. 1978. "Communications Technologies of the 1980s (II)." Paris: Unesco. Document No. 82 submitted to the MacBride Commission.

Kroloff, George M. 1979. The View From Congress. *Journal of Communication* 29(1): 165–169.

Lamb, David. 1982. *The Africans*. New York: Random House.

Larson, James F. 1979. International Affairs Coverage on U.S. Network Television. *Journal of Communication* 29(2): 136–147.

Larson, James F. 1984. *Television's Window on the World: International Affairs Coverage on the U.S. Networks*. Norwood NJ: Ablex.

Lawhorne, Clifton O. 1982. "The Egyptian Press: An Official Fourth Estate." Paper presented to the Association for Education in Journalism and Mass Communication, meeting in Athens, OH.

Le Duc, Don R. 1980. Transforming Principles into Policy. *Journal of Communication* 30(2): 196–203.

Le Duc, Don R. 1981. East-West News Flow "Imbalance": Qualifying the Quantifications. *Journal of Communication* 31(4): 135–141.

Lee, Chin-Chuan. 1980. *Media Imperialism Reconsidered*. Beverly Hills: Sage Publications.

Lee, Chin-Chuan. 1982. The International Information Order. *Communication Research* 9(4): 617–636.

Lee, William E. 1977. "The Shaping of An American Empire: Negotiating the Interim Intelsat Agreements." Paper presented to the Association for Education in Journalism and Mass Communication, meeting in Madison, WI.

Legum, Colin, and John Cornwell. 1978. *A Free and Balanced Flow*. Lexington, MA: Lexington Books.

Lent, John A., ed. 1971. *The Asian Newspapers' Reluctant Revolution*. Ames, IA: The Iowa State University Press.

Lent, John A. 1975. The Price of Modernity. *Journal of Communication* 25(2): 128–135.

Lent, John A. 1977. Foreign News in American Media. *Journal of Communication* 27(1): 46–51.

Lent, John A. 1979. "The Unesco Debate on the Role of Mass Media in the Third World: An Assessment of the Issues, Fora and Literature." Paper presented at the Conference on Culture and Media, meeting in Philadelphia.

Lent, John A. 1979. "Third World Media: Issues, Theory and Research." Publication No. 9, Studies in Third World Societies. Williamsburg, VA: College of William and Mary.

Lerner, Daniel. 1958. *The Passing of Traditional Society: Modernizing the Middle East*. Glencoe IL: Free Press. Paperback edition published in 1964.

Lerner, Daniel, and Wilbur Schramm. 1967. *Communication and Change in the Developing Countries*. Honolulu: University Press of Hawaii.

Lerner, Daniel. 1978. *Communication, Development and World Order*. Medford MA: Tufts University.

Link, Jere H. 1982. "A Test of the Cultural Dependency Theory in Seven Latin American Newspapers." Paper presented to the Association for Education in

Journalism and Mass Communication, meeting in Athens, OH.

Liu, Han C., and Shelton A. Gunaratne. 1972. Foreign News in Two Asian Dailies. *Gazette* 18(1): 37–41.

Lomax, Alex. 1977. Appeal for Cultural Equity. *Journal of Communication* 27(2): 125–138.

MacBride, Sean. 1978. "Shaping a New World Information Order." Paris: Unesco. Document No. 33ter submitted to the MacBride Commission.

Makagiansar, Makaminan. 1977. Unesco and World Problems of Communication. *Unesco Courier*, April: 4–10.

Martelanc, Tomo, et al. 1977. *External Radio Broadcasting and International Understanding*. Paris: Unesco.

Martin, L. John, and Anju Grover Chaudhary. 1983. *Comparative Mass Media Systems*. New York: Longman.

Martin, Thomas H. 1977. Balance: An Aspect of the Right to Communicate. *Journal of Communication* 27(2): 159–162.

Marvin, Carolyn. 1978. Computer Systems: Prospects for a Public Information Network. *Journal of Communication* 28(4): 172–183.

Masmoudi, Mustapha. 1978. "The New World Information Order." Document No. 31 submitted to the MacBride Commission.

Masmoudi, Mustapha. 1979. The New World Information Order. *Journal of Communication* 29(2): 172–185.

Massing, Michael. 1979. Inside the Wires' Banana Republics. *Columbia Journalism Review*, Nov./Dec.: 45–49.

Massing, Michael. 1984. UNESCO Under Fire. *The Atlantic Monthly* 254(1): 89–97 (July).

Mateu, Pablo E. 1985. "Latin America's New Media." Paper presented to the International Communication Association, meeting in Honolulu HI.

Mathur, Pradeep, and K. M. Shrivasatava. 1984. *Non-Aligned Movement: New Dehli and Beyond*. New Dehli: Sterling.

Matovu, Jacob. 1982. "Comparative Study of Radio and the Talking Drums of Uganda: In Search of New Communication Strategies." Paper presented to the International Communication Association, meeting in Boston.

Matta, Fernando Reyes. 1979. The Latin American Concept of News. *Journal of Communication* 29(2): 164–171.

Mattelart, Michele, and Armand Mattelart. 1982. "Small" Technologies: the Case of Mozambique. *Journal of Broadcasting* 32(2): 75–79.

McAnany, Emile G. 1978. Does Information Really World? *Journal of Communication* 28(1): 84–90.

McAnany, Emile G. 1980. *Communication in the Rural Third World: The Role of Information in Development*. New York: Praeger.

McAnany, Emile G., and Joao Batista A. Oliveira. 1980. *The SACI/EXERN Project in Brazil: An Analytical Case Study*. Paris: Unesco.

McCrone, Donald J., and Charles F. Cnudde. 1967. Toward a Communications

Theory of Democratic Political Development: a Causal Model. *American Political Science Review* 61: 72–79.

McMartin, Pamela A. 1974. A Cross-Lag Test of Lerner's Model of Modernization. *Journalism Quarterly* 51(1): 120–2.

McNelly, John T. 1979. International News for Latin America. *Journal of Communication* 29(2): 156–163.

McPhail, Thomas L. 1981. *Electronic Colonialism: The Future of International Broadcasting and Communication.* Beverly Hills: Sage Publications.

Media Crisis, The. No Date. Reston, VA: World Press Freedom Committee.

Media Crisis: A Continuing Challenge, The. No Date. Reston, VA: World Press Freedom Committee.

Mehra, Achal. 1983. "International Program for the Development of Communication: Death of a Meteor?" Paper presented to a Northwestern University conference on communication and development, meeting in Chicago.

Mehta, D. S. 1979. *Mass Communication and Journalism in India.* Beverly Hills: Sage Publications.

Melkote, Srinivas Rajagopal. 1982. "In Search of Alternative Communication Strategies for Rural Development in the Third World: A Critique of the Diffusion of Innovations Research." Paper presented to the Association for Education in Journalism and Mass Communication, meeting in Athens, OH.

Mellor, John W. 1976. *The New Economics of Growth.* Ithaca, NY: Cornell University Press.

Mendelsohn, Harold. 1979. Delusions of Technology. *Journal of Communication* 29(3): 141–143.

Merrill, John C. 1983. *Global Journalism: A Survey of the World's Mass Media.* New York: Longman.

Merrill, John C. and Whitney R. Mundt. 1981. "U.S. Daily Newspaper Coverage of Mexico." Paper presented to the International Association for Mass Communication Research, meeting in Paris.

Middleton, Karen P., and Meheroo Jussawalla. 1981. *The Economics of Communication.* New York: Pergamon Press.

"Missing Link, The." 1984. Report of the Independent Commission for World-Wide Telecommunications Development (The Maitland Commission). Geneva: International Telecommunications Union.

Miyo, Yuko and M. Mark Miller. 1982. "Government Control of the Press and Factors Influencing International News Flow." Paper presented to the International Communication Association, meeting in Boston.

Mody, Bella. 1983. "First World Technologies in Third World Contexts." Paper presented to a Northwestern University conference on communication and development, meeting in Chicago.

Monographs I. 1978. Paris: Unesco. Document No. 13 submitted to the MacBride Commission.

Monographs II. 1978. Paris: Unesco. Document No. 14 submitted to the MacBride Commission.

Monographs III. 1978. Paris: Unesco. Document No. 15 submitted to the MacBride Commission.

Mosco, Vincent. 1979. Who Makes U.S. Government Policy in World Communications? *Journal of Communication* 29(1): 158–164.

Mosher, Steven W. 1983. *Broken Earth: The Rural Chinese.* New York: Free Press.

Mowlana, Hamid. 1975. Who Covers America? *Journal of Communication* 25(3): 86–91.

Mowlana, Hamid. 1979. Technology versus Tradition: Communication in the Iranian Revolution. *Journal of Communication* 29(3): 107–113.

Mowlana, Hamid. 1983. "International Flow of Information in National and International Development: A Conceptual Model for Theory and Policy." Paper presented to a Northwestern University conference on communication and development, meeting in Chicago.

Mueller, M. L. 1982. *Warnings of a Western Waterloo.* Medford, MA: Tufts University.

Murthy, T. Rama, and Andrea Ngai. 1979. "Radio Peking: What it Says About the U.S. and the U.S.S.R." Paper presented to the Association for Education in Journalism and Mass Communication, meeting in Houston, TX.

Mytton, Graham. 1983. *Mass Communication in Africa.* London: Edward Arnold.

Nam, Sunwoo. 1978. The Taming of the Korean Press. *Columbia Journalism Review,* Mar./Apr.: 43–45.

Nasser, Munir K. 1981. "Mass Media in the Third World: Which Why to Go?" Paper presented to the World Media Conference.

"New Foreign Correspondence, The." 1980. *Washington Journalism Review* 2(2): 39–49.

Newspaper Enterprise Association, 1986. *World Almanac and Book of Facts 1985, The.* New York.

Nihon Shinbun Kyokai Research Institute. 1981. "Coverage of Foreign News by the Japanese Media: A Survey." Tokyo: The Nihon Shinbun Kyokai Research Institute.

Nonaligned on Information — Documents. 1979. Volumes prepared for the second conference of the Non-Aligned News Agencies Pool, Belgrade.

Nordenstreng, Kaarle. 1979. Behind the Semantics — A Strategic Design. *Journal of Communication* 29(2): 195–199.

Nordenstreng. Kaarle. 1982. U.S. Policy and the Third World: A Critique. *Journal of Communication* 32(3): 54–59.

Nordenstreng, Kaarle. 1984. *The Mass Media Declaration of Unesco.* Norwood NJ: Ablex.

Nordenstreng, Kaarle, and Markku Salomaa. 1978. "Studying the Image of Foreign Countries As Portrayed By the Mass Media: A Progress Report." Paper presented to the International Association for Mass Communication Research, meeting in Warsaw.

Nordenstreng, Kaarle, and Herbert Schiller. 1979. *National Sovereignty and Inter-*

national Communication. Norwood NJ: Ablex Publishing.

Nwosu, Ikechukwu E. 1979. "The Global News Flow Imbalance: A Comparative Study of the Reportage and Image of Black Africa in Four British and American Newspapers." Paper presented to the Association for Education in Journalism and Mass Communication, meeting in Houston, TX.

Ogan, Christine L. 1982. Development Journalism/Communication: The Status of the Concept. *Gazette* 29(1/2): 3–14.

Ogan, Christine L., and Jo Ellen Flair. 1984. "A Little Good News": The Treatment of Development in Selected Third World Newspapers. *Gazette* 33(3): 173–192.

Onu, P. Eze. 1981. The Use and Misuse of Scarce Newsprint: Mortuary Advertisements Compete for Space in African Newspapers. *Gazette* 27(1981): 105–121.

Organization for Economic Co-operation and Development. 1981. *Information Activities, Electronics and Telecommunications Technologies*, Volume 1. Paris: OECD.

Ortega, Carlos and Carlos Romero. 1977. *Communications Policies in Peru*. Paris: Unesco.

Palmer, Edward L., et al. 1976. Sesame Street: Patterns of International Adaptation. *Journal of Communication* 26(2): 109–123.

Parker, Edwin B. 1978. An Information-Based Hypothesis. *Journal of Communication* 28(1): 81–83.

Phillips, Joseph D. 1975. Film Conglomerate "Blockbusters." *Journal of Communication* 25(2): 171–182.

Pierce, William, and Nicolas Jequier. 1983. *Telecommunications and Development*. Geneva: International Telecommunications Union.

Pinch, Edward T. 1977. "The Third World and the Fourth Estate: A Look at the Non-Aligned News Agencies Pool." Paper prepared for the U.S. Department of State Senior Seminar in Foreign Policy.

Pinch, Edward T. 1978. *A Brief Study of News Patterns in Sixteen Third World Countries*. Medford, MA: Tufts University.

Pingree, Suzanne, and Robert Hawkins. 1981. U.S. Programs on Australian Television: The Cultivation Effeet. *Journal of Communication* 31(1): 97–105.

Pipe, G. Russell. 1979. National Policies, International Debates. *Journal of Communication* 29(3): 114–123.

Pollock, John Crothers. 1978. *An Anthropological Approach to Mass Communication Research: The U.S. Press and Political Change in Latin America*. New Brunswick, NJ: Rutgers University, Latin American Institute.

Pool, Ithiel de Sola, et al. 1973. *Handbook of Communication*. Chicago: Rand McNally.

Pool, Ithiel de Sola. 1977a. The Changing Flow of Television. *Journal of Communication* 27(2): 139–149.

Pool, Ithiel de Sola. 1977b. *The Social Impact of the Telephone*. Cambridge, MA: MIT Press.

Pool, Ithiel de Sola. 1978. "Technology and Change in Modern Communications."

Paris: Unesco. Document No. 84 submitted to the MacBride Commission.

Pool, Ithiel de Sola. 1979. The Problems of WARC. *Journal of Communication* 29(1): 187–196.

Pool, Ithiel de Sola. 1983. *Technologies of Freedom.* Cambridge, MA: The Belknap Press.

Pool, Ithiel de Sola, and Stephen Dizard. 1978. *International Telecommunications and the Requirements of News Services.* Medford, MA: Tufts University.

Pool, Ithiel de Sola, and Herbert I. Schiller. 1981. Perspectives on Communications Research: An Exchange. *Journal of Communication* 31(3): 15–23.

Porat, Marc Uri. 1978. Global Implications of the Information Society. *Journal of Communication* 28(1): 70–80.

Power, Philip H., and Elie Abel. 1980. "Third World vs. the Media." *New York Times Magazine.* Sept. 21.

Power, Sarah Goddard. 1981. The U.S. View of Belgrade. *Journal of Communication* 31(4): 142–149.

Pratt, C. B. 1980. The Reportage and Images of Africa in Six U.S. News and Opinion Magazines: A Comparative Study. *Gazette* 26(1): 31–45.

Rachty, Gehan. 1978. *Foreign News in Nine Arab Countries.* Medford, MA: Tufts University.

Raghawan, G. N. S., and V. S. Gopalakrishnan. 1978. "Toward a National Policy on Communication in Support of Development: The Indian Case." Paris: Unesco. Document No. 43 submitted to the MacBride Commission.

Ranganath, H. K. 1978. "Not a Thing of the Past: Functional and Cultural Status of Traditional Media in India." Paris: Unesco. Document No. 92 submitted to the MacBride Commission.

Rawley, Joseph P. 1980. "International Press Telecommunications Tariffs and Recent Unesco Recommendations." Report to the ANPA Telecommunications Committee.

Rawley, Joseph. 1982. "Communication Needs and Priorities in Developing Countries." Paper presented to the International Association for Mass Communication Research, meeting in Paris.

Read, William H. 1976. Global TV Flow: Another Look. *Journal of Communication* 26(3): 69–73.

Read, William H. 1979. Information as a National Resource. *Journal of Communication* 29(1): 172–178.

Reed, David L., and Carolyn Garrett Cline. 1981. "The Israeli Invasion of Southern Lebanon: An Expanded Directional Analysis of Middle East Crisis Coverage on ABC, CBS and NBC." Paper presented to the Association for Education in Journalism and Mass Communication, meeting in East Lansing, MI.

"Reporting of International News and Roles of the Gate-Keepers." 1979. Paris: Unesco.

"Communication in the Community: An International Study on the Role of the Mass Media in Seven Communities." 1982. Paris: Unesco.

Richstad, Jim, and Tony Nnaemeka. 1980. "Information Regions: Context for International News Flow Research." Paper presented to the Association for Education in Journalism and Mass Communication, meeting in East Lansing MI.

Richstad, Jim, and Michael H. Anderson. 1981. *Crisis in International News: Policies and Prospects.* New York: Columbia University Press.

Riffe, Daniel, 1982. "The Origins of Borrowed News." Paper presented to the Association for Education in Journalism and Mass Communication, meeting in Athens OH.

Riffe, Daniel. 1984. International News Borrowing: A Trend Analysis. *Journalism Quarterly* 61(1): 142–149.

Righter, Rosemary. 1978. *Whose News? Politics, the Press and the Third World.* New York: Times Books.

Righter, Rosemary. 1979. Who Won? *Journal of Communication* 29(2): 192–195.

Roach, Colleen. 1982. Mexican and U.S. News Coverage of the IDPC at Acapulco. *Journal of Communication* 32(3): 71–85.

Robinson, Glen O. 1979. The U.S. Position. *Journal of Communication* 29(1): 150–157.

Rogers, Everett M. 1969. *Modernization Among Peasants: The Impact of Communication.* New York: Holt, Rinehart and Winston.

Rogers, Everett M. 1976. *Communication and Development: Critical Perspectives.* Beverly Hills: Sage Publications.

Rogers, Everett M. 1978. The Rise and Fall of the Dominant Paradigm. *Journal of Communication* 28(1): 64–69.

Rogers, Everett M., and F. Floyd Shoemaker. 1971. *Communication of Innovations; a Cross-Cultural Approach* [2d Ed.]. New York: Free Press.

Rogers, Everett M., and Jorge R. Schement [Eds.]. 1984. Media Flows in Latin America. *Communication Research* 11(2). [Special issue].

Rosenblum, Mort. 1979. *Coups and Earthquakes.* New York: Harper and Row.

Rosengren, Karl Erik. 1977. Four Types of Tables. *Journal of Communication* 27(1): 67–75.

Rostow, Walt W. 1960. *The Stages of Economic Growth.* Cambridge, UK: Cambridge University Press.

Rugh, William A. 1979. *The Arab Press.* Syracuse, NY: Syracuse University Press.

Russett, Bruce M., et al. 1968. *World Handbook of Political and Social Indicators.* New Haven, CT: Yale University Press.

Rutkowski, A. M., et al. 1978. "Communications Technologies of the 1980s (I)." Paris: Unesco. Document No. 81 submitted to the MacBride Commission.

Sahin, Haluk, et al. 1981. "Television News as a Source of International Affairs Information: What Gets Across and What Doesn't." Paper presented to the Association for Education in Journalism and Mass Communication, meeting in East Lansing, MI.

Salvaggio, Jerry L. 1983. *Telecommunications: Issues and Choices for Society.* New York: Longman.

Saunders, Robert J., and C. R. Dickenson. 1979. Telecommunications: Priority Needs for Economic Development. *Telecommunications Journal* 46(2): 78.

Saunders, Robert J., et al. 1983. *Telecommunications and Economic Development.* Baltimore: Johns Hopkins University Press.

Saur, Ricardo A. C. 1979. Protection Without Protectionism. *Journal of Communication* 29(3): 138–140.

Savio, Roberto. 1981. Statement presented to the Subcommittee on Human Rights and International Organizations. Committee on Foreign Affairs, U.S. House of Representatives, July 16.

Schiller, Herbert I. 1971. *Mass Communications and American Empire.* Boston: Beacon Press.

Schiller, Herbert I. 1974. Freedom From the "Free Flow." *Journal of Communication* 24(1): 110–117.

Schiller, Herbert I. 1976. *Communication and Cultural Domination.* White Plains, NY: International Arts and Sciences Press.

Schiller, Herbert. 1981. *Who Knows: Information in the Age of the Fortune 500.* Norwood, NJ: Ablex.

Schiller, Herbert. 1982. Information: America's New Global Empire. *Channels* 2(3): 30–33 (Sept.–Oct.).

Schiller, Herbert. 1984. *Information and the Crisis Economy.* Norwood, NJ:Ablex.

Schmitt, Harrison. 1979. One Senator's View. *Journal of Communication* 29(1): 170–171.

Schramm, Wilbur. 1964. *Mass Media and National Development.* Stanford, CA: Stanford University Press.

Schramm, Wilbur. 1978. "Mass Media and National Development — 1978." Paris: Unesco. Document No. 42 submitted to the MacBride Commission.

Schramm, Wilbur, and Daniel Lerner. 1976. *Communication and Change; the Last Ten Years — and the Next.* Honolulu, HI: University Press of Hawaii.

Schramm, Wilbur, and Erwin Atwood. 1981. *Circulation of News in the Third World — A Study of Asia.* Hong Kong: The Chinese University of Hong Kong.

Schwartz, Louis B. 1976. The Cultural Deficit in Broadcasting. *Journal of Communication* 26(1): 58–66.

Sebaei, Osama A. 1980. "The Non-Aligned News Agency Pool." Freedom of Information Center Report No. 421, University of Missouri School of Journalism.

Second Conference of Broadcasting Organizations of the Non-Aligned Countries. 1980. Belgrade, Yugoslavia: Jugoslovenska Radiotelevizija.

Shaw, Donald L., and Robert L. Stevenson. 1981. "World of Conflict — World of Peace: Foreign Affairs News In Newspapers From Stable vs. Pluralistic Political Systems." Paper presented to the Association for Education in Journalism and mass Communication, meeting in Athens, OH.

Sinclair, John. 1982. "Television Advertising and Taste Transfer in Mexico." Paper presented to the International Association for Mass Communication Research, meeting in Paris.

Singh, Indu B. 1983. *Telecommunications in the Year 2000: National and International Perspectives.* Norwood, NJ: Ablex.

Sivard, Ruth Leger. 1982. *World Military and Social Expenditures 1982.* Leesburg, VA: World Priorities.

Skurnik, W. A. E. 1981. Foreign News Coverage in Six African Newspapers: The Potency of National Interests. *Gazette* 28: 117–130.

Smith, Anthony. 1980. *The Geopolitics of Information.* New York: Oxford University Press.

Smith, Datus C. 1977. *The Economics of Book Publishing in Developing Countries.* Paris: Unesco.

Snow, Marcellus S. 1980. Intelsat: An International Example. *Journal of Communication* 30(2): 147–156.

Solomon, Douglas, et al. 1979. *The Role of Communication in Health.* Stanford, CA: Institute for Communication Research, Stanford University.

Soloski, John. 1981. *Foundations for Communications Studies.* Iowa City, IA: Center for Communication Study, University of Iowa.

Sowell, Thomas, 1983a. *Economics and Politics of Race An International Perspective.* New York: William Morrow.

Sowell, Thomas. 1983b. Second Thoughts About the Third World. *Harper's Magazine* 267 (1602): 34–42 (November).

Spain, Peter L., et al. 1977. *Radio for Education and Development: Case Studies.* Washington: The World Bank.

Sreberny-Mohammadi, Annabelle, et al. 1980. "The World of the News: The News of the World." Final Report of the "Foreign Images" Study, International Association for Mass Communication Research. Leicester, England: Centre for Mass Communication Research, University of Leicester.

Stevenson, Robert L. 1983a. The MacBride Commission Report Reconsidered. *Political Communication and Persuasion* 2(2): 147–158.

Stevenson, Robert L. 1983b. "The Record of Communication Development in the 1970s." Paper presented to the conference on communication and development sponsored by Northwestern University.

Stevenson, Robert L. 1985a. "New Actors, New Institutions in World Communications." Paper presented to the International Communication Association, meeting in Honolulu, HI.

Stevenson, Robert L. 1985b. "New News for the New World Information Order." Paper presented to the International Communication Association, meeting in Honolulu, HI.

Stevenson, Robert L. 1985c. "Third World Development in the 1970s." Paper presented to the International Communication Association, meeting in Honolulu, HI.

Stevenson, Robert L., and Stevan Marjanovic. 1984. "A Look at Alternative News Sources." Paper presented to the International Association for Mass Communication Research, meeting in Prague.

Stevenson, Robert L., and Donald Lewis Shaw. 1984. *Foreign News and the New World Information Order.* Ames, IA: Iowa State University Press.

Story of NAN, The. No Date. Lagos: News Agency of Nigeria.

Stovall, James Glen. 1982. "Foreign Policy News in the 1980 Presidential Election Campaign." Paper presented to the International Communication Association, meeting in Boston.

"Strengthening the Press in the Third World." 1978. Paris: Unesco. Document No. 73 submitted to the MacBride Commission.

Strobl, Rudolf. 1980. "Recent European Critical Thought: Emergence of a Theory of Communication." Prepared for the Seminar on Communication Theory from Eastern and Western Perspectives in Honolulu, HI.

"Survey of International Structures for Policy and Decision-Making in the Communications Field." 1978. Paris: Unesco. Document No. 29 submitted to the MacBride Commission.

"Survey of National Legislation (1): Constitutional Provisions." 1978. Paris: Unesco. Document No. 23 submitted to the MacBride Commission.

"Survey of National Legislation (2): Media Enterprises." No Date. Paris: Unesco. Document No. 24 submitted to the MacBride Commission.

Sussman, Leonard. 1978. "An Approach To The Study of Transnational News Media In a Pluralistic World." Document No. 18. Submitted to the MacBride Commission. Paris: Unesco.

Sussman, Leonard R. 1980. "Press Control: Is There Middle Ground?" Paper presented to World Communications Conference II meeting in Athens, OH.

Sussman, Leonard. 1981. The Third World and the Fourth Estate. *Washington Journalism Review* 3(5): 36–39.

Sussman, Leonard. 1982. *The World Information "Order": A Status Report and How Fares World Press Freedom?* Baton Rouge, LA: Louisiana State University School of Journalism.

Symphonie Experiment Study Group. 1978. A Unesco Experiment. *Journal of Communication* 28(3): 149–156.

Tatarian, Roger. 1978. *The Multinational News Pool.* Medford, MA: Tufts University.

Tehranian, Majid. 1978. "Communication and International Development: Some Theoretical Considerations." Paris: Unesco. Document No. 41 submitted to the MacBride Commission.

Tehranian, Majid. 1983. "Communications and International Development: History, Theory, Policy." Paper presented to a Northwestern University conference on communication and development, meeting in Chicago.

"Telecommunication Tariffs for the Mass Media." No Date. Paris: Unesco. Documents on the News Communications Order No. 8.

Till, Don. 1983. "A Study on the Feasibility of the Installation and Organization of Satellite Earth Stations for Broadcasting Organizations, New Agencies." Paris: Unesco. Documents on the New Communication Order No. 10.

Towards a New World Information and Communication Order. 1981. *Development*

Dialogue, 1981: 2. Uppsala, Sweden: Dag Hammarskhold Foundation.

"Transnational Corporations and Data Flows: A Technical Paper." 1982. United Nations Centre on Transnational Corporations. New York: United Nations.

"Transnational Corporations In Advertising." 1979. Centre on Transnational Corporations. New York: United Nations.

Tuchman, Gaye. 1976. Telling Stories. *Journal of Communication* 26(4): 93–97.

Tunstall, Jeremy. 1977. *The Media Are American.* New York: Columbia University Press.

Uche, Luke Uka. 1982. "Communication Habits of the Urban and Rural Opinion Leaders in Nigeria During Major Crises." Paper presented to the International Communication Association, meeting in Boston.

Ugboajah, Frank Okwu. 1980. *Communication Policies in Nigeria.* Paris: Unesco.

Unesco's New World Information Order. 1982. *Political Communication and Persuasion* 1(4).

Unesco Statistical Yearbook 1982. 1982. Paris: Unesco.

Union of National Radio and Television Organizations of Africa. 1980. "Rural Radio in Anglophone Africa: The Objectives, Policies and Models of 13 Countries." URTNA Review Special Edition.

U.S. Development Communications Assistance Programs. 1984 Chronicle of International Communication, 5(9): 1–5.

U.S. Development Communications Assistance Programs. 1985. Final Report prepared for the National Security Council by the Senior Inter-Agency Group for International Communication and Information Policy.

Utomi, Patrick. 1981. Performance Under Constraints: The Nigerian Press Under Military Rule. *Gazette* 28(1981): 51–54.

Vaiddya, K. D. 1979. Development of Telecommunications. *Telecommunications Journal* 46(2): 78.

Valdez-A., M. Isabel. 1982. "Third World and the Conflicting Ideologies of the Information Age." Paper presented to the International Association for Mass Communication Research, meeting in Paris.

Varis, Tapio. 1974. Global Traffic in Television. *Journal of Communication* 24(1): 102–109.

Varis, Tapio. 1984. The International Flow of Television Programs. *Journal of Communication* 34(1): 143–152 (Winter).

Vittachi, Tarzie, 1979. Why News Values Must Change. *Journalism Studies Review.* July: 15–20.

Voices of Freedom: A World Conference of Independent News Media. 1981. Medford MA: Tufts University.

Weaver, David H., and G. Cleveland Wilhoit. 1981. Foreign News Coverage in Two U.S. Wire Services. *Journal of Communication* 31(2): 55–63.

Wells, Alan. 1974. *Mass Communications: A World View.* Palo Alto CA: National Press Books.

White, Robert A., and James M. McDonnell. 1982. *Priorities for National Communi-*

cation Policy in the Third World. London: Centre for the Study of Communication and Culture.

Whitney, D. Charles, et al. 1982. *Mass Communication Review Yearbook* Vol. 3. Beverly Hills: Sage Publications.

Wigand, Rolf T. 1980. The Direct Satellite Connection: Definitions and Prospects. *Journal of Communication* 30(2): 140–146.

Willings, John A. 1977. Cross-cultural Communication: Possibility or Pipe-dream? *Unesco Courier* April: 12–15.

Winham, Gilbert F. 1970. Political Development and Lerner's Theory: Further Test of a Causal Model. *American Political Science Review* 64: 810–818 (September).

The World Bank, 1981. "Educational Use of Mass Media, The." World Bank Staff Working Paper No. 491. Washington.

World Communications. 1975. New York: Unipub.

"World of News Agencies, The." 1978. Paris: Unesco. Document No. 11 submitted to the MacBride Commission.

"World of the News" Study, The. 1984. *Journal of Communication* 34(1): 120–142.

Yadav, Dharam. 1984. "Twenty Years of Technological and Social Change in Two Indian Villages." Paper presented to the International Communication Association, meeting in San Francisco.

Yadava, Jaswant S. [Ed.]. 1984. *The Politics of News*. New Delhi: Concept Publishing Co.

Yao, Ignatius Peng. 1963. The New China News Agency: How It Serves the Party. *Journalism Quarterly* 40(1): 83–86.

Zasursky, Yassen N. and Yuri I. Kashlev. 1977. A Soviet Viewpoint. *Unesco Courier*, April: 24–27

Index